HISTORY OF LINCOL
Edited by
JOAN THIRSK

VOLUME V

CHURCH AND SOCIETY IN MEDIEVAL LINCOLNSHIRE

by
DOROTHY M. OWEN

PREFACE

*

LINCOLNSHIRE is not one of the favoured regions of England. Unlike many other counties it has never had its own history produced by an industrious eighteenth- or nineteenth-century antiquary. It is not that there have been few students of history within the county. Rather the size of the county, among other factors, has presented problems in bringing together all this material into a comprehensive historical and topographical account of Lincolnshire, a basis for all future work; and the Victoria County History proceeded no further than one volume.

For some time the Lincolnshire Local History Society has been concerned at this lack, and after discussions it set up in 1966 the History of Lincolnshire Committee to plan and publish such a History of Lincolnshire. The volumes were to be scholarly but of general interest, a summary of recent research work written by specialists already engaged in work on the particular periods or subjects but nevertheless aimed at the general reader as well as at the scholar. It was hoped to provide a more or less comprehensive account of the history of the region from prehistoric times until the 1960s.

Initial support was immediately forthcoming. Dr Joan Thirsk of St Hilda's College, Oxford, accepted the Committee's invitation to become General Editor for the series. Contributors for most of the volumes planned were not hard to find. As with the first of the series to be published, a number of bodies have given willing financial assistance to this volume. Among those to whom the Committee is most indebted for financial help are the Pilgrim Trust, the Marc Fitch Fund, and the Willoughby Memorial Trust. Through its Department of Adult Education, Nottingham University has helped with many of the administrative costs. The Lincolnshire Association has maintained its interest in many ways; while the Lincoln City Library and Museum, the Lincolnshire Archives Office, and the Lincolnshire Local History Society (the Committee's parent body) have also helped the work of the Committee. Above all, the Committee acknowledges the support of its printers, The

PREFACE

Broadwater Press, who for more than four years have given unstinted help and advice more willingly than we deserve. It is largely owing to the support of these bodies that the Committee is able to continue publication of

THE HISTORY OF LINCOLNSHIRE
in twelve volumes

ALAN ROGERS (*Chairman, History of Lincolnshire Committee*)

F. T. BAKER (*Chairman, Lincolnshire Local History Society*)

PREFACE TO REPRINT

Ten years after the appearance of Mrs Owen's volume it must be reprinted; this is a well-deserved compliment to the author and a source of gratification to the Committee. The success of the volume is not surprising; it has proved to be of both local interest and general value. No other local study of the Church in medieval England presents it so effectively, as a collection of human beings, with all their strengths and weaknesses, creating and running an organization of great power and diverse activities. The shades of those older scholars to whom she dedicated her book must be smiling at her achievement.

From page ix onwards the reprint is exactly as the original publication. The Committee acknowledges the assistance of the Marc Fitch Fund and of Lincolnshire County Council in financing the reprint.

DENNIS MILLS (*Chairman, History of Lincolnshire Committee*)

April 1981

MAURICE BARLEY (*General Editor*)

LIST OF VOLUMES

General Editors: Mrs Joan Thirsk, M.A., Ph.D., Reader in Economic History, University of Oxford, and Fellow of St Hilda's College; Maurice Barley, M.A., F.S.A., Emeritus Professor of Archaeology, University of Nottingham

- ★I PREHISTORIC LINCOLNSHIRE: J. May, M.A., F.S.A., Senior Lecturer in Archaeology, University of Nottingham
- ★II ROMAN LINCOLNSHIRE: J. B. Whitwell, M.A., Ph.D., F.S.A., Director of Humberside Archaeological Unit
- III ANGLO-SAXON LINCOLNSHIRE: P. H. Sawyer, M.A., Professor of Medieval History, University of Leeds
- IV MEDIEVAL LINCOLNSHIRE: ITS SOCIAL AND ECONOMIC HISTORY: G. Platts, M.A., Ph.D.
- ★V CHURCH AND SOCIETY IN MEDIEVAL LINCOLNSHIRE: Mrs D. M. Owen, M.A., F.S.A., Fellow of Wolfson College, Cambridge
- ★VI TUDOR LINCOLNSHIRE: G. A. J. Hodgett, M.A., Reader in History, King's College, University of London
- ★VII SEVENTEENTH-CENTURY LINCOLNSHIRE: C. Holmes, M.A., Ph.D., Associate Professor in History, Cornell University, New York
- ★VIII THE AGRICULTURAL REVOLUTION IN LINCOLNSHIRE: T. W. Beastall, M.A
- IX CHURCH, CHAPEL AND COMMUNITY IN NINETEENTH-CENTURY LINCOLNSHIRE: R. W. Ambler, B.A., Lecturer in History, Department of Adult Education, University of Hull
- ★X RURAL SOCIETY AND COUNTY GOVERNMENT IN NINETEENTH-CENTURY LINCOLNSHIRE: R. J. Olney, M.A., D.Phil., Assistant Keeper, Royal Commission on Historical Manuscripts
- XI URBAN AND INDUSTRIAL DEVELOPMENTS IN LINCOLNSHIRE, 1700–1914: N. R. Wright, D.M.A.
- XII LINCOLNSHIRE IN THE TWENTIETH CENTURY: A. Clark, M.A., Ph.D.

★Already published

All titles are provisional and the series will not be published in numerical order.

View of remains of Newstead-on-Ancholme Priory by Thomas Espin, 1814. LAO, EXLEY 32/3/15

HISTORY OF LINCOLNSHIRE

V

Church and Society in Medieval Lincolnshire

by

DOROTHY M. OWEN, M.A., F.S.A.
Fellow of Wolfson College, Cambridge

LINCOLN

HISTORY OF LINCOLNSHIRE COMMITTEE
for the Society for Lincolnshire History and Archaeology
1981

FIRST PUBLISHED IN 1971, REPRINTED IN 1981 BY
THE HISTORY OF LINCOLNSHIRE COMMITTEE
47 NEWLAND, LINCOLN

© THE HISTORY OF LINCOLNSHIRE COMMITTEE

ISBN 0 902668 04 8 (cased)
      0 902668 13 7 (limp)

PRINTED IN GREAT BRITAIN BY
W. S. MANEY AND SON LTD, HUDSON ROAD, LEEDS LS9 7DL

*This book is dedicated to the memory of
Charles Wilmer Foster, Alexander Hamilton Thompson, and
Frank Merry Stenton, without whose work
it would not have been possible.*

CONTENTS

Preface	page iii
Plates	xii
Text-figures	xiii
Acknowledgements	xv
Bibliography and List of Abbreviations	xvii
Foreword	xxi

Chapters

I. Setting the scene	1
II. The administrative pattern	20
III. The cathedral	37
IV. Religious houses: foundation, endowment, and economic life	47
V. Religious houses: religious and domestic life	71
VI. The mendicants	84
VII. Chantries and collegiate foundations	92
VIII. The church and the laity	102
IX. The parochial clergy	132

Appendices 1. Numbers of clergy in 1376 and 1526 in the Deanery of Holland	143
2. Numbers of religious in 1376	144
3. Religious houses	146
4. The medieval bishops of Lincoln	154
Index	157

PLATES

Frontispiece View of remains of Newstead-on-Ancholme priory by Thomas Espin, 1814

Between pages 74 and 75

    I. Chapel at Bulby in Irnham

    II. The funeral of St Hugh

    III. The Close wall at Lincoln

    IV. Monastic records
        (a) Benefactors of Crowland
        (b) A book from Kirkstead

    V. Monastic records: a page of the Thornton stock-keeper's account

    VI. Chapel of St Leonard outside the gates of Kirkstead

    VII. Bench-end in Osbournby church

    VIII. Rood-loft at Coates by Stow

TEXT-FIGURES

1. Cliff parishes divided on the line of the High Dyke   *page* 3
2. South Beltisloe in the twelfth century   7
3. South Lindsey in the twelfth century   9
4. South Holland in the twelfth century   11
5. Ecclesiastical divisions of Lincolnshire   23
6. Religious houses in the Witham Valley   59
7. Wool-producing religious houses in Lincolnshire   67
8. Token of the Good Rood at Boston   156

ACKNOWLEDGEMENTS

Plates I and VI are reproduced by permission of the Library and Art Gallery Committee, Lincoln; Plate II by permission of Mr Leslie Hare; Plate III by permission of my brother, Mr Frank Williamson; Plate IVa by permission of the Trustees of the British Museum; Plate IVb by permission of the Syndics of the University Library, Cambridge; Plate V by permission of the Curators of the Bodleian Library, Oxford; Plate VII by permission of the Lincolnshire Old Churches Trust; and Plate VIII by permission of Mr Peter Grey. Figure 8 was photographed in the University Library, Cambridge, from Pishey Thompson's *Boston*, p. 300. The frontispiece is reproduced by permission of its owner, Mr G. R. Exley, from a watercolour deposited by him in the Lincolnshire Archives Office, and photographed in the University Library, Cambridge. The coloured plate for this illustration has been given by an anonymous donor.

Permission to quote from copyright material has been given by Professor C. N. L. Brooke, Professor M. M. Postan, Dr D. L. Douie, Mr Hugh Farmer, Sir Francis Hill, Lady Stenton, the Lincolnshire Archives Office, the Lincoln Record Society, the Northamptonshire Record Society, and the Royal Historical Society.

D.M.O.

This volume has been published with the help of grants from the Marc Fitch Fund and the Pilgrim Trust. The maps have been drawn, as in the previous volume, by Mrs M. Simpson of Leicester. Mrs E. Mattingly of Leeds has helped in the design of the dustjacket. To all of these we express our sincere thanks.

A.R.

BIBLIOGRAPHY AND LIST OF ABBREVIATIONS

Abbreviation	Full Title
AASRP	Associated Architectural and Archaeological Societies' Reports and Papers
Abbrev. Plac.	W. Illingworth, Placitorum in domo capitulari Westmonasteriensi asservatorum abbreviatio, temporum regum Ric. I, Johann., Henr. III, Edw. I, Ed. II, Record Commission, 1811.
Anglo-Saxon England	F. M. Stenton, Anglo-Saxon England, Oxford, 1943.
Arch. J.	Archaeological Journal
BM Add.	British Museum Additional Manuscript
BM Cott.	,, ,, Cotton ,,
BM Harl.	,, ,, Harleian ,,
Bod.	Bodleian Library
Brid. Cart.	W. T. Lancaster, Chartulary . . . of Bridlington, Leeds, 1912.
Burn	R. Burn, Ecclesiastical Law, London, 1763.
CCCC	Corpus Christi College, Cambridge
Cal. Misc. Inq.	Calendar of Miscellaneous Inquisitions
Cal. Pap. Reg.	Calendar of Papal Registers: Letters
Cal. Pat. Rolls	Calendar of Patent Rolls
Camden Soc.	Camden Society Publications (Royal Historical Society)
Cant. Adm.	I. J. Churchill, Canterbury Administration, London, 1933.
Chantry Cert.	C. W. Foster and A. Hamilton Thompson, 'The Chantry Certificates for Lincoln and Lincolnshire', AASRP XXXIV–XXXV, 1922–5.
Counc. & Syn.	F. M. Powicke and C. R. Cheney, Councils and Synods with other documents relating to the English Church, II, 1205–1313, 2 vols, Oxford, 1964.

BIBLIOGRAPHY AND LIST OF ABBREVIATIONS

Abbreviation	Full Title
DLC	F. M. Stenton, *Documents illustrative of the social and economic history of the Danelaw*, British Academy, 1920.
EETS	Early English Text Society Publications
English Clergy	A. Hamilton Thompson, *The English Clergy in the Later Middle Ages*, Oxford, 1947.
EHRn	Information of Mrs E. H. Rudkin
F.L.	Foster Library (Lincolnshire Archives Office)
FNQ	*Fenland Notes and Queries*
G. & C.	Gonville & Caius College, Cambridge
Gomme, *Manners*	G. L. Gomme, *Gentlemen's Magazine Library, Manners and Customs*, 1883.
Gomme, *Top. Hist.*	G. L. Gomme, *Gentlemen's Magazine Library, Topographical History of Leics., Lincs., Middlesex, Monmouth*, 1896.
Goxhill Leiger	Peterborough Dean & Chapter MS. 23, transcript in F.L.
Huntingfield Cartulary	LAO 3 Anc. 2/1.
Hundred Rolls	W. Illingworth, *Rotuli hundredorum temp. Hen. III et Edw. I in turr' Lond' et in curia . . . asservati*, Record Commission, 1812–18.
HMCR	*Reports of the Historical Manuscripts Commission*
JEH	*Journal of Ecclesiastical History*
K.M.	Transcripts made by Professor Kathleen Major
LAASRP	*Lincolnshire Architectural and Archaeological Society's Reports and Papers*
LAO (R)	Lincolnshire Archives Office (Report)
LH	*Lincolnshire Historian*
Lib. Ant.	A. Gibbons, *Liber Antiquus Hugonis de Welles*, Lincoln, 1888.
LCS	H. Bradshaw and C. Wordsworth, *Lincoln Cathedral Statutes*, 3 vols, Cambridge, 1892–7.
LMP	*Lincoln Minster Pamphlets*
LNQ	*Lincolnshire Notes and Queries*

BIBLIOGRAPHY AND LIST OF ABBREVIATIONS

Abbreviation   *Full Title*
LRS   Lincoln Record Society Publications.

The following volumes of the Lincoln Record Society's publications are referred to frequently in the notes:

1. R. E. G. Cole, *Lincolnshire Church Notes made by Gervase Holles, A.D. 1634-42*, 1911.
3, 6, 9. W. P. Phillimore, F. N. Davis, and others, *Rotuli Hugonis de Welles*, 1912–14.
5, 10, 24. C. W. Foster, *Lincoln Wills*, 1914–30.
7, 14, 21. A. Hamilton Thompson, *Visitations of Religious Houses*, 1914–29.
11. F. N. Davis, *Rotuli Roberti Grosseteste*, 1914.
17. C. W. Foster, *Final Concords of the county of Lincoln...*, *1244–72*, 1920.
18. F. M. Stenton, *Transcripts of Charters relating to the Gilbertine houses...*, 1922.
19. C. W. Foster and T. Longley, *Lincolnshire Domesday and the Lindsey Survey*, 1924.
20. F. N. Davis and others, *Rotuli Ricardi Gravesend*, 1925.
30. R. Sillem, *Records of Some Sessions of the Peace for Lincolnshire, 1360–75*, 1936.
33, 35, 37. A. Hamilton Thompson, *Visitations in the diocese of Lincoln, 1517–31*, 1940–47.
36. W. S. Thomson, *A Lincolnshire Assize Roll for 1298*, 1944.
39, 43, 48, 52, 60, 64. R. M. T. Hill, *The Rolls and Register of Bishop Oliver Sutton, 1280–99*, 1948 etc. in progress.
47. W. Holtzmann and E. W. Kemp, *Papal Decretals relating to the diocese of Lincoln in the twelfth century*, 1954.
49. E. G. Kimball, *Records of Some Sessions of the Peace in Lincolnshire, 1381–96*, 1955.
55. W. D. Simpson, *The Building Accounts of Tattershall Castle*, 1960.
57, 58. M. Archer, *Bishop Repingdon's Register*, 1963.
67. M. Bowker, *An Episcopal Court Book, 1514-20*, 1967.
   See also below: RA.

Abbreviation   *Full Title*
Magna Vita   D. Douie and H. Farmer, *Magna Vita Sancti Hugonis*, 2 vols., London, 1961.
Med. Lin.   J. W. F. Hill, *Medieval Lincoln*, Cambridge, 1948.
Mon. Ang.   W. Dugdale, *Monasticon Anglicanum*, ed. B. Bandinel, J. Caley, and H. Ellis, 6 vols., 1846.
PBGB   Information of Canon P. B. G. Binnall
PCC   C. W. Foster, 'Lincolnshire Wills in the Prerogative Court of Canterbury', AASRP XLI, 1932–3.

Abbreviation	Full Title
Pevsner	N. Pevsner and J. Harris, *Buildings of Lincolnshire*, Penguin Books, 1964.
Plac. de Q. W.	W. Illingworth, *Placita de quo warranto temporibus Edw. I. II et III. in curia . . . asservata*, Record Commission, 1818.
PRO	Public Record Office
PRS	Pipe Roll Society Publications
RA	*Registrum Antiquissimum* (LRS 27, 28, 29, 32, 34, 41, 42, 46, 51, 62).
Reg.	LAO Episcopal register
RS	Rolls Series
Sempring. Char.	E. M. Poynton, 'Charters relating to the Priory of Sempringham', *The Genealogist*, new ser. XVI, etc.
U.L.C.	University Library, Cambridge
Val. Eccl.	J. Caley and J. Hunter, *Valor Ecclesiasticus temp. Henr. VIII auctoritate regia institutus*, Record Commission, 1810–34.
VCH	Victoria County History
White 1872	W. White, *History, Gazetteer and Directory of Lincolnshire*, Sheffield, 1872.
Wrest Park	Cartulary of Crowland Abbey, Spalding Gentlemen's Society.

FOREWORD

No one who has spent ten years of her life, as I did, working within sight and sound of the cathedral at Lincoln can fail to be aware of the part played by the medieval past, and especially by the medieval church, in moulding the present Lincolnshire scene. The physical presence of so many of its buildings reminds us constantly of this, for they are patchworks of many medieval styles of architecture, with innumerable signs of the uses to which they have been put by successive generations. They were built where they are, and as they are, because a manorial lord wanted his church close at hand, or a new and growing settlement required extra provision, or a wealthy individual or community wished to express their devotion or demonstrate their wealth. The cathedral itself is the most impressive of witnesses to the impulse of devotion felt by the hundreds of Lincolnshire men and women who endowed it in the twelfth and thirteenth centuries, and to the attractions of the cult of St Hugh. Ways of life and thought which left behind them such substantial memorials can hardly have failed to influence the land and its development, and this book is an attempt to analyse the organizations within which such activities were possible.

At the very beginning, there is, I am conscious, some difficulty, for it has not always proved easy to decide when, or how, some of them appeared: setting the scene for the medieval development of the church was much the hardest part to write, and remains, for the writer, the least satisfactory. In the succeeding chapters I have made no attempt to write a chronological summary: there is little material for such a study, and no space for it here. Instead I have tried to depict and analyse the various convenient sections into which the medieval church can be divided, never, I hope, forgetting that these are artificial and arbitrary divisions of an organization which is a unified whole. In doing this I have necessarily described something of the economic and social scene within which the church operated, and where I could find traces of individual men and women in action, I have tried to depict them.

This book is, therefore, a study of Lincolnshire society in one of its facets during the medieval period, and an attempt to see how the habits and attitudes which were then generated have influenced the county as we know it today. By far the most important legacy of the medieval church to the secular world which succeeded to it seems to be the habit

FOREWORD

of communal action within the parishes, which originated sometimes in the group's need to provide and endow the actual church, and was always nourished by its responsibility for the fabric and ornaments, and by the experiences of the semi-secular gilds. All these activities provided a training-ground for the parochial officials of local government as it was to evolve in the post-medieval period. During the time with which we are concerned here, and for long after, the parish church and its officers performed many secular functions, and the church buildings and church-yards were for many years the only meeting places for every type of private and communal activity, so that a study of the development of the church within the county is to a very great extent a study of the development of the county.

I have dedicated this book to the memory of three great historians whose work revolutionized medieval studies in Lincolnshire and elsewhere, but it owes a great deal to the Lincolnshire Archives Office, and to its past and present staff, and to my many friends and associates in Lincolnshire, with whom, over the last twenty-two years, I have bicycled, driven, and talked. Some particular debts I have acknowledged, quite inadequately, I am aware, in the footnotes, and I must make special mention of the help I have received from Professor Major, Mrs Rudkin, Mrs Varley, Mr E. Gillett, and Canon Binnall. I cannot close without further mention of the education in Lincolnshire matters, past and present, which I have received at various times from my friends F. T. Baker, Maurice Barley, G. S. Dixon, C. L. Exley, Eva Farmery, Sir Francis Hill, and Flora Murray. My husband's knowledge of the county and his inexhaustible patience have been a greater help than I can well express here. Most of all, this book is a personal expression of love for an adopted homeland where I have been very happy; I am grateful to the Lincolnshire Local History Society, and to Dr Rogers, for enabling me to make it.

DOROTHY M. OWEN

CHAPTER I
SETTING THE SCENE

THE Lincolnshire ecclesiastical scene at the death of the Conqueror was almost completely Anglo-Saxon. The cathedral of the bishop of Lincoln had not yet been transferred from Dorchester to Lincoln; the great burst of monastic foundation and donation was still to come; its holy places and churches were, for the most part, those which had existed for three hundred years; many of the parish churches, and most of the chapels, were still not founded. Perhaps the earliest sites of Christian worship surviving into this period were the chapels and hermitages associated with holy wells, which seem to have been taken over by the first missionaries from some pre-Christian culture, and vestiges of which could still be seen in the nineteenth century. They form part of a much larger tradition which will be discussed later, but it is important to remember that well chapels like St Pancras, on the cliff at Scampton, St Helen near the seven springs at Hemswell, Shadwell (Chad's well) at Barton, and St Mary's at Ancaster, probably formed a significant portion of the ecclesiastical provision of the late eleventh century.[1] Alongside this early missionary tradition there had grown up an ecclesiastical organization which was to be formalized by Aethelred II and Cnut. It was based upon a series of large churches, or 'head minsters', which were often the seat of a bishop, and had each its large dependent area, or diocese.[2] In Lincolnshire, after the Danish devastation, the system had disintegrated; no head minster and no bishop survived, and from early in the eleventh century Lincolnshire had formed part of the Mercian see of Dorchester. Within the head minster's area there had been set up a series of smaller, but still important, churches, known as 'old minsters' or 'mother churches', which seem to have been founded in existing settlements or to have provided focal points for settlement, and vestiges of such foundations were still to be seen in Lincolnshire despite the Danish activities. The church on whose site the cathedral was subsequently built was almost certainly of this type and three other churches at Caistor, Grantham, and Horncastle seem to have had sufficient local importance before the Conquest to be probably of the same type. Each was on the royal

[1] LNQ XIX, pp. 42–77; White 1872, *passim*; EHRn. & PBGB.
[2] *Anglo-Saxon England*, pp. 148–50, 652–61.

demesne, and each had its dependent chapels in the vills which were outlying members of the royal manor. Louth, and possibly even Stow, also have features which suggest early importance, and Castle Bytham, which seems to have been served by a group of prebendaries who formed a college, was characteristic of many pre-Conquest foundations elsewhere. No doubt Caistor, Grantham, and Horncastle may have had some such arrangement, which did not survive their transfer early in the Norman régime to the cathedrals of Lincoln and Salisbury and the bishop of Carlisle.[3]

Around the old minsters lay considerable areas in which they must at first have exercised some sort of religious care of the inhabitants, but their supervision can never have been very close, and the wide area was gradually divided into smaller and more convenient sections or parishes. The boundaries of these smaller areas were determined by the location of centres of population, the lie of the land, the location of such natural features as rivers, streams, and estuaries, and the occurrence of prominent landmarks like the Roman road known as High Dyke. How a feature like this last could determine the parish boundaries is demonstrated very well by the pattern of the cliff parishes north of Lincoln shown in Figure 1.

In the parishes there seems first to have been no more than an open-air mission station marked by a cross, where the gospel was preached and mass was celebrated. Many of these crosses survived well into the medieval period and even later, standing at the centre of the settlement, but not necessarily in the churchyard. There was one at Rand in the mid-thirteenth century; Stukeley mentions one on Aunby heath, "now called Robin Hood's cross;" and others still existed in 1872 at Gelston, Quarrington, Swinstead, and Old Sleaford.[4] These open-air meeting places can scarcely have lasted long. Small churches soon supplemented or replaced them, and kings and bishops were urging landowners to put up such buildings and provide burial grounds for them before the end of the tenth century. Until the Danes settled finally in the county, and were themselves converted to Christianity, few of these parish churches can have been built in Lincolnshire, and it seems likely that the movement was scarcely felt there before the second or third decade of the eleventh century.

By Anglo-Saxon law the upkeep of all churches was obligatory on the populations they served, and money was at first raised in three principal forms: plough-scot, an annual levy of one penny for each plough team; church-scot; and soul-scot, which last is the corpse-present or mortuary of a later period. Church-scot was perhaps the earliest of all these levies;

[3] LRS 19, 1/9–25, 65, 91; RA II, p. 274.
[4] RA IV, p. 40; CCCC ms. 618, p. 28; White 1872.

SETTING THE SCENE 3

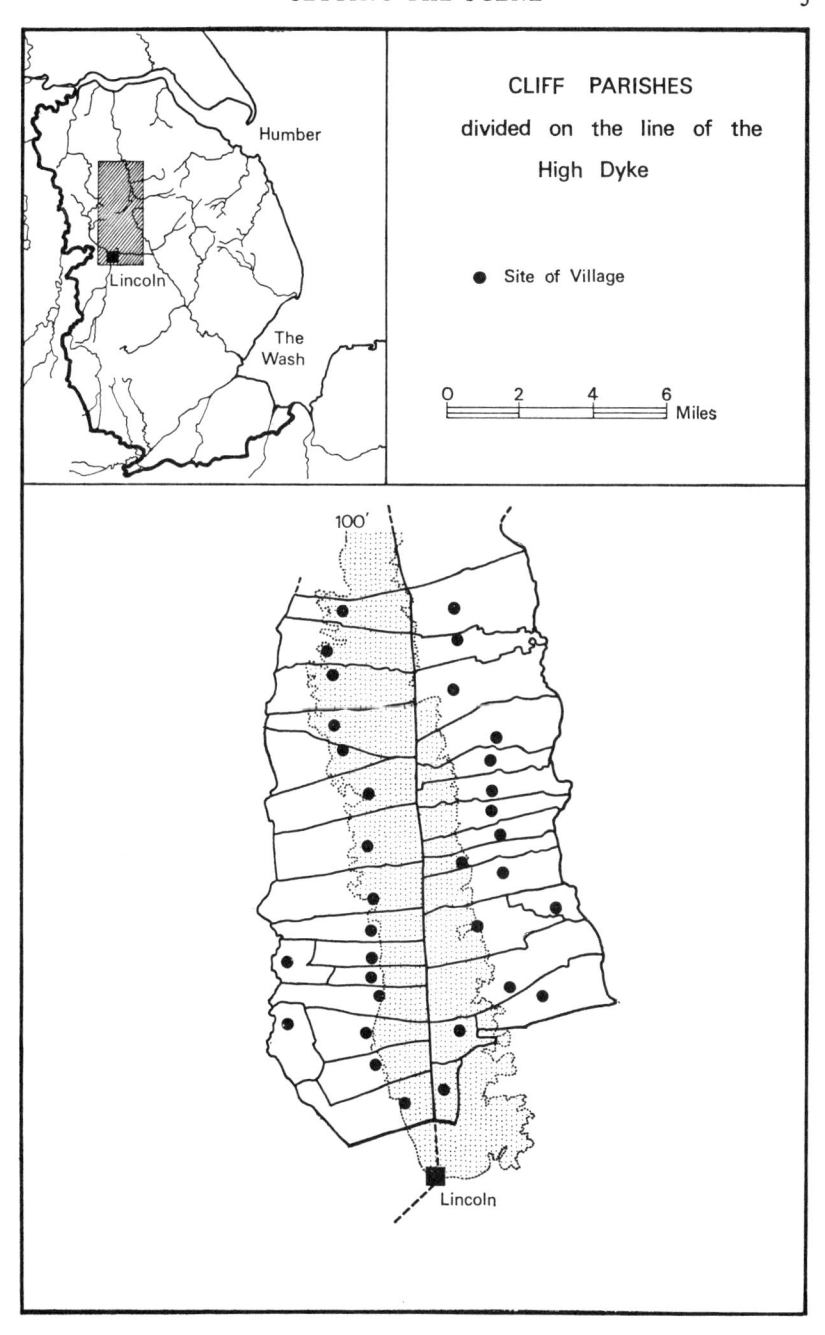

Fig. 1

it was paid in kind, not to the parish church but to the old minster, and in Lincolnshire it was certainly paid by some parishes to the cathedral in the twelfth and thirteenth centuries.[5] The contribution of a tenth, or tithe, of all produce to the support of the church had also been introduced into the Anglo-Saxon church, and by the tenth century was already incorporated in the legal codes. From the very beginning of most of the parish churches it provided the major portion of the funds which supported their priests, and the customary offerings, important though they were, can never have yielded so much except in city parishes.

These parish churches were being founded in increasing numbers in the county, especially from the first half of the eleventh century, usually by one or more landowners who paid for the erection of the building and endowed it with land (glebe) and a house site (toft) for the priest, and who, thereafter, 'owned' the profits of the church, that is the profits of the obligatory tithes and offerings. If a number of landowners were involved in the venture, they would sometimes share the right of choosing a priest (the advowson), and they always divided the profits. This sometimes accounts for the half, quarter, and sixth parts of churches, which are recorded as attached to some fees in Domesday. On the other hand, if there were only two principal landowners in an area, each might build his own church, and paired churches of this type survived throughout the medieval period at Bilsby, Swaby, and Binbrook. Even when the under-tenants dwelling in the parish contributed to the endowment of the church, and this seems to have happened fairly often, the advowson and the profits remained with the principal owner. This proprietary and territorial way of regarding the parish churches continued very strong throughout the twelfth century; it is well illustrated by the lawsuit in which, when the principal fee in Wyberton was divided between two brothers, one of the heirs claimed the parish church because it was "situated on his fee."[6] The multiple parishes of Lincoln and Stamford seem to have arisen in the same way: a single landowner founded a church for himself and his men, or a group of neighbours in a street or quarter collaborated for the same purpose.

The same 'territorial' attitude allowed landowners to endow monasteries with churches and with lands, including even those lands which had been given to the churches by their men. Early in the twelfth century Crowland, for example, received from Emecina of Gedney, "the churches of my lands of Gedney and Whaplode," from William of Roumara, "the church situated on the fee of Raithby by Spilsby," and from Ketelbern of Keal, "the two churches of my fee" (East and West Keal). Small gifts of land made by local residents to the church of Thurlby by Bourne when it was consecrated in 1112, later passed with the church to Peter-

---

[5] *Med. Lin.*, p. 67.   [6] DLC, Introduction, p. lxx; *Abbrev. Plac.*, p. 97.

borough Abbey. The owner of a church might even decide to change its site, as William son of Ernis did when he gave the church of Sutton in Holland to Castleacre Priory before 1180: "three acres of land in Sutton, in the field called Heoldefen next the road, to build a parish church there. And my wish is that the earlier wooden church of the same vill, in place of which the new church will be built, shall be taken away and the bodies buried in it shall be taken to the new church."[7]

Once the parochial boundaries had been laid down and a church with a burial ground established in the principal settlement, Anglo-Saxon law seems to have been clear that subsequent churches in the same parish would be subordinate to the first, and should not deprive it of parochial offerings, particularly of burial fees and mortuaries. The term 'mother church' (*matrix ecclesia*) now begins to be used to describe not an old minster, but a parish church in its relation to these younger foundations, and disputes occur in which the owner of a chapel, like that at Towthorpe in Grantham, attempted to prove its independence by declaring it to be a *matrix ecclesia*.[8]

These lesser churches tended to be founded in areas of the parish only recently available for cultivation, where a newly settled population required the services of a priest. To the Anglo-Saxons they were 'field churches', but the post-Conquest name for them was 'chapels of ease' or sometimes 'parochial chapels'. Like the parish churches themselves, they were often provided by the principal owner of the newly cleared land, who, before his reclamation was completed, reserved the space for it, and made sure of the concurrence of the owner of the parish church. Baldwin Wake did this when he was preparing to reclaim the area of Frognal in Deeping St James.

A chapel of this sort often began in a temporary licence by the bishop for services to be held in a room or building in the landlord's homestead, which might well be the first permanent building on the newly cleared land. Grosseteste gave licences for such chapels at South Kelsey and Little Hale; one founded by Alexander of Pointon in his house at Wrangle was described as "a certain chapel within the enclosure of his house, forty feet long and twenty feet broad, without font or burial ground." Chapels like this had no endowment. They were served by a stipendiary priest who was employed by the landlord, and they might easily disappear if he ceased to live in the house. At best the service in them was provided only while he was fully resident, and the owners of the parish churches often took care to stipulate this before agreeing to their foundation. The prior and convent of Bridlington, who were owners of the parish church of

---

[7] Wrest Park, ff. 106, 193*v*; Peterborough Swaffham Register, f. VIII. 15.27 (K.M.); BM Harl. 2110, f. 70*v*.

[8] F. W. Maitland, *Bracton's Notebook*, Cambridge, 1887, no. 357.

Edenham, permitted Roger of Huntingfield to have service in his chapel at Southorpe within that parish only between St Edmund's day and Christmas, or Epiphany if he stayed there so long. Where the owner of the parish church had omitted to restrict the services, or neglected to establish his right to the offerings and tithes of those who frequented the chapel, its founder and his successors might well claim that it had become a 'free chapel' which lay outside the parochial system. This occurred in St Katherine's grange at North Hykeham, at Wykes in Donington in Holland, and at Barthorpe in Swineshead.[9]

If the new land prospered and people settled there in some numbers, some more permanent and independent chapel outside the landlord's homestead might become desirable. Then the landlord and his villeins often cooperated to build and endow it, especially in the twelfth century. Peter of Goxhill and his men did this at Roxholme in Leasingham; so did Robert, son of Hugh of Tattershall, and his men at Great Sturton in Baumber; so also did William of Stockwith with his men at Stockwith in the parish of Gainsborough.[10] The Stockwith foundation was licensed late in the thirteenth century, and by this time the landlords seem to have played a less conspicuous part than before. Chapel foundations now tended to be the work of the inhabitants acting alone (as at Cowbit, in Spalding parish, first licensed by the bishop in 1363) or even of the rector of the mother parish. William of Langwath, rector of Bottesford, for example, founded and endowed a chapel for the inhabitants of the outlying hamlet of Burringham in 1302. But whoever founded the chapel, it seems to have been regarded, like the parish church, as part of the property of the lord on whose fee it stood. During the twelfth century a parish church with its chapels could be, and often was, granted by a lord to a monastic house, which claimed the tithes and offerings of all the inhabitants of the fee. Complicated legal battles were sometimes fought in parishes where a fee crossed a parochial boundary, or when the mother parish of a chapelry was in dispute.[11]

Detailed examination of several contrasting areas of the county throws further light on the church as it existed in the localities in the first three centuries after the Conquest. Much of the evidence for this comes, apart from later entries in the episcopal registers, from the cartularies and registers of monastic houses which had acquired parish churches or manors with attached chapels, and which were themselves often reclaiming land for cultivation and planting new chapels on it. The south-west corner of the county, which forms the southern half of the rural deanery

[9] BM Harl. 3658, f. lv; LRS 11, pp. 12, 37; Goxhill Leiger, F. L., no. 197; *Brid. Cart.*, p. 364; *Val. Eccl.* IV, pp. 31, 93.
[10] Goxhill Leiger, F. L., no. 211; *Brid. Cart.*, p. 352; LRS 52, p. 38.
[11] Reg. 12, f. 36; Reg. 3, f. 44v.

SETTING THE SCENE 7

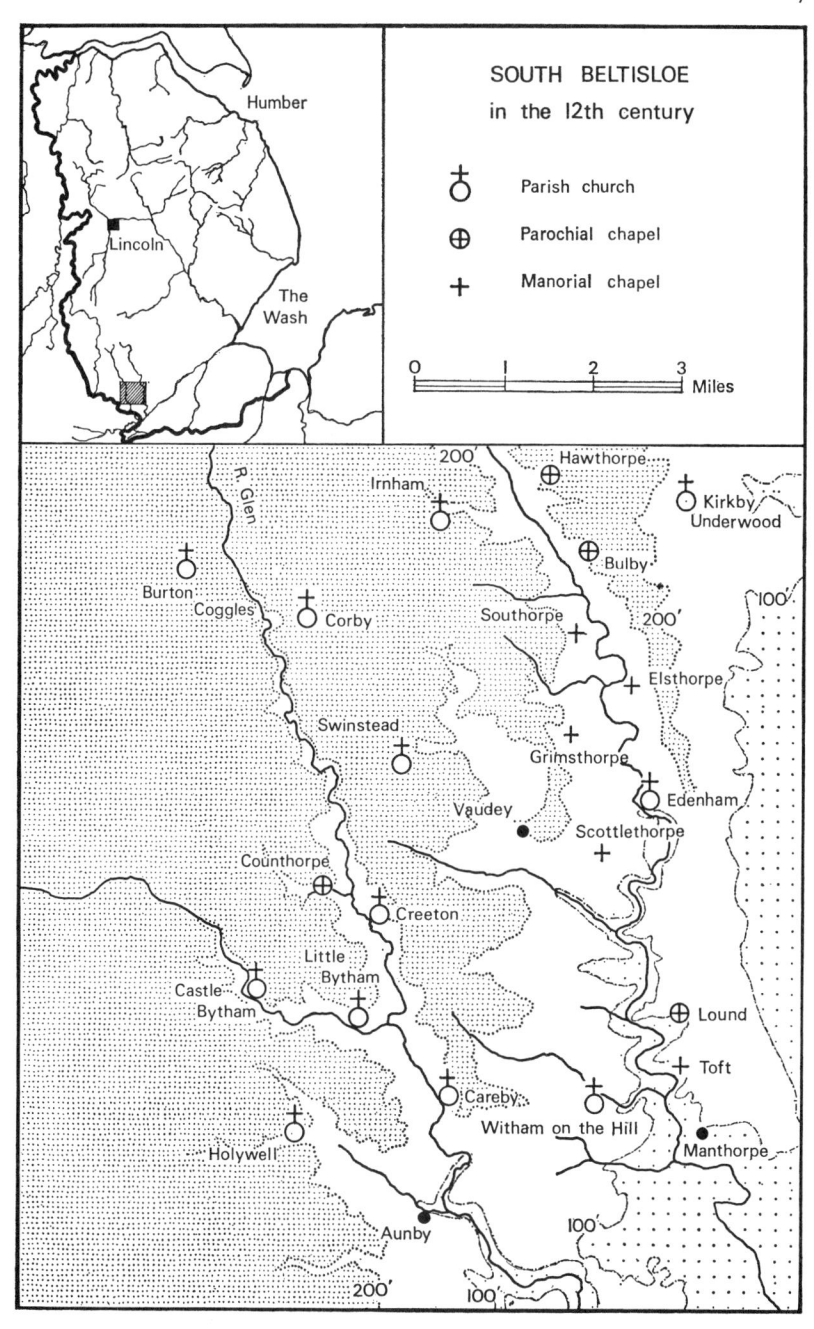

Fig. 2

of Beltisloe, is a well-wooded region where the place-names suggest that much of the settlement was made in clearings in the woods (Fig. 2). In the twelfth century it was still so uncleared and remote as to attract Cistercians to settle there, at Vaudey in the western end of the large parish of Edenham. Edenham was, indeed, characteristic of the whole region. The parish church was already owned by the Austin canons of Bridlington. During the twelfth century four manorial chapels were set up, to serve the families of Huntingfield, De Baiocis, Neville, and Amundeville, whose manor houses lay in the secondary settlements of Southorpe, Elsthorpe, Grimsthorpe, and Scottlethorpe. Of these, only Scottlethorpe survived into later centuries as a parochial chapel. In Grimsthorpe, at least, land reclamation was still going on when the chapel was first mentioned, and all four chapels probably represent an early stage in the process of settlement.

North of Edenham lay Irnham, again a fairly large parish, with two substantial settlements at Bulby and Hawthorpe on its eastern boundary, each with a long-established parochial chapel. These seem to represent early colonization of land lying opposite the main settlement on the east bank of the stream. Further south, in Witham on the Hill, the situation is more involved. The principal settlement, and the parish church, lay on high land west of the river Glen, and across the river, in small valleys opening on it, are Toft, Lound, and Manthorpe. Lound seems to have had a parochial chapel from the first, but there is no sign of any chapel in Manthorpe, and at Toft, relatively late in the twelfth century, a manorial chapel was set up by Robert, son of Hugh of Tattershall.

The large parish of Castle Bytham had complicated arrangements of a different kind, for until 1284 it preserved something of its pre-Conquest collegiate status, with three canonries, or portions, in the churches of Castle Bytham, Little Bytham, and Holywell. In addition, in two secondary settlements at Counthorpe and Aunby there was at least one parochial chapel and a preaching cross. Finally, within the main village and serving the castle, which was at the height of its importance during the twelfth century, was a bewildering array of lesser chapels: St Mary in the Castle, St Thomas in the Barbican, St Mary Magdalen below the Castle, and St John Baptist belonging to the hospital of "Herberdist." The parish churches here survive still, but the chapels have almost vanished, and it is hard to decide what they were like. A Romanesque west doorway from Scottlethorpe, which is now in Edenham church, and the drawing of Bulby chapel reproduced in Plate I suggest that they were built during the twelfth century in good local stone. Stukeley's drawing and description of Toft, however, if they represent an original building, suggest that the earliest buildings of the area were perhaps of wood: "A very pretty front of stone of the oldest manner . . . the body of the church

SETTING THE SCENE 9

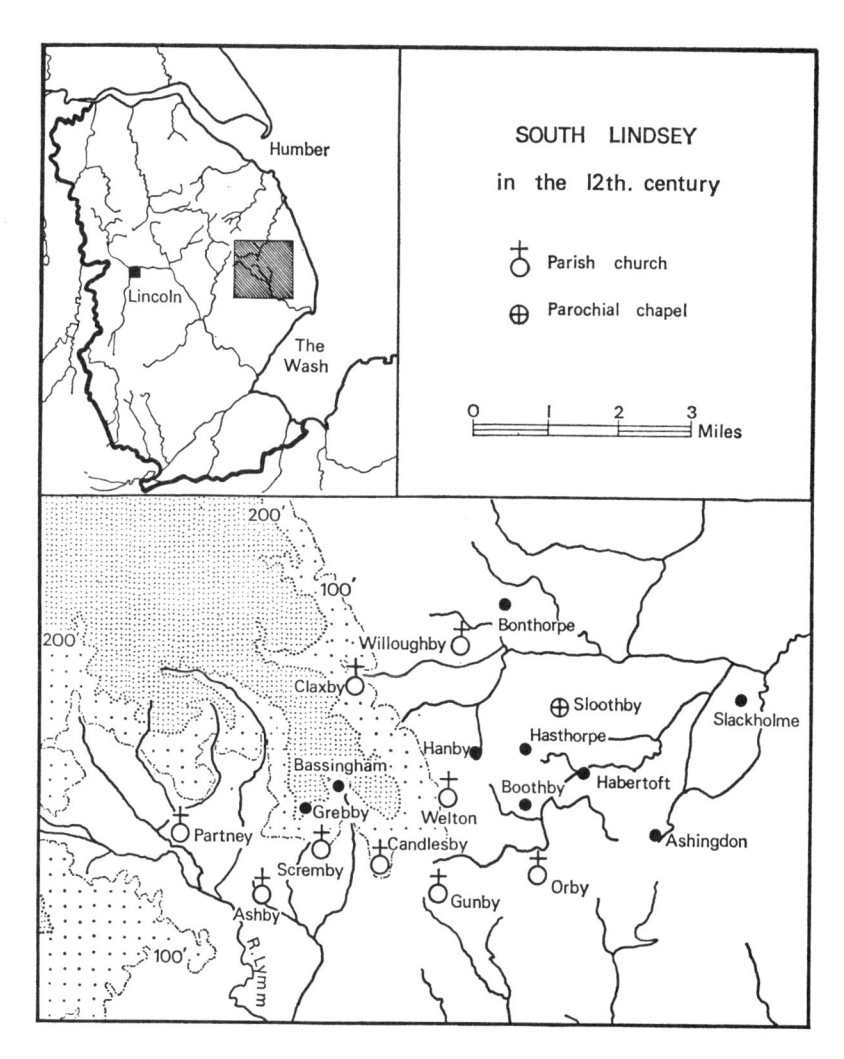

Fig. 3

is studwork of timber ... it grieved us much to see it unworthily converted into a blacksmith's shop.[12]

An area in Lindsey to the north-east of Spilsby provides a considerable contrast (Fig. 3). Here, on the north bank of the river Lymm, and rounding the eastern corner of the high land to the north, is a group of thickly planted settlements, Partney, Ashby, Scremby, Candlesby, Welton, and Claxby, while to the east and south lie the parishes of Gunby, Orby, Burgh, and Willoughby. Ashby, Candlesby, Gunby, Orby, and Claxby are small, nucleated parishes, with no evidence of secondary settlements. Scremby, equally small, had two hamlets, Grebby and Bassingham, neither, it seems, large enough or far enough from the centre to require a separate chapel; Partney, where there had been an Anglo-Saxon monastic settlement which seems to have lingered into the twelfth century, or been revived as a hospital dedicated to St Mary Magdalen, was more thickly populated than any of its neighbours at an early period. Welton had two subordinate settlements at Hanby and Boothby, which appear to have been clearings in the woods which covered much of the parish, but neither was large enough to call for separate ecclesiastical provision. The true marshland parish, Willoughby, is a very different thing, for here the original village and the parish church are on the high marsh, but there are also two substantial settlements in the lower marsh, at Sloothby and Bonthorpe. Sloothby already had a parochial chapel in the twelfth century and a gild chapel was founded during the thirteenth century. The men of Bonthorpe, on the other hand, continued to go to the parish church, and their church path for carrying corpses to burial there was well defined in the late thirteenth century. Other yet smaller settlements appeared still further to the east, at Ashingdon, Habertoft, and Slackholme; as early as 1332 the men of Ashingdon also had their church path, for Thomas Pilat was said to have obstructed it by raising a bank.[13]

Finally, in the parishes of south-east Holland, in Spalding, Moulton, Whaplode, Holbeach, Fleet, Gedney, and Sutton, we come to the most elaborate parochial arrangements which we shall meet in Lincolnshire (Fig. 4). As Professor Hallam has demonstrated, it was in the eleventh and twelfth centuries an area of intensive reclamation, outwards to the sea, and backwards to the fen, from the ridge on which the original settlements stand. On the seaward reclamations were the parochial chapels of Holbeach Hurn (St Nicholas), Fleet Hargate, and Lutton (also St Nicholas), and the 'hospital' of St John Baptist in Fleet, which was to become

[12] *Brid. Cart.*, pp. 363–421; LAO, Huntingfield Cart., no. 107; Gomme, *Top. Hist.*, p. 83; CCCC ms. 618, p. 29; LRS 39, pp. 156–7; RA I, pp. 81–3; RA III, pp. 343–59; Bod. Top. gen. d. 14, f. 33; Surtees Soc., 76, p. 324.
[13] BM Cott. Vesp. E xx, ff. 57v, 68; G. G. Walker, *Historical Notes on the Parish of Partney*, Spilsby, 1898, p. 52; LAO, 2 Anc 1/14/5, 2 Anc 2/21/1; LRS 5, p. 43.

SETTING THE SCENE

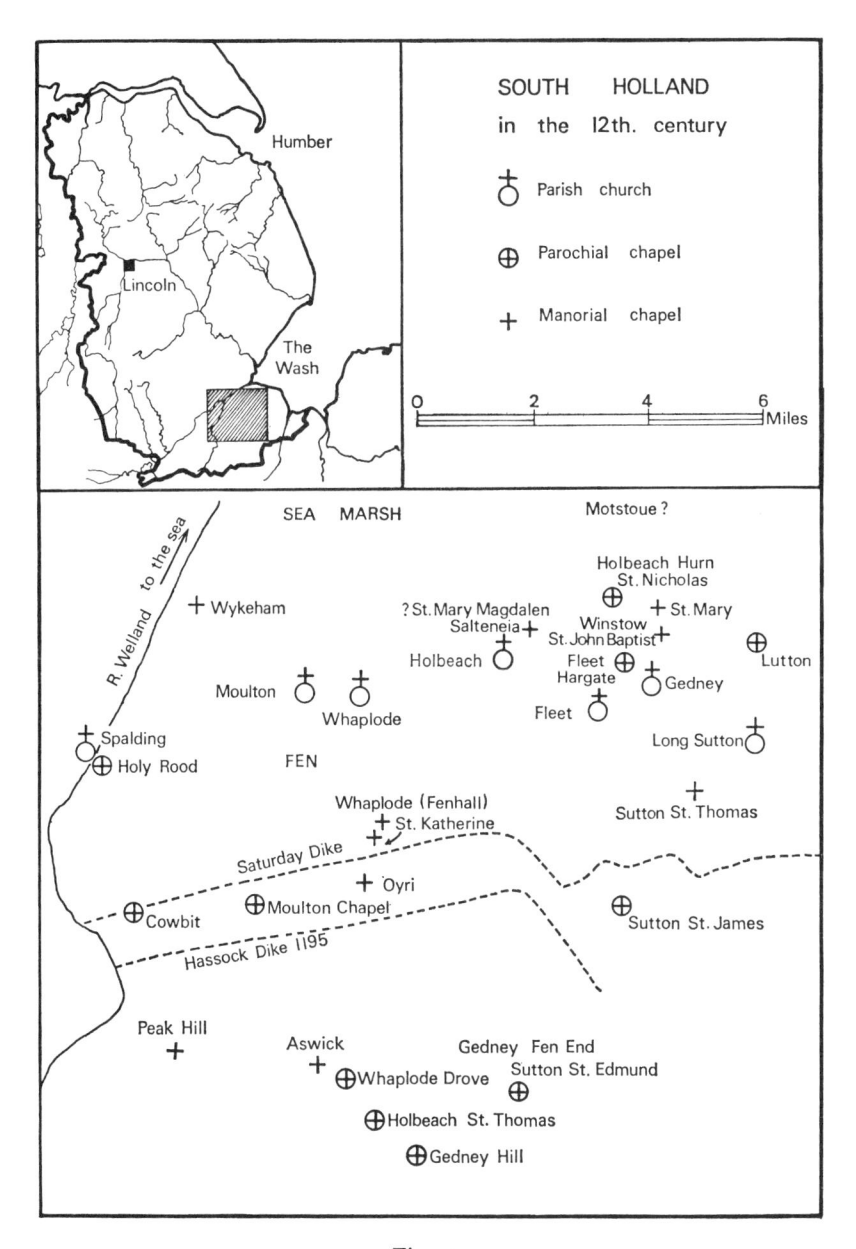

Fig. 4

the manorial chapel of the Hospitallers' estate at Winstow. It is possible that there was also a hospital of St John Baptist at Salteneia; the single reference to it, in the Crowland cartulary, suggests that it lay to the northeast of Saltney Gate which links Holbeach and Whaplode. A holy place, probably marked by a cross, lay at Hurnfleet on the seaward edge of Holbeach; it seems to represent not a precursor of St Nicholas's chapel, but a still further extension of settlement.[14]

In the direction of the fen, settlements were already made before the end of the twelfth century, when the parallel banks of Saturday Dike and Hassock Dike had been completed and the chapels of Whaplode St Katherine (Fenhall), Moulton St James, Sutton St James, Sutton St Thomas Martyr, and Holbeach St Thomas (seven miles from the parish church) had already been established. There would soon be in addition a manorial chapel between the two banks in Whaplode parish, used to endow a short-lived friary, a chantry chapel of St John, a manorial chapel in Crowland's grange at Aswick, and a parochial chapel at Whaplode Drove for "the easement of those who guard the banks of the rivers and ring the bells as a warning."[15] The known chapels at the remotest ends of the parishes, in Cowbit and Peak Hill, Sutton St Edmund, and Gedney Hill, followed during the thirteenth and early fourteenth centuries. There were also a number of unidentified chapels, presumably in the newlands, such as Gedney St Thomas and Holy Trinity Sutton, which lie somewhat close together, Sutton St Katherine, and a hospital in Gedney fen (in John d'Oyry's manor) which in 1256 was given to the Norfolk abbey of Creake.[16]

By the twelfth century, the maintenance of churches was provided from a three-fold source which had come to replace the Anglo-Saxon scot. An endowment, of land or rent charges on land (the glebe), had been made by the founders and tenants at the time of consecration, and this was sometimes increased by later gifts. Tithes (tenth parts, payable annually), of corn, hay, and wood (the greater tithes), of other crops and young animals, and of the profits of trade, milling, fisheries, salt-making, and other personal activities (the lesser tithes), were becoming customary during the twelfth century. Finally there were the customary offerings made by parishioners to the church or the priest, which, though they differed widely from parish to parish, everywhere formed a substantial portion of the priest's endowments.[17]

[14] H. E. Hallam, *Settlement and Society*, Cambridge, 1965, *passim*; N. Neilson, *A Terrier of Fleet*, British Academy, 1920, pp. 32, 83; Camden Soc., old ser. 65, p. 60; Wrest Park, f. 192v.

[15] Reg. 5, f. 173v; Reg. 7, f. 175; AASRP 41, pp. 139-54; LAO, institution indexes, *passim*; Chantry Cert., *passim*; *Val. Eccl.* IV, pp. 91-5.

[16] LRS 5, p. 128; PCC, 53; LRS 17, p. 145.   [17] Burn, II, p. 375 *et seq.*

Between 1100 and 1300 many of the churches of the county were given either to the cathedral or to various monastic houses, and since these were concerned to record and establish their rights, almost all our detailed information about the revenues of these churches comes from their surviving archives. The coverage is therefore incomplete. We have few details about the revenues of the churches remaining in lay patronage. Nevertheless few religious owners were interested in surveying or recording the land given to their churches, and not all parishes disputed their tithe or declined to make the customary offerings. When the time came, as it did in the thirteenth century, to value the revenue of all parish churches for purposes of taxation, all that can really be said is that the Lincolnshire benefices varied enormously in value.[18]

At the consecration of a new church or chapel it was customary for the specific founder and other interested persons to make gifts of land for its maintenance and for the support of the priest, and to provide a toft or house site close to the church as a dwelling for him. When in 1112 Bishop Robert Bloet consecrated the church at Thurlby by Bourne, Bencelina, the mother of Ralf de la Mare, endowed it with half a bovate of arable land, an acre of meadow, and a toft, to which one of her knights added two more acres of arable and one of meadow. When the church of Deeping St James was consecrated, Gerald *Pincerna*, whose lord, Baldwin Wake, had founded it, offered on the altar in the presence of Bishop Alexander, on the day of its dedication, a charter giving to the church six acres of meadow. On the other hand, some land had already been given "before it was hallowed," to St Andrew, Utterby. This must often have happened, but it is not always clear when, and how, the properties casually mentioned in charters had been given. Eight acres of arable were thus given by the *rustici* of the vill to the chapel of Great Sturton, twenty acres to Lound, a man and his chattels at Wellingore, and a mill to the chapel of St Mary Hartsholme. Often there are brief mentions of additional gifts; before 1130 the endowment of Thurlby by Bourne, which had now been given to Peterborough, had increased to a bovate of demesne, three acres of arable, and two acres of meadow. It is clear that such additional gifts were often made by the villeins associated with their lord in a foundation, or by free peasants or sokemen. Thus the men of Keddington gave to the endowment of their church one acre from every bovate of their holdings.[19]

Later endowments were made less to the church as a whole than for some specific object within it. From the late twelfth century onwards

[18] W. E. Lunt, *The Valuation of Norwich*, Oxford, 1926, pp. 228–314.
[19] Peterborough Swaffham Register f. VIII. 15.27 (K.M.); BM Harl. 3658, f. 5; LRS 18, p. 40; *Brid. Cart.*, pp. 352, 364; RA II, pp. 87–97; BM Cott. Vesp. E XX, f. 207; Camden Soc., old ser. 47, p. 160; DLC, p. lxxi, note.

gifts were made for particular altars or lights, such as the two acres given by William Berners to the church of Habrough, which were earmarked for the upkeep of the altar of the Blessed Katherine, or the rent charge of fivepence which was paid by the holder of three acres of land in Fleet to St Mary's altar in Fleet church. As time passed the gifts made in wills, or in return for a specific privilege, became even more detailed in their provisions. Sir Simon of Hale, for example, in acknowledgement of permission to have mass in his private chapel, gave two wax candles, each weighing two pounds, to the church of Hale at its patronal festival; and in the early sixteenth century Quadring Eaudike chapel had bequests of a saltern to provide wine and 'singing bread' (blessed bread for distribution to the congregation), and a cow to pay for the maintenance of an organist.[20]

It is very rare to see mentions of disputes about the identity of land given to the churches: clearly the priest was like other landholders in the vill: his holding was well known in the collective memory of his neighbours, and there was little need to set it down. Hence, medieval surveys or terriers of the church land, which would at a later time be called the glebe, are fairly rare, even in the records of religious houses. It was otherwise with tithes, the collection and ownership of which were continually in dispute. Collection was a piecemeal affair, as the valuation of the rectory of Grayingham, made for the purposes of a lawsuit in 1450, shows: the annual tithe yield for half the rectory was on the average two quarters of corn, two quarters of rye, twenty quarters of barley, ten quarters of peas, four quarters of oats, twelve lambs, six stones of wool, milk and calves worth four shillings and sixpence, and hay worth eighteenpence.

It is hardly surprising that special agents had often to be appointed to collect tithe, and special buildings acquired in which to house them. Such 'tithe barns' were to be particularly necessary where religious houses owned many churches: two-thirds of the demesne tithe of Rigsby, for example, were given to the nuns of Stixwold "with a toft in the vill in which they can lay the tithe." Even more important to religious houses, where it was possible, was to persuade their parishioners, often it seems with difficulty, to ease the burden of collection by paying money in lieu of tithe. Post-reformation examples of ancient tithe 'compositions' suggest that this may often have been done, but only one example, made apparently in the mid-fourteenth century, is known to the writer. By this the parishioners of Friskney agreed with the Gilbertine houses of Bullington and St Katherine's, who were rectors of the parish, to pay twopence for each quarter-acre of meadow in lieu of tithe hay.[21]

[20] DLC, 270; Neilson, *Terrier of Fleet*, p. 43; BM Cott. Vesp. E xx, f. 222; LRS 5, pp. 141, 169.
[21] Reg. 20, f. 7; BM Add. 46701, f. 57; BM Add. 32101, f. 50v.

Other and even more acute problems were raised by tithe collection and there was much litigation about it from the twelfth century onwards. Much of the trouble was caused by the gifts of tithes of the demesne, which many Norman lords made in the century or so after the Conquest to Norman religious houses. A good example of the situation created by these gifts is found at Torrington, where William Mustel, granting to Bullington Priory all the tithes of the parish, specifically excepts "two sheaves [i.e. two-thirds] from my ploughs from the land I cultivate myself, of wheat, beans, and peas, which the monks of Angers have." There were inevitably disputes when these excepted demesne tithes were claimed, especially after the English possessions of French monasteries were confiscated by the Crown and regranted to an English owner. As early as 1238 the canons of Bridlington, as rectors of Edenham, and the monks of Westminster took to the papal court their dispute about the demesne tithe of Elsthorpe. Parishes like Edenham, with their many subordinate chapelries, were continual sources of trouble and Bridlington spent much time and money in establishing its claims to demesne tithe at Elsthorpe and Grimsthorpe.[22]

It was often very hard, in an area of small, closely settled parishes, or in parishes of extensive settlement, to decide on which side of a parish boundary people lived, and, consequently, to whom their tithe should be paid. At Deeping it was found necessary in 1299 to define the boundaries between the two parishes of St Guthlac and St James. The boundary ran in part:

"Namely from Robert of Wryde's ditch, on the path going north through Grimeston, as far as the ditch opposite Andrew Marsh's house... St Guthlac is [also] to take tithe in Northmede, from all the land bordering the headlands on both sides, as far as the moor called Peyntourland, and from Lenge headland up to Caresdyk, and from each side of Lambard Hefdlond and in Longefurlong to the meadow and the marsh."

Many fourteenth- and fifteenth-century boundary definitions were concerned with the tithe of land recently brought into cultivation, where no exact line had ever been known. Leadenham and Fulbeck, Holbeach and Whaplode, and Tattershall and Kirkby on Bain all had troubles of this sort. Further difficulties were caused by the claim of the Cistercian order to exemption from tithe payments on their newly reclaimed land, the area of which was extensive in Lincolnshire. The thirteenth century saw many disputes on this topic, in which they successfully established their rights: Kirkstead, for example, was able to do this for its grange at Linwood in Kesteven, and Vaudey for its assarts in Eden-

[22] *Brid. Cart.*, pp. 419–20.

ham.²³ Meanwhile, less dramatically, and more cheaply, annual parochial processions at Rogationtide, of which more will be said later, served the eminently practical purpose of defining the tithe-paying area.

The definition of the parochial area was equally important to secure that part of the church's income which derived from the offerings of its parishioners. There were many disputes about offerings made in manorial chapels, and in chapels on bridges or on a great road which lay between two parishes. Most ordinations by the bishop of private chapels safeguard very strictly the right of the parish church to the offerings made there, and similar clauses were included in the licences of dependent chapels within a parish. At a later date, when the friars were preaching and acting as confessors in many town parishes, the mainspring of the incumbents' case against them was their appropriation of the penitents' offerings, which belonged to their parish churches. Disputes about burials in places other than the parish, and insistence on the duty of burials in the mother parish of corpses from outlying hamlets, have the same origin. It is hardly surprising that in 1349 the surviving inhabitants of Stragglethorpe should have complained to the bishop during his visitation of the difficulties they had experienced in carrying corpses through the floods, during the recent pestilence, for burial at the mother church of Beckingham.²⁴

The offerings thus claimed fall into several distinct categories. There were in the first place the so-called voluntary offerings made during mass at the three major festivals of Christmas, Easter, and Whitsuntide, at the church's dedication feast, and often, also, at All Saints. At Deeping St James these were threepence at Christmas, twopence at Easter and Whitsuntide, one penny at St James and All Saints. For other sacraments, burials, marriages, and churchings one penny was also paid; baptisms were free. Since Anglo-Saxon times there had also been two compulsory payments required from parishioners, wax-scot and soul-scot. Wax-scot (*ceragium*) was an annual levy which supposedly supported the lights of the church and which varied in amount. Soul-scot, corpse-present, or mortuary, was a gift customarily made at each burial by the successors of the deceased. Local custom had fixed this, long before the time we are discussing, but it often took the form of the dead man's best beast. The sacrist of Peterborough claimed this, as owner of Scotton, when John Neville died there in 1328: "The executors agreed that the Sacrist was entitled to John's best horse, saddled and bridled, but because his best horse was not good enough for so great a lord as the abbot, they agreed to give the sacrist an additional forty shillings . . ." From Sir Philip

---

²³ BM Harl. 3658, f. 9; Reg. 8, f. 6v; Reg. 12, f. 95v; LRS 58, pp. 303–6; BM Vesp. E xviii, f. 39v; *Brid. Cart.*, p. 416.

²⁴ Reg. 9, f. 36.

Neville's executors, after his burial at Scotton in 1362, a fully armed horse was claimed, but one hundred shillings were paid instead.[25]

The range of offerings, and the difficulties caused by uncertainties about parish boundaries, are well illustrated in a composition made in the mid-twelfth century between the incumbents of Barkston and Honington and the priory of Stixwold about the offerings of the priory's tenants in their grange at Honington. All baptisms and churchings were to take place at Honington; after a death, the first bequest (the mortuary, that is) was also to go to Honington, where the burial was to take place, but a second bequest was to be made to Barkston. The husband and wife from each house were to go to Honington to confession in Lent, to pay wax-scot there at Easter and Candlemas but at Barkston at All Saints, and to visit the church at Honington with their offerings at Easter and on the patronal festival of St Wilfred, though their households might go to Barkston.[26]

These offerings were collected everywhere, but many parishes had in addition their own customs, often associated with Easter. Thus the payment to the church at Easter, when the bishop consecrated the holy oils, of 'chrism pennies' was forbidden by Bishop Robert de Chesney as an abuse. Oliver Sutton, however, was concerned to maintain other "laudable" local customs, perhaps at the incumbents' request, when he visited Kelstern and Bradley in 1295, and he particularly enforced, at Ranby and Kirkby-on-Bain, a custom called 'meinport', known also in Bishop Norton, by which women brought gifts of bread to the church at Easter. The Easter offerings do perhaps look a little like paganism; certainly John Buckingham thought so when in 1396 he forbade a long-established Nettleham custom by which hard-boiled eggs and "swine's flesh called bacun" were brought to the church on Easter morning for blessing and later distributed to the parish. Old customs die hard and Nettleham incumbents were in trouble later for selling cakes called 'flauns' to their people at Easter. The enterprising, or plainly unscrupulous, incumbent could exploit the whole system of offerings very profitably, if he chose. No doubt the scandalous drinking feasts called 'church-ales', which Grosseteste forbade in 1239, were in essence compulsory sales to parishioners, and a vicar of Langtoft later in the same century was found to be successfully demanding double and treble offerings at funerals, churchings, and weddings.[27]

The religious needs of the settled population were reasonably well served, by the end of the twelfth century, by this system of parish

[25] BM Harl. 3658, f. 44; LH 4, p. 139; LAO Asw 2/1/10.
[26] BM Add. 46701, f. 102.
[27] BM Vesp. E xx, f. 38; LRS 48, pp. 149–50; LRS 60, pp. 55, 140; Reg. 12, f. 450; LH 2, no. 10; Counc. & Syn. I, 274; LRS 60, p. 190.

churches and dependent chapels, but travellers, merchants, and the frequenters of markets and fairs were overlooked by it. So were the pioneers of land reclamation, living in booths or shacks out in the fen, far down the sea-marsh, or on the wild heathland, and those who settled, for the sake of employment or trade, at the gates of the Cistercian monasteries, in areas which were then very far from civilization. To meet the needs of all these people there grew up, outside the parochial system, a number of chapels, some of which were clearly for temporary accommodation only. Some, often dedicated to St Thomas Beckett (as at Amcotts, and Wyberton marsh) or St Leonard (as at Farlesthorpe and Holme-in-Beckingham) began as private chapels founded by reclaiming lords in new territories during the twelfth century. A chapel on Brakenholme island, far out in Farlesthorpe marsh, for which Louth Park Abbey assumed responsibility in 1207, was like this, and in such a remote spot can hardly have lasted long. The chapel of St James Rodemill, which Robert son of Turketin gave to Newhouse Abbey about 1150, lay on the Witham at the boundary between Bassingham and Norton Disney, and was clearly intended to serve the small community gathered about the watermill there.[28]

But the process was continuous, for the hermitage of St Katherine at Saltfleethaven in Skidbrook, which was founded about 1337, marked a stage in the seaward spread of the parish; and the chapel in Fulstowmarsh (Marshchapel), to which gifts were already being made in the late thirteenth century, was a comparable case. All of these seem to have been the work of laymen living in the newlands, but many new chapels can be attributed to monastic founders. Chapels were built to serve the resident lay communities and travellers, at the gates of Revesby, Kirkstead, and Louth; the Hospitallers founded chapels in their reclaimed land at Swinderby Moor (1378) and Eagle (1407), and the Templars had set up a chapel of St John in Aslackby, which was still served in 1514.[29]

Many of these chapels were intended at first to serve only an outlying monastic community and its lay servants, and have left little trace in records, unless they so expanded as to become a threat to nearby parishes. One such was the chapel in the Bury St Edmunds settlement on Sailholme in Wainfleet, which lay on a site to the south of Salem Bridge, where the A154 road now crosses Wainfleet Haven. This island of land had been given by Matthew de Praeres to the monks of Bury about 1165, with turf to heat any buildings they erected on it. By 1184 a chapel had been built in Sailholme, and its priests were forbidden to exercise parochial

[28] PRS 29, no. 228; DLC, p. 230.
[29] Chantry Cert., no. 42; LRS 5, p. 177; Reg. 8, f. 45; LAASRP IV, 1951–2, p. 37; Reg. 7, f. 85; E. Venables, *Chronicon Abbatie de Parco Lude*, Horncastle, 1891, p. 13; LRS I, p. 220.

duties outside it, in the parish of Wainfleet St Mary, which belonged to Stixwold Priory. In 1256 no monks were resident in Sailholme, and the chapel was adjudged to belong to the mother church of Wainfleet St Mary, whose chaplain kept the key. A century later it was ruinous, but bids to restore it, after the encouragement of a series of miracles, seem to have succeeded, and it was still in existence in 1527. Another chapel, on a similar site in the same parish, St John Baptist at Holme, is recorded only once, but the chapel of St Thomas Northolme, in Kyme Priory's parish of Wainfleet All Saints, seems to have survived until the mid-seventeenth century.[30]

During the Middle Ages, any large community, wherever sited and however temporary, might reasonably expect to have daily mass said for its benefit. This explains the need for manorial chapels to be in use during the lord's residence, for the castle chapels at Bolingbroke and Bytham, and, even more, for the market chapels. On Stow Green near Threekingham, where from the mid-thirteenth century Sempringham Priory held a fair, the remains of a chapel could still be seen in 1791. At Castle Carlton the chapel of St John served a market set up there about 1230 by Robert Lupus, but it, and the market too, disappeared long before the Reformation. It seems very probable that the chapel of St James at Spilsby (now the parish church), was first founded by a Bek, living at Eresby during the thirteenth century, to serve his market there. In the same way Glanford Brigg, the new community which settled at the foot of the bridge over the Ancholme, and which lay in Wrawby parish, was served by a hermit in an oratory built in honour of Holy Cross and the Blessed Virgin. There were similar bridge chapels on Northdyke causeway in Stickney, at the west end of Holland Bridge causeway, and at Langworth Bridge, while the Dogdike chapel was evidently founded to serve a settlement which grew up around the terminus of a ferry over the Witham. Such small foundations were set up to satisfy the spiritual needs of groups lying outside the parochial system. They demonstrate not only the extent to which the medieval church was firmly entwined with every aspect of life, but also the continuing needs of the population for spiritual provision, which the chantries and gilds of later centuries would go much further towards satisfying.[31]

[30] D. Douglas, *Feudal Documents of the Abbey of Bury St Edmunds*, London, 1932, pp. 173, 181–2; BM Add. 46701, ff. 93, 47–8; Karl Horstmann, *Nova Legenda Anglie*, Oxford, 1901, II, p. 677; LNQ 3, pp. 46–7; Reg. 7, ff. 27v, 166; E. Oldfield, *A Topographical and Historical Account of Wainfleet and the Wapentake of Candleshoe*, 1829, p. 84.
[31] *Val. Eccl.* IV, p. 102; RA III, p. 346; Gomme, *Top. Hist.*, p. 180; LRS 11, p. 66; LRS 9, p. 205; Reg. 2, f. 45; Reg. 13, f. 19v; LRS 20, pp. 24–6; Reg. 12, f. 314; Chantry Cert., no. 112.

CHAPTER II

THE ADMINISTRATIVE PATTERN

THE network of Lincolnshire churches and chapels which we have just described lay within the much larger unit of the newly established diocese of Lincoln, which extended over nine and a half counties of eastern and midland England and inherited from its forbears many varying traditions and customs. When, in the late eleventh century, Bishop Remigius had removed his cathedral from Dorchester to Lincoln, the Bishop himself must have been the only unifying element in the diocese. Local custom, and the proprietary rights described in Chapter I, probably made his influence weak enough. The next four centuries, and particularly the first of them, were to see a spectacular increase in the strength of episcopal government everywhere, and nowhere was this more marked than in Lincoln. Here an elaborate administrative machine was quickly created, and by 1250 had assumed the form which it was to keep until the Reformation and beyond. The centre and fount of authority was the bishop, who was at once pastor, judge, and disciplinarian of his entire flock. He moved perpetually through his diocese, from one to another of his estates, or to London to his residence in the Old Temple.[1] Miss Hill has given us a vivid picture of Bishop Oliver Sutton, travelling rapidly on horseback with registrar and scribes, his armed escort of knights, and his baggage train which bore, among other necessaries for the journey, the records of the see. A century and a half later the itinerary of Bishop William Alnwick was even more breathless, and although both spent some time in Lincoln, it is clear that there were inevitably long periods when Lincolnshire never saw its bishop.[2]

It is important to remember that the medieval bishop's threefold functions embraced more than the pastoral duties symbolized by the crozier with which he was invested at his consecration. He was a landholder, holding much land for which his responsibilities were no different from those of other landholders. Much of his time and energy must have been absorbed by the management of his estates, the maintenance of his

[1] For a list of the medieval bishops of Lincoln, see Appendix 4.
[2] LRS 48, pp. xxvi–xxvii; LRS 14, pp. xxxiv–xxxv.

position as a landed magnate, and the performance of his feudal duties, especially the giving of counsel to the king. Equally, he was often required by the Crown to perform administrative duties connected with the collection of taxation from the clergy, or with the execution of writs relating to criminous clerks: many of the episcopal registers contain large sections devoted to royal writs connected with these and similar types of business, which suggest that much time and energy were absorbed by these secular duties.

The Domesday entries show that the bishop of Lincoln was a fairly important landowner in the county, with large estates at Sleaford, Stow, and Louth. He and his successors, like other great landowners, built many manor houses, palaces at Lincoln, Stow, and Nettleham, and a castle and a new town at Sleaford; they drained and reclaimed waste lands, assisted in the development and population of the growing commercial port of Torksey, and established a number of religious houses on their Lincolnshire estates. By the mid-thirteenth century, when much of this work had already been done, and a great survey of the episcopal estates was compiled, the bishop's position in the county seemed scarcely different from that of other landowners whose tenants owed suit of court and services of various kinds. The Louth tenants of bovates and half-bovates supplied forage for the bishop's horses whenever he came there between Martinmas (11 November) and the Invention of Holy Cross (3 May), while the men of Nettleham malted and brewed for his needs, and carried the liquor into the Palace cellars at Lincoln.[3]

The archbishop of York and the bishop of Durham were far more considerable tenants-in-chief of Lincolnshire land than the diocesan. Archbishop Thomas of York had indeed claimed after the Conquest not only that the northern half of the county lay within his province, but also that some of the episcopal manors, Stow, Louth, and Newark (Notts.), were the property of his see. The claim as to the province was settled in 1072 in favour of Lincoln by the Council of Winchester, while the more specific demands on properties were countered by King William II, who in 1093 "redeemed" the disputed lands from York as a favour to Remigius' successor Robert Bloet, who had been his Chancellor.[4] The area disputed with York, which formed the western half of Lindsey, seems to have been difficult of assimilation with the rest of the diocese. Remigius had originally divided his see into seven archdeaconries corresponding roughly to the shires which composed it: Lincoln, Leicester, Huntingdon (including Cambridge and north Hertford), Bedford, Buckingham, Northampton (including Rutland), and Oxford, but at some date before

[3] LRS 19, pp. 47–54; AASRP XXIV, p. 473, citing BM Cott., Ch. ii, 14, 1 & 2; Queen's Coll. Oxford ms. 366, ff. iii, iii*v*.
[4] RA I, p. 11.

the mid-twelfth century an "archdeacon of Lindsey" is found, whose territory was gradually defined as the former disputed area in the west of the county which would eventually be known as Stow archdeaconry, and which presumably was thought to need special attention from the diocesan authorities (Fig. 5).[5]

The pastoral function of the bishop was no easy one in an area the size of Lincoln, especially at the outset of our period, when conditions in the parish churches, and among the men who served them, must have been far from satisfactory. The proprietary nature of the church was a marked obstacle to the efficient performance of pastoral duties in the parochial units. Endowments and tithes of a parish church might be divided by its 'owner' among several incumbents or portioners, or granted, wholly or in part, to a religious house, which might, or might not, concern itself with the quality and behaviour of the clerk who served the church. If a lay owner retained control of the right to present clerks to his church, he did not necessarily ask whether the clerk he presented understood his duties and resided in the parish, provided that the sacraments were available when he and his family needed them: the clerk might be married, or keep concubines, regularly get drunk, and debauch his female parishioners, so long as the church was served. If most of the revenues of the parish churches were diverted to religious houses, only the parochial offerings remained for the priest; the type of clerk attracted by such poor remuneration was not surprisingly of a low educational and moral standard. At the same time the revenues of parish priests were further diminished by the proliferation of unlicensed private chapels, often in manor houses remote from the parish church, which provided mass and diverted offerings. Such chapels not only threatened the income of the parish priest but tended to depress still further the educational and economic standards of the whole priesthood, being served by cheap stipendiary clerks who could be removed at will. Clerical marriage presented its own problems, for churches passed from father to son and the removal of an unsatisfactory priest claiming to hold by hereditary right was extremely difficult. It is scarcely surprising that the bishops came to regard the practice as a serious obstacle to the welfare of the church and although there is little surviving evidence of their interference with it in the twelfth century, when many cases are known from charters and other sources, the thirteenth century saw its gradual extinction. As late as 1278, nevertheless, an incumbent of Thorganby confessed that he was married, and was deprived.[6]

The problem presented by the state of the parochial clergy, repeated in every archdeaconry of the diocese, was a formidable one for the bishops of the twelfth century. Standards of episcopal conduct had been

[5] RA IX, Appendix I, pp. 256–62, 'The Archdeacons of Stow'.   [6] LRS 20, p. 79.

THE ADMINISTRATIVE PATTERN 23

Fig. 5. *Ecclesiastical divisions of Lincolnshire*

rising steadily under the influence of the Hildebrandine reformation inspired by Pope Gregory VII and his associates, and the result is to be seen in the strenuous attack on the fundamental abuses of the parochial system which was mounted in the diocese from 1180 onwards. The bishops were greatly helped in their efforts to repress abuses and enforce suitable standards of service and conduct by the increasing influence of the papacy in England, and by the willingness of the Popes to support, with their whole authority, all measures of reform. They most often did this by decrees made in General Councils (especially those held at the Lateran in 1179 and 1216) which became law binding upon the whole church, and enforceable in the church courts. Individual bishops or their archdeacons might also submit difficult problems of law or discipline to the Pope and receive in reply authoritative judgments, as did Walter of Coutances in 1183-4.[7]

"Lucius III to Walter, bishop of Lincoln.

"It has come to our ears on your showing, that very often deans, archdeacons, precentors or others who hold ecclesiastical dignities, when they ask through deputies for letters of appointment to lesser benefices suppress the name of their dignity and call themselves by a plain name as if they had no title, and therefore you have asked for a rescript from us to show whether such concealment of title ought to prejudice their application. We therefore reply briefly to your consultation that as it is not our intention that persons who already have a considerable income should through our letters injure poor clerks in respect of minor benefices, we desire that letters in which the petitioner has suppressed the name of his dignity shall have no force.

"Concerning rectors of churches who are infected with leprosy in such wise that they cannot reasonably serve the altar nor go into church without grave scandal to those who are whole, we wish to keep your fraternity to this that a coadjutor be given to them who shall have the cure of souls and shall receive a suitable portion of the revenues of the church for his maintenance.

"Lastly we inform your fraternity by these present letters that if a case has been delegated to anyone who is a relation of the petitioner or of the advocate in the case, or is suspect for any other just cause, such a delegate can be rightly refused even though the matter had been delegated without appeal."

At the same time the twelfth century saw the full growth of the system of appeals to the papacy by which parties to suits in local church courts might appeal to the papal Curia for reconsideration of their sentences. Many appeals arose from attempts by the diocesan authorities and others

[7] LRS 47, p. 53.

to enforce improved standards upon local churches or to resist the vested interests of clerical inheritance. One example from the volume of Lincoln *decreta* collected by Dr Walther Holtzmann must suffice to indicate the sort of support provided by the papacy to the cause of reform. It concerns the church of Bilsby, the patron of which was the Augustinian priory of Markby, and into which the son of a previous incumbent had fraudulently inserted himself.[8]

"Alexander, bishop, servant of the servants of God, to our beloved son G., archdeacon of Lincoln, greeting and apostolic blessing:

"On the information of the prior and brethren of Markby it has come to our ears that R. priest of Bilsby, concealed the truth that he was the son of a priest when he came to us and got letters by fraud that he might be established as chaplain in the church of Bilsby which is known to belong to the aforesaid prior and brethren, in which his father ministered. Because indeed fraud or deceit ought not to be a protection to anyone we command your discretion by letters apostolic that within forty days of the receipt of these letters you shall diligently enquire into the truth of the matter, and if it is established before you that the aforesaid R. was born in the priesthood and that his father ministered in the same church, you shall then, despite our above-mentioned letters, remove him, all excuse and appeal notwithstanding, and you shall freely and peacefully restore the said church to the above named brethren."

The fundamental pastoral problems faced by the twelfth-century bishops of Lincoln inevitably recurred, in different forms, throughout the medieval period, but at no time were they again so acute. Later bishops had to concern themselves less with reforming the entire way of life of the clergy than with the removal of certain specific evils. Oliver Sutton was concerned with enforcing rigid obedience to the precepts of Canon Law, John Dalderby and Henry Burghersh spent much time on the problems created by the use of friars in parochial life, John Gynwell tried, not wholly successfully, to deal with non-residence and other evils which followed the Black Death, and John Buckingham was deeply concerned to stamp out superstitious usages and pagan practices.[9] At the same time these bishops and their successors were perpetually engaged in maintaining the standards set by their twelfth-century predecessors and in operating the machinery which they had created for the purpose.

The pastoral duty of the bishop made him responsible for the spiritual care of all his subjects, lay and clerical. It was incumbent on him to see

[8] LRS 47, p. 11.
[9] LRS 48, pp. 52, 60, 64, *passim*; Reg. 3, ff. 387 *et seq.*; Reg. 5, ff. 1–33; Reg. 8, 11, 12, *passim*.

that churches and chapels were regularly and continuously served by suitably qualified literate clerks. The first step to achieving this object was to insist that all clerks presented to benefices should be examined, approved, admitted, and instituted by the bishop or his representative. Those failing to convince the examiner of their literacy could be, and were, rejected, or 'referred', like the Eustace whom Hugh of Wells refused to institute to the benefice of Langton-by-Spilsby until he had spent five years in the schools, or Reginald Otley, who in 1274 was instituted to Bicker on condition that he kept there with him "a companion who will instruct him in letters, from whom he is to learn with all diligence," or Geoffrey de Fontinello who was to employ a priest to serve his parish of Broxholme until he was sufficiently instructed "*in ydyomati Anglicano.*"[10] An oath to reside in the benefice, or to provide a suitable substitute, was sometimes exacted from a clerk at institution and although episcopal and papal licences could, and did, permit non-residence for special purposes, such as education, or government service, the payment of a suitably qualified substitute was generally a condition of their acceptance. At the same time unlicensed non-residents might be deprived of their benefices, as was a rector of Scrivelsby in 1467, and regular reminders of the duty of permanent residence were issued throughout the period.[11]

It was equally necessary to protect those serving the cures, and to ensure that they received a suitable share of the revenues of the benefice. This was particularly necessary when monastic houses or other religious foundations, like the cathedral, had been given churches whose entire profits they monopolized, while causing the cure to be served only by a stipendiary who received a small wage, or an allowance of food and lodging, and could be dismissed at will. To prevent abuses, and ensure security of tenure and a reasonable income for the clerk, the later twelfth-century bishops of Lincoln devised a series of agreements by which stipulated pensions, or portions of the fruits of a benefice, with a suitable house, were set aside for a *vicar* or substitute for the rector. He was to be admitted and instituted formally by the diocesan, was to reside in the parish, and was to be incumbent in perpetuity, while the religious house which 'owned' the benefice appropriated to its own uses the remainder of the fruits. It has often been thought that such arrangements began in Lincoln only in the time of Hugh of Wells, after Pope Innocent III's decrees concerning them in the fourth Lateran Council, but a number of vicarages, in the sense of vicars' portions, were already ancient when they were approved and recorded by Hugh in his *Liber Antiquus*.[12] One such early

[10] LRS 3, p. 166; LRS 20, pp. 58, 96.   [11] Reg. 20, f. 86.
[12] C. R. Cheney, *From Becket to Langton*, Manchester, 1956, Appendix ii, pp. 182–5.

arrangement was recorded in 1185 by a vice-archdeacon of Lincoln in Bardney Abbey's church of Edlington: "Know that I found the church of Edlington totally in the possession of the Abbot and Convent of Bardney, apart from a vicarage of three marks which they have assigned to William of Stigedbi, clerk."[13]

One hundred and eighty Lincolnshire vicarages are recorded in the *Liber Antiquus* and it is clear that many of them had been arranged or approved by Hugh himself. The process continued, although more slowly, until the Reformation and as time went on more elaborate provisions are recorded. Thus when a vicarage was ordained for Revesby Abbey's church of Theddlethorpe in 1397, the monks undertook to allot to the vicar a portion of glebe, "shut in with dykes according to the custom of the country," and to build for him on the glebe a hall with two chambers over it and two cellars below, the whole to be twenty-four feet by eighteen, a kitchen, brewhouse, bakehouse, a stable for three horses and a sty for twelve pigs, all roofed with reeds or straw.[14] At the same time earlier arrangements were often revised in the light of changing economic conditions and, especially after the mid-fourteenth century, vicars are found appealing to the bishops for new ordinations or augmentations of their vicarages.

The bishops also controlled the church at parochial level by the performance of their duty to consecrate new buildings and altars and to seek out and consecrate those not previously so set aside for the service of God. Early examples of such consecrations by Robert Bloet (Thurlby-by-Bourne, 1112) and Alexander the Magnificent (Newhouse, St Martial's chapel, and Deeping St James) show that it was customary for the bishop to witness, and even to receive at the altar, charters of endowment made during the course of the ceremony, and it was evidently usual, as the surviving example at Old Clee shows, to commemorate the ceremony by an inscription in a prominent position.[15] Once the bishops began to insist on the need for consecration of all buildings where mass was celebrated, they could, and did, claim their right to license those who wished for celebrations in unconsecrated buildings. Licences for celebration occur throughout the medieval registers for new church buildings and for small quasi-temporary chapels. In 1359, for example Bishop Gynwell issued temporary licences of this sort for a new chancel at Covenham St Mary and a chapel at Osgodby in Lenton.[16] Parallel with these licences for celebration are those which permit the diversion to other uses of a consecrated building, or an alteration to its fabric, which modern dio-

---

[13] BM Cott. Vesp. E xx, ff. 32–32*v*, cited in RA VII, p. 206. [14] Reg. 12, f. 461*v*.
[15] Peterborough Swaffham Register, *loc. cit.*; DLC 313; BM Harl. 3658, f. 5; LRS 1, *passim*.
[16] Reg. 8, ff. 136*v*, 141.

D

cesan authorities know as a faculty. Only one example of the medieval exercise of this power seems to have survived in Lincolnshire, the licence of 1342 to transmit to Brant Broughton the stones of the disused chapel of Little Stapleford, but others must have occurred.[17] Other extensions of episcopal interest in pastoral care can be seen in the licences to unite poor or depopulated livings, which have been extensively used by the students of depopulation, and in the insistence that incumbents should not lease their tithes and glebe to a layman without the permission of the diocesan authorities.

Administrative action like this had, by the early fourteenth century, been welded into a compact system of which the neatly classified bishops' registers at Lincoln, with sections of institutions and licences of different sorts, are the outward evidence. Records of the ordinations of clerks fill large sections of these registers and bear witness to the bishops' fundamental duty to provide clerks for the service of the church by ordaining men to the priesthood. Until the provisions of the Council of Lyons of 1273 made it necessary for beneficed clerks to proceed to the priesthood within twelve months of their institution there had been many cases of incumbents who remained in minor orders until their death, leaving to a hired curate those duties of their benefice which could be discharged only by a priest. The same decree enjoined a stricter observance of the canonical age for ordination, and from this time on there are many signs that bishops were requiring proofs of age before ordaining a man, and enforcing more strictly other requirements such as celibacy, legitimacy, and freedom from physical disabilities.

Actions of this type were usually taken as part of the regular business of the see, once they had become familiar, but acquiescence in them could only, in the first place, be assured by a public announcement. Many of the measures were, as we have seen, based on the Canon Law and backed by papal authority, but still they had to be made known as such before they could be implemented, while others, devised to meet particular local needs and problems, required specific publication in the area where they would apply. The means of publication varied considerably at different times: there might be a solemn legislative pronouncement in a meeting known as a synod, visitations might be accompanied by series of precepts or injunctions from the bishops, embodying their orders, or an injunction on a single subject might be embodied in a mandate sent out to rural deans for publication in the churches of their deaneries.

The synod was a consultative assembly of the clergy of a diocese, which evolved from the body of priestly helpers who surrounded the bishops in earlier times. Once at least, in the diocese of Lincoln in the

[17] Reg. 7, f. 20.

twelfth century, the laity seem also to have been present, to witness a grant to Stixwold Priory, but this was obviously unusual.[18] In Lincoln the synod was used from the twelfth century onwards for a variety of pastoral and judicial purposes, and it was still evidently active in 1387 when John Buckingham convoked it to discuss a dispute between two claimants for the archdeaconry of Lincoln, and to announce the relaxation of a sequestration on all clergy of the archdeaconry.[19] It seems unlikely that a synod of the entire diocese of Lincoln can ever have been held, and the early meetings recorded are clearly for the clergy of a single archdeaconry. Bishop Alexander, for instance, successfully asserted his right to hold an assembly in Peterborough Abbey "as they are used to be held in other parochial [i.e. leading] churches of the diocese." The Peterborough meeting was presumably intended for the Northampton clergy and before 1166 Robert de Chesney presided at a general synod at Lincoln where a grant of land to Kirkstead Abbey was recognized, which was obviously intended for the two Lincolnshire archdeaconries. Similar meetings are said to have been held about 1186 by St Hugh, for the announcement of "certain precepts and injunctions," throughout the diocese.[20]

The early statutes of the cathedral make it clear that two synods had been held there annually, from some distant period, on the morrow of Trinity Sunday and after Michaelmas, when seats were prepared for them by the cathedral carpenters. Payment for this work was to be made by the archdeacon of Lincoln, who was clearly associated very closely with the synodal organization, "by whomsoever the synod is celebrated, be it the bishop, the archdeacon, or the official."[21] A letter of excuse sent by the Master of Nuncoton Priory to William de Thornaco, archdeacon of Lincoln after 1219, seems to show that synods, presided over by the archdeacon on the bishop's account for all the clergy in the county, were regular events. This is borne out by Bishop Buckingham's statement during the dispute of 1387 that for various reasons the holding of synods had been long deputed to the archdeacons, who nevertheless acted with the bishop's authority, and whose duty it was to transmit to him the payments they collected from the clergy during the synods.[22] A truly archidiaconal assembly seems to have been known as a 'provincial chapter' and to have been held outside Lincoln: there is evidence that one such was held for Stow at West Halton in the last fifteen years of the

[18] C. R. Cheney, *English Synodalia*, 2nd edn, Oxford, 1968, Introduction; BM Add. 46701, f. 69v.

[19] Reg. 12, ff. 341v, 349.

[20] C. R. Cheney, *From Becket to Langton*, p. 143, citing RA I, p. 36; *Gesta Henrici* I, p. 357; BM Cott. Vesp. E xviii, f. 82v.

[21] LCS I (Black Book), p. 293.   [22] Bod. ms. Top. Linc. d. 1, f. 43; Reg. 12, f. 239v.

twelfth century, where arrangements about the patronage of churches in which Nuncoton was interested were ratified by Mr Alexander the archdeacon.[23]

The synod was used by the bishops to carry out their pastoral, disciplinary, and judicial work. They used it for the hearing of important cases between parties, and for the publication and recording of grants, compositions, and other outstanding public acts. Most of our evidence for this sort of activity comes from monastic cartularies and belongs to the mid-twelfth century, when donors offered a knife on the altar before the whole synod in token of their grant, or made their gift into the hands of the presiding bishop or archdeacon.[24] There is no direct record at any time of a bishop personally announcing to his synod any code of legislation, apart from St Hugh's activities, but a single statute might well be published at the synod. As late as 1397 John Buckingham forwarded to "synods, chapters, and honourable meetings" in the diocese statutes ordering a weekly commemoration of St Hugh, and denouncing unregistered collectors.[25] Moreover the president, whoever he was, used the sermon, with which the proceedings opened, for a series of general pastoral exhortations; and one such example, composed, but possibly not delivered, by Robert Grosseteste, has been preserved.[26] There is no sign at Lincoln that actual detection and correction of offenders took place in the synod, as it is known to have done elsewhere: possibly the early development in the diocese of a system of visitation, which performed such functions considerably more efficiently, made this unnecessary. On the other hand, cases of dispute between parties about matters like tithe must often, at first, have been heard and settled in the synod.

As the episcopal administration became more elaborate, much of the judicial business passed to regularly constituted courts, and the pastoral duties of exhortation and correction were performed during the visitation, in which injunctions and a sermon soon played an important part. Meanwhile the public record of gifts and agreements before an assembly of collective witnesses can no longer have been necessary when a diocesan registry, modelled distantly on the papal pattern, contained registered documents embodying such acts, and a staff of notaries public was able at any time to produce authenticated copies for public use.

The more complicated legal problems, once submitted to the collective judgment of the synod, were increasingly heard in private by the bishops themselves, or their legally qualified advisers or auditors, to whom some business was deputed. Difficult matrimonial suits, especially those which involved parties of distinction or raised awkward legal problems, all

---

[23] Bod. ms. Top. Linc. d. 1, f. 15.
[24] BM Add. 46701, f. 69v; LRS 18, p. 5; BM Cott. Vesp. E xvIII, f. 82v.
[25] Reg. 12, f. 387.   [26] *Counc. & Syn.* I, p. 266.

cases concerning the discipline of clerks, heresy, and many of the tithe disputes which turned on parish boundaries and the status of parochial chapels, were already by Bishop Sutton's time determined by the bishop or his advisers in his 'court of audience'. Often the bishops acted as arbitrators, as when St Hugh judged between rival heirs at Saleby. Their decisions in tithe disputes, like those which ended in the definition of the boundaries between Holbeach and Whaplode, or Old Sleaford and Kirkby Laythorpe, were of this nature.[27] Matters like this were dealt with wherever the bishops chanced to be, and were recorded in their registers along with all their other business; only in the fifteenth century did the auditors begin to keep a separate record of their proceedings.[28] In much the same way the bishops and their auditors began to hear and prove the wills of the clergy and prominent lay people of the diocese, and to record their acts and copies of the wills in the episcopal registers. Alfred Gibbons published a selection of such wills proved before the bishops, which included wills of cathedral dignitaries, wealthy incumbents, local noblemen, and leading citizens of Lincoln, Boston, and Stamford.[29]

More commonplace disputes about matters belonging to the episcopal jurisdiction, such as tithe and church property, as well as the straightforward probate of the wills of lesser laymen, soon came to be deputed by the bishops to an official, who, from the late twelfth century onwards, acted for them in certain types of business under a permanent commission, and who by the mid-thirteenth century was holding regular courts or 'consistories' for their despatch. Records of these courts were in existence in Oliver Sutton's time, and Professor Morris has published a sole survivor from a slightly later period, but for the most part the official's importance can scarcely be appreciated from the remaining records. Something can be inferred from a document of about 1450 preserved by the continuator of the Crowland chronicle in which a dispute about the ownership and nature of a chapel founded in the waste at Baston was resolved by the testimony of Richard Dyklon, "president of the consistory of Lincoln," to the endowment and consecration of the chapel, and to the order that its dedication was to be celebrated on the festival of St Anne.[30]

The size of the diocese made it difficult, and indeed virtually impossible, for one man to be responsible in one consistory court for all the legal business likely to arise, and before 1300 officers known as 'commissaries'

[27] *Magna Vita*, II, pp. 20-3; BM Add. 5845, f. 48; Reg. 8, f. 96.
[28] A. H. Thompson, *English Clergy*, pp. 206-46; LRS 61, *passim*.
[29] *Early Lincoln Wills*, privately printed, Lincoln, 1888.
[30] C. Morris, 'A Consistory Court in the Middle Ages', JEH XIV, 1963; H. T. Riley, *Crowland Chronicle*, Bohn Classics, 1854, p. 414.

were holding courts in each of the archdeaconries and dealing with what in a smaller diocese would have gone to the official's consistory. In the same way testamentary business grew so much, and the diocesan authorities attached so much importance to it during the thirteenth century, that the administrative official called the 'sequestrator' was deputed in each archdeaconry to collect all wills for probate.[31]

Pastoral exhortation, and the issue of instructions and rules of conduct, which had once been heard in the synod, continued to form part of episcopal government. Now, however, they were embodied in mandates sent by the bishops for publication to archdeacons, rural deans, or parish priests. Thus did Richard Fleming communicate to his subjects a mandate forbidding barbers and merchants to operate on Sundays and feast days, "wherever markets and fairs are customary, and especially at Sempringham, Holbeach, and Le Merschechapel."[32] Denunciations by the bishops of breakers of sanctuary, and of those who interfered with church property, refused to pay tithe or take part in Whitsun processions, or failed to serve their cures are particularly common during the social upheavals of the later fourteenth century. Two centuries before, the major problems of episcopal legislators had been survivals of paganism, commercialization of the sacraments, 'church-ales', and churchyard fairs, and denunciations of these evils recurred until the end of the fifteenth century, along with condemnations of specific "new" evils, like the revival about 1360 of the old Lincolnshire heresy of observing Saturday as a feast day.[33]

Parallel with exhortations and orders like this the diocese of Lincoln developed from the early thirteenth century a machinery for the oversight of its lay and clerical subjects and for the discovery and correction of their faults, which has come to be known as 'visitation'. So far as this procedure is concerned with religious houses discussion of it can be postponed until later, but the dealings with secular clergy and laymen require some comment here. It seems certain that in the late twelfth century, alongside the clerical synods, there grew up a system of meetings of clergy and people, in small convenient groupings, to which the bishops or their representatives came, and where inquiry was made into faults and the guilty were punished. Grosseteste describes very clearly what happened at his visitations:

"After this I began to go about my diocese, into each of the rural deaneries, causing the clergy of each deanery to be summoned together at certain times in certain places, and warning the lay people to appear on

---

[31] C. Morris, 'The Commissary of the Bishop in the Diocese of Lincoln', JEH x, 1959; D. M. Owen, 'A Lincoln Diocesan Book', LAASRP x, 1963-4.
[32] Reg. 22, f. 229.   [33] Reg. 7, f. 49.

the same days, for the confirmation of their children, to hear the word of God preached and to make their own confessions. When all were assembled I myself preached the word of God to the clergy and a friar preacher or minor spoke to the laity and afterwards four friars heard confessions and assigned penances. When on that and the next day I had finished confirmation I and my clerks went on with inquiries, corrections, and reforms, as is fitting for a visitation."[34]

Professor Cheney has suggested that it was in meetings such as this, rather than in the synods, that Grosseteste's diocesan legislation was announced. Later, in the fourteenth and fifteenth centuries, the sermons preached at the visitation were a recognized vehicle for the reiteration of such legislation and of suitable moral precepts for the guidance of the clergy.[35]

There is not much evidence for the detailed machinery of episcopal visitation before the early sixteenth century, but it is possible to see in the registers of Oliver Sutton and his fourteenth-century successors how the bishops, having received during the visitation reports as to things wrong in a parish (known as *detecta*) from the clergy, churchwardens, or specially appointed inquisitors, would decide which matters called for further action (*comperta*) and would proceed to immediate trial and condemnation, or else to further inquiry. Thomas Bek's register has a whole series of orders for further inquiry into matters like the missing fabric fund of Northolme chapel in Wainfleet, or the failure of the abbot and convent of Torre (Devon) to arrange for the distribution to the poor of their appropriated church of Skidbrook of corn which "according to episcopal constitution and long-established custom" was their due, which had come to his notice during a visitation of north-east Lindsey in 1342-3.[36] Along with such cases there were persistent adulterers and fornicators, reluctant executors of wills, infrequent attenders at church, witches, slanderers, and scolds to be judged, and if found guilty, punished. A good list of offenders meriting excommunication, which was proclaimed throughout the diocese in the vulgar tongue after the London council of 1433, illustrates the business likely to be heard in a visitation:[37]

    1. Those taking away the rightful property or rights of a church, or church court
    2. Disturbers of the King's peace
    3. Perjurers
    4. Slanderers
    5. Those failing to execute royal writs
    6. Those stealing church property
    7. Breakers of sanctuary

[34] *Counc. & Syn.* I, p. 265.   [35] Owst, *op. cit.*   [36] Reg. 7, ff. 27v, 62.
[37] Reg. 17, f. 172v.

8. Witches, usurers, simoniacs, sacrilegious persons, heretics, lollards, and those who sheltered them.

The bishops cannot always have conducted all their visitations in person, even if they attempted to visit no oftener than every three years, and there is no doubt that they used the commissaries, and many *ad hoc* auditors, for the purpose. Much of the judicial business brought to the visitation could not be decided summarily. If investigations were to be made and witnesses sought and produced, special sessions of the consistory, or prorogued (extended) visitation sessions were used for them. In either case a variety of assistants was called for, most of them with legal training.

At first there was about the bishops a group of men learned in the law, a council, such as St Hugh is said to have gathered on his first coming to the diocese, most of them members of the cathedral chapter. Soon, however, individual men begin to do specific jobs, to 'specialize', as it were, in certain branches of work. The earliest to emerge was the official who in the early thirteenth century is found not only presiding in the consistory, but also witnessing institutions and other episcopal acts, or performing administrative acts such as the assessment of pensions payable by the appropriator of a parish church.[38] The strict observance in English church courts of the procedural rules of the papal courts, especially after the fourth Lateran Council, had made it compulsory to conduct all court business by authenticated written acts. This led to an expansion of the episcopal 'civil service' to include notaries public, who were qualified to authenticate and register such acts, and one of whom was to become in due course the registrar or scribe of the acts, in the courts. These, and a number of other *iuris periti* (men skilled in the law) formed the backbone of the episcopal service: they heard and decided cases on commission from the bishops; they held permanent appointments as commissaries, sequestrators, or auditors of causes; they often began as pleaders (proctors) in the consistory courts of the diocese, and very often they had migrated with the bishops from some other diocese.

These men of legal training formed the immediate entourage of the bishops, but within the diocesan administration there were other, more independent, persons, on whose assistance the bishop might rely, but who might well threaten his powers. The archdeacon, "the eye of the bishop," was inevitably an important figure in a diocese so large as Lincoln, and he was undoubtedly the bishops' principal channel of communication with their subjects, and a person of great power, until the

---

[38] Magdalen Coll., Oxford, mun. II, 14 (K.M.); BM Cott. Vesp. E xx, f. 197*v*; LRS 11, p. 77.

episcopal commissaries emerged. So we find Robert of Hardres issuing a licence for sermons to be preached, soliciting contributions to the repair of Nordyke causeway in Stickney, and Robert of Hayles acting as the official.[39]

The archdeacon of Lincoln in the twelfth century often discharged his duties by a deputy, the vice-archdeacon, whom we find hearing a tithe cause, certifying a proof of age, and inducting clerks to benefices.[40] Even when the commissaries were well-established organs of episcopal policy the archdeacons continued to be used as the first stage in the transmission of episcopal injunctions to the parishes, but their primary business was, and continued to be, the parochial clergy and the property of the churches. It was they who inducted approved clerks into corporeal possession of benefices, in obedience to mandates from the bishops. It was they who surveyed, and reported on, the state of church fabrics and property, and conducted visitations for the purpose. At the visitations the churchwardens appeared and took oaths to perform their duties faithfully, defects in fabric and furniture were noted, and criminals presented and punished. The records of such a visitation, held in the archdeaconry of Stow in 1287, have by chance survived among the chapter muniments, and the entry made for Hibaldstow is characteristic of the work done in these visitations.[41]

"Defects of the church: it lacks two grails, a processional, two psalters, a troper, an antiphoner, two frontals, two surplices, two rochets, a festal vestment with two towels, a chrismatory, a processional cross with a painted staff, two phials and a thurible. There are also wanting iron bars for the chancel window and for the little cupboard where the body of Christ is put. Rain falls between the chancel and the church. The eastern gable of the chancel should be reconstructed and almost all the books rebound. They are ordered to make good the defects before Michaelmas 1287."

This was work done in conjunction with the bishops, but in Lincoln, as elsewhere, the archdeacons set themselves up as rivals of the bishops, especially in jurisdiction. Attracted, no doubt, by the profits of court keeping, they attempted to draw business of all sorts into the courts they held, and because they were often easier to reach than the distant consistory, these courts were successful in securing a good many probate and small tithe cases, in addition to the work of correction resulting from their visitations. There is little evidence of rivalry between the episcopal and archidiaconal courts in Lincolnshire, although this is not true else-

[39] N. Neilson, *Terrier of Fleet*, London, 1920, pp. 154–5; BM Cott. Vesp. E xx, f. 266v.
[40] Wrest Park, f. 78v; BM Add. 46701, f. 102; *Brid. Cart.*, p. 355.
[41] LAO D & C Dij/64/2, no. 7.

where in the diocese, and the two sets of courts apparently existed side by side without trouble.

In the early twelfth century the parishes were arranged in administrative groups (deaneries) which corresponded very closely with the civil groupings known as wapentakes. Thenceforth communication between the archdeacon and the parish was generally made through a representative clergyman, a rural dean, who was used as an organizer and spokesman for the deanery. He convened the clergy of his deanery in chapters where collective witness was given to charters, and episcopal injunctions and archidiaconal mandates were read. At times in the thirteenth century, visitation and correction went on there too, perhaps in the manner of a monastic chapter, for it was in the chapter that the incumbent of Thorganby had confessed to his marriage.[42] Later on the chapter meetings were used chiefly to publish such announcements as Archbishop Arundel's constitution of 1409, which Bishop Repingdon ordered to be read "in all synods and chapters."[43] Though the chapter meetings had become empty formalities the rural deans had acquired many new functions, which made them important links in diocesan administration. It was they who were called on to serve, and to certify the service of, citations (summonses) in ecclesiastical courts, to publish schedules of excommunications, to conduct inquiries into the vacancy or dilapidation of benefices, to assess benefices for taxation, to collect money penances for transmission to the courts, and even to prove wills, where no legal difficulties were involved. It is hardly surprising that an unscrupulous dean, in a position of local influence, should abuse his powers. In 1382 Edmund, vicar of Saleby and dean of Calceworth, took forty shillings for corrections from Joan of Schorwood and Joan of Ulceby, and had altogether extorted £10 from the lay people of his deanery in the previous six years; in the same year Gregory, the dean of Manlake, was accused of extorting £20 in all.[44]

The diocesan administration, from the bishop down to the lowliest of officials, formed a vigorous, active, pervasive influence in the life of the county. It had come gradually to touch the lives of the inhabitants at so many points that, without the framework it provided, many of their activities would have seemed impossible. It is within this framework that we must now consider, in greater detail, the way in which the church performed its many functions.

[42] LRS 20, p. 79.   [43] LRS 57, p. 153.   [44] LRS 56, pp. 74, 157.

CHAPTER III

THE CATHEDRAL

THE ring given to the bishop at his consecration is often said to symbolize his marriage to his cathedral church, and the connection between diocesan bishops and the great churches in which their chairs were placed was undoubtedly a very close one. Such a church came to be thought of as the bishop's 'own' church, the 'mother church' of the diocese, in which, in the earliest times, he performed almost all his episcopal functions, and ministered to his flock, and where the clerks who served it with him formed his immediate family or council. In Lincolnshire itself, at the point where our study begins, there had been no episcopal church for the past hundred years, while the diocese was centred on Dorchester. There may of course have been memories of the earlier Lindsey cathedral at Caistor or Louth, or even in Lincoln itself, but they can have been only faint when in 1072 the new Norman bishop of Dorchester, Remigius, who had succeeded Bishop Wulfwig in 1067, was authorized by King William I to transfer his see from the small town of Dorchester to the ancient and important regional capital of Lincoln. Here he was to build a cathedral fit to be "the mother church of the whole diocese," and, to finance the building, he was given new properties, the large manors of Sleaford and Welton by Lincoln, and the churches of St Laurence and St Martin in Lincoln as well as the churches on the royal manors of Kirton Lindsey, Caistor, and Wellingore.

There was already at Lincoln a large church dedicated to St Mary which seems to have been the mother church of a considerable area (*parochia*) in Lindsey and Kesteven, the inhabitants of which made to it a traditional payment called 'Mariecorn'. The lords of many churches founded in this *parochia* made annual payments to St Mary of two-thirds of the tithe of their demesne lands, and it had been given, besides this, a number of estates throughout the county which were now to be grouped in a special fund, which was distinguished from the new endowments of the Norman bishops by the name of 'Old Minster Fee'.[1] This church, like the minsters of Beverley and Southwell, was probably served by a small body of clerks known as canons, who, while holding their property in common and living under a species of loose rule, were not bound by strict

[1] LCS Black Book, ff. 31 *et seq.*; RA I, p. 2; *Med. Lin.*, p. 67 *et seq.*

vows like those of the Benedictine monks. It seems likely that they were at most seven or eight in number; they would scarcely have sufficed for the needs of the cathedral of a large diocese; and Remigius raised their number to twenty-one and imposed on them an organization which would ensure that in his own absence the cathedral continued to function smoothly.

There is no certain evidence as to what rules Remigius laid down, or exactly how he divided the duties of the cathedral among his twenty-one canons, who were from this time known as the cathedral chapter. The main lines were undoubtedly laid down by the first half of the twelfth century, when Archdeacon Henry of Huntingdon recorded that the twenty-one canons included four dignitaries (*persone*): the dean, who was the leader or chairman of the chapter; the precentor, whose duty was to maintain the *Opus Dei*, the daily round of praise and prayer; the chancellor or secretary of the chapter; and the treasurer. Besides these the chapter included a deputy, or sub-dean, and the seven archdeacons (to be eight when Stow was created), who were the bishop's principal agents in diocesan matters. Soon the total number of canons rose to forty-two, and Alexander added two more. All of these dignities and canonries, except for the deanery, which was at first elective, were in the gift of the bishop.

The chapter very quickly developed customary rules by which its actions were governed; but it was not until the early thirteenth century that these were set down in writing, and nothing resembling an orderly and coherent body of regulations was known before the fifteenth century. At various times before this, however, *ad hoc* decisions made by the whole chapter had dealt with problems as they arose, and the principles thus agreed on had become binding on the chapter. One of the earliest of these was the division of the Psalter among the canons, each of whom recited daily the psalms assigned to his prebend, as the inscriptions on their stalls in the choir still bear witness. A similar decision was probably taken when the chancellor was entrusted with the care of the library; by about 1150, when Hamo became chancellor, he received and noted in the Great Bible of the cathedral a library of thirty-nine volumes, for which he was held responsible until he relinquished his office and handed them on to his successor.[2] In the same way the chancellor came to have responsibility for the flourishing schools at Lincoln, in which during the twelfth century teachers of law and theology lectured, and where, in the time of Giraldus Cambrensis, "theological study was more favoured than anywhere else in England." The chancellor was also concerned with a school in which grammar and singing were taught to promising young clerks, but not to the boys of the choir, for whom a separate provision

[2] R. M. Woolley, *Catalogue of the Manuscripts of Lincoln Cathedral Library*, Oxford, 1927, pp. v–vi.

was made. Other schools for the elementary education of clerks existed below hill in Lincoln and probably in such early centres as Barton, Caistor, Grantham, Louth, Partney, and Stamford. All of these schools eventually came under the supervision of the chancellor, who nominated their masters and exercised a vague control over them.[3]

We have seen that the cathedral clergy had from the earliest times provided a reserve of personnel and expertise on which the bishops could draw at need. As the chapter grew and developed it came to provide administrators, lawyers, and theologians, who could be used either in the detailed business of the diocese, as registrars, judges, commissaries for visitation, and so on, or in the teaching, preaching, and penitentiary work by which the medieval bishops endeavoured to elevate their flocks. At first the whole chapter acted as witnesses of the bishops' formal acts, but soon we find individual canons acting on their behalf as official, auditor of causes, or treasurer, instituting clerks to benefices, examining them before ordination, and receiving their confessions. St Hugh, it seems, gave fresh impetus to this by adding to the chapter a number of learned men:

"Such men gave the church of Lincoln a greater fame and reputation than that of any other in the whole world, and on them he conferred prebends and benefices whenever they fell vacant, and promoted to different ecclesiastical dignities and offices. He sought for them throughout England and even in other countries and the schools on the continent, and made them members of his cathedral chapter."[4]

Throughout the thirteenth century the chapter continued to be the primary source of lawyers and administrators for the diocese. The career of John of Schalby, the registrar and faithful servant of Oliver Sutton, and a member of the chapter for more than thirty years, is typical of many.

The whole chapter came also to have a formal and corporate place in diocesan affairs. During the twelfth century it witnessed as a body the bishops' solemn acts, such as St Hugh's arbitration in the dispute between St Gilbert and the lay brothers of Sempringham (1186-9).[5] At the same time it provided a setting of due solemnity for the public ceremonial which accompanied many of the gifts made to religious houses. Roger Basuin gave twenty acres of land in Bassingthorpe to the nuns of Stixwold "and this gift and grant he made in the church of St Mary, Lincoln, with a knife laid upon the altar there, in the presence of many clerks and laymen." At another time the chapter itself testified that "Thorald son of Ralf of Stixwold, and Gerard and William his sons, came into our

---
[3] K. Edwards, *English Secular Cathedrals in the Middle Ages*, 2nd edn, Manchester, 1968, pp. 187-8; VCH *Lincs.* II, 421-84.
[4] *Magna Vita*, I, p. 110.   [5] R. Foreville, *Le Livre de Saint Gilbert*, Paris, 1947, p. 82.

presence and laid in the hands of Humphrey the Subdean, for himself and all his kin, his entire claim and right to the lands held by the nuns in Stixwold."[6] Such events must often have occurred at the times when the synod was meeting in the cathedral, or the bishops were at Nettleham or Stow. Then, too, the cathedral provided a suitable setting for a solemn ceremonial such as St Hugh's funeral:

"On the sixth day of our journey we were already near, and when we arrived at the foot of the hill almost a mile outside the city, we were met by the kings of England and Scotland, the archbishops, bishops, magnates, abbots and nobles and an immense crowd of clergy and people, such as had scarcely ever been seen in England before this gathering. The king of Scotland who had a deep affection for Hugh, was so overcome that he could not approach the coffin, but remained behind weeping bitterly, although if his sorrow had been less intense he would have realized that he had more cause for rejoicing. The king of England and the rest of the magnates raised the illustrious load on to their shoulders. It was no small matter of congratulation for anyone to be granted the privilege of carrying the body of one whose merits could save from destruction the souls and bodies of those who rendered him this service and secure their admission into the kingdom of Heaven."[7]

In such a ceremony a leading place was obviously taken by the cathedral clergy, for they, with their prayers and devotions, their multitude of lights, "making night into day," their vestments and altar vessels, "the palls all of silk, the copes embroidered with gold, the reliquaries, crosses and copies of the sacred texts bound in gold and silver," were the visible expression of the devotion of the diocese to its great bishop.[8] So, in due course, when St Hugh was canonized, the eastern end of the cathedral was gradually adapted to serve as a shrine and a place of pilgrimage, to which devotion was paid throughout the diocese until the very end of the medieval period. Lesser 'unofficial' shrines, like those of Dalderby and Grosseteste, also added distinction and attracted pilgrims, so that by the mid-fourteenth century the cathedral had attained great importance as a devotional centre for the diocese and beyond it. Meanwhile it was used for synods, visitations, and ordinations, for the sanctifying of chrism (the baptismal oil consecrated by the bishop on Holy Thursday), the conduct of solemn processions of intercession, and the preaching of important sermons, for the city and county of Lincoln, at least.

The chapter's role in diocesan administration had gradually developed from the giving of counsel, and the witnessing of solemn grants, to the confirmation, by the addition of its seal, of many episcopal acts, especially

[6] BM Add. 46701, ff. 69v, 14.   [7] *Magna Vita*, II, p. 225. Plate II depicts this scene.
[8] LMP 2, p. 6.

those concerned with grants of land or of offices, and to the care of the spiritual duties of the bishops during vacancies of the see. This latter function, which the chapter had been claiming since the late twelfth century, in the face of opposition from the archbishops of Canterbury, was finally regularized in 1261 by a composition which allowed the chapter to submit to the archbishop the name of one of their number to act as official of the see whenever a vacancy occurred.[9]

The new church which Remigius set out to build was completed by 1092, in the style of the Conqueror's own church of St Étienne of Caen. Its west front, further embellished by Bishop Alexander, and encased by the later work of St Hugh, survives to show how imposing it must have seemed, and how worthy a centre for the new diocese.[10] It was not until Alexander began to enrich the west front, and replace the wooden roofs with stone vaults, that the new cathedral seems really to have captured the imagination of the people of the county. When in 1185 the church of Remigius and Alexander was almost wrecked by an earthquake, the work began again under the inspiration of St Hugh, who spurred on the subjects of his diocese to still further efforts by organizing regular offerings, granting indulgences, and founding a gild for the raising of a cathedral building fund. This was, as Canon Foster has said,

"especially the day of smaller men. On either side of the year 1200 there is a truly astonishing number of grants of land, often of very small pieces of land, to God and St Mary and the Church of Lincoln. A charter will state that a peasant has placed upon the altar of St Mary half an acre of land—no doubt by laying there a sod or some other sacramental token. In some charters God is cited as the first of the witnesses. Frequently these grants are the gifts of very humble people, peasants whose names prove them to be descendants of the Danish army which re-settled this county in 879."[11]

The original endowments of the cathedral and the gifts made in the twelfth and thirteenth centuries were by no means its only sources of income. There were, for example, the Pentecostals, or 'smoke farthings', paid during the Whitsun processions by each household in the diocese, in token of obedience to the mother church of the diocese. This was already a well-established custom in the time of Robert de Chesney, when it was laid down that, except in Lincolnshire, the processions and collections could be held not in the cathedral, but in suitable large

[9] *Cant. Adm.* I, pp. 170–1.
[10] LMP 2, pp. 6–7; for the latest survey of the architecture of the cathedral see Pevsner, *op. cit.*, and F. Saxl, 'Lincoln Cathedral: The Eleventh-century design for the West Front', *Arch. J.* CIII, 1946, pp. 105–18.
[11] A sermon for St Hugh's Day, 1932, cited in *Med. Lin.*, p. 112.

churches within the archdeaconries. An agreement by which the abbey of St Albans was allowed to appropriate to its own use the pentecostal offerings from some of the parishes in its neighbourhood tells us that the ancient days for pentecostal processions were the sixth day after the Ascension and the sixth day before Pentecost. St Hugh, and his successor William of Blois, found it necessary to order parish priests to arrange for the regular payment of the offerings by a representative from each household in the parish (possibly, it has been suggested, because of the increased need for money during the rebuilding of the cathedral). From then on pentecostals formed a regular item in the chapter's income, which the archdeacons transmitted to the treasury during the Pentecostal synod.[12]

Another source of income which originated in the late twelfth century under St Hugh's inspiration was the Works Chantry, which was founded to provide continual prayers for the souls of all benefactors of the cathedral fabric. These were not so much the donors of land as the testators all over the diocese who, throughout the medieval period, bequeathed money and jewels to "the red chest of the fabric," as automatically as they provided for their mortuary, for the tithes they had forgotten, and for the disposal of their own corpses.[13] These continuing bequests, as well as the offerings made at the shrines of St Hugh, show for how much the cathedral had come to stand in the religious life not only of the county, but of the whole diocese.

The financing of the new work at the cathedral led in the late twelfth century to the completion of a series of financial arrangements which were to remain almost unaltered until the nineteenth century. In the earliest days of the cathedral its estimates and revenues had not been separated from those of the bishops, and many of the early privileges and grants of land were made to "the bishop and St Mary of Lincoln." But the inconvenience of this arrangement and the need for a strong chapter gradually led to an apportionment of the estates between the bishopric and the cathedral. The cathedral estates seem almost at first to have been divided again, to form a Common Fund which met general expenses, and a series of prebends or endowments for the support of individual dignitaries and canons.

Some of these prebends included manors, or portions of manors, like the five which shared the great manor of Welton by Lincoln, but more of them received churches, or portions of tithes. Such parochial prebends often had residences in the parish, and were estates of considerable importance: at Glentham a taxation of dilapidations during a vacancy of the prebend about 1307 mentions a hall (ceiled) with a north porch; a

[12] RA I, p. 265; RA II, pp. 13-15, 58-60; Reg. 12 f. 339v.
[13] C. Wordsworth, *Notes on Medieval Services*, London, 1898, p. 302; A. F. Cirket, *English Wills 1498-1526*, Beds. Hist. Rec. Soc., XXXVII, 1957, *passim*.

chamber, a little chamber, a principal chamber and a private chamber; a bakehouse, kitchen, and servant's chamber; an ox-house, cow-house, hay-house, cart-house, and long sheepfold, all walled about with mud and stone walls, and all thatched.[14] Other poorer prebends depended for their income on pensions payable by the bishop: *Decem Librarum* and *Sexaginta Solidorum* are of this type. There were obviously vast differences in value, and a scale of preferences, among the prebends, and canons awaiting an endowment, without which they had no vote in chapter, might at first take one of the small pensions, only to exchange it for a more valuable manorial or rectorial prebend as soon as a vacancy occurred.

Finally, at some time before 1200 a Fabric Fund was set up. It not only received all the legacies and offerings specifically made to the fabric, but also came to be endowed with much land given by wealthy individuals for the financing of obits (prayers on the anniversaries of their day of death), or chantries, which provided daily masses for the soul of the founder. One example of this type of fabric endowment was a row of houses in Wigford, called St Andrew's Rowe, or Sutton rents, which originated in the obit of John of Sutton, citizen of Lincoln, and which remained as part of the fabric estate until it was commuted in the nineteenth century. When the *Valor Ecclesiasticus* was compiled in 1534 the Common Fund yielded, clear of all payments, £579 16s. 10⅞d., the Fabric Fund £575 7s. 2⅞d., and the Deanery £196 10s. 8d., while the prebends varied in value between £4 and £38.[15]

So many members of the chapter were engaged on the bishop's affairs, and were travelling about the diocese with him, as John of Schalby did, that from the earliest days of the cathedral there can rarely have been a full chapter in residence. Besides, the archdeacons must have been away in their 'provinces' for long periods, and the prebendaries had to attend to their prebendal estates. Then there were the clerks in royal service, for whom a prebend was a desirable endowment, and who might well be away in the exchequer or chancery for almost the whole of their time. Such men, in the manner of non-resident fellows, provided for a substitute, received the revenues of their prebends, and interfered scarcely at all in the chapter's domestic affairs.

Meanwhile, some fifteen or sixteen canons, to be reduced by the end of the fifteenth century to eight or nine, were in more or less continual residence. They lived in some state in the large and comfortable residence houses around the cathedral, the best surviving examples of which are, perhaps, the Chancery, the Sub-deanery, and Atherstone Place in Eastgate, part of which is now the Bishop's House. New and probationary canons were obliged to make a continuous residence of three years, after which they might, if they chose, continue as minor residentiaries for one-

[14] LAO D & C A/2/21, f. 8.   [15] LAASRP 6, pp. 118–20; *Val. Eccl.* IV, pp. 8–22.

third of the year only, or become greater residentiaries who were at Lincoln continually for thirty-four weeks and four days in each year. All residentiaries received from the Common Fund twelve pence daily and varying amounts of food during their residence, and were entitled to the benefits of obit payments, in money or food, if they attended the special obit and anniversary masses. Those making the greater residence were also entitled to a dividend of the surplus of the Common Fund, at each year's end, and to leases of the property of the Common, as they fell in.

The residents' duties were primarily the maintenance of divine worship, beginning with midnight matins, and going on through high mass and the canonical hours. All took their turn as hebdomadary (the canon who for one week at a time celebrated mass), and as ruler of the choir. Then there were the onerous posts of fabric master, auditor, and provost of the Common, which eventually passed annually from one to another of the greater residentiaries. All kept up a liberal hospitality, especially on entrance, when they "paid their footing" by giving bread and drink to all who were present, during their hebdomadary week, by giving breakfast daily to deacons and subdeacons, vicars, and bell-ringers, and at the greater feasts of the church's year.

Despite the numbers of residentiaries the burden of cathedral services was undoubtedly borne not by the canons, but by the lesser clergy. These were principally the vicars, or substitutes, of the canons, who partly supported them. These vicars were already important in cathedral worship by the end of the twelfth century. Oliver Sutton organized them in a self-governing, property-owning corporation, provided a common residence for them, with hall and kitchen, which survives on the south side of Minster Yard, and founded a hospital at St Giles to provide a refuge for them in illness and old age. The lesser clerks, known as 'poor clerks of the second form' or 'young vicars', who were still pupils in the chancellor's grammar school, also had a common hall endowed by Bishop Sutton, on the east side of Minster Yard.

From the late twelfth century onwards there were also many chantry priests who served a variety of minor altars in the cathedral and helped the vicars in choir. They were maintained out of the large chantry and obit funds accumulated by the dean and chapter, and some but by no means all of them were housed and regulated by the detailed statutes of corporations such as the Burghersh and Cantelupe chantries, in houses which survive today. The number and variety of the masses said by these priests are well illustrated by Canon Wordsworth, who calculated that in the early sixteenth century, between the three morrow masses said at five a.m. and high mass at ten or eleven, no fewer than thirty-seven masses were celebrated in the cathedral every day.[16]

[16] Wordsworth, *Medieval Services, passim.*

Finally there were twelve choristers, for whom Richard Gravesend in 1264 provided a master and a house, next to the present Chancery, and who attended a school of grammar and song provided by the precentor. Many of the vicars and other clerks in the employ of the cathedral served, outside their liturgical duties, as clerks, copyists, accountants, and schoolmasters, but their numbers could scarcely supply all the personnel required by the intricate, costly, cathedral establishment. There were an organist, vergers, bell-ringers, carpenters, sweepers, a glazier, the constable of the Close, a night watchman with a flute to mark the hours, a candle-lighter, searchers and watchers of the shrines, a tailor, a sempstress, a laundress, and many messengers, all, no doubt, with their assistants and 'servers'.

The cathedral's neighbourhood housed most of these people, and it soon became a densely populated area, with innumerable problems of administration and discipline. The endowment of the cathedral in the early twelfth century was accompanied by a grant of judicial autonomy, which virtually freed the dean and chapter, their manors and churches, and Minster Yard from all interference by the episcopal authority. Grosseteste, it is true, successfully re-asserted the bishop's right to visit the cathedral church, but the dean and chapter retained sole jurisdiction over the parishioners of churches which formed part of the cathedral endowment, such as Hainton and Heydour, and of the churches within the cathedral close (St Margaret and St Mary Magdalen).

Breaches of discipline among the vicars or poor clerks, choristers, or servants were punished by the chapter itself, and the outlying parishes were visited in an annual tourn conducted by the provost of the common, at which presentments were made, and punishments adjudged for lesser spiritual offences. Cases of tithe or defamation involving these same people were heard in the chapter's own court, before its auditor of causes, who also proved their wills. At the same time the dignitaries (notably the subdean in Kirton Lindsey) and some of the prebendaries had jurisdiction over the parishioners of their prebendal churches, where they held visitations, heard cases, and proved wills on their own account.

This ecclesiastical privilege was matched by a civil autonomy, which apparently existed from the earliest years of the cathedral's history. At first the cathedral had lain wholly within the city wall, but the last eastward extension, when the Angel Choir was built to house the new shrine of St Hugh, was made only by breaking through the eastern wall. This left the cathedral and its surrounding dwellings without protection and open to the outside world. To maintain its ecclesiastical immunities, and to exclude all agents of the secular power the cathedral authorities now obtained (in 1327) from the Crown the right to wall and crenellate the entire area, thus creating a city within a city, running from Winnowsty

Lane on the east to Steep Hill on the west.[17] Here then, until the Reformation, lived a thriving community which was at once a centre of diocesan life and an independent, self-sufficient, self-regarding entity. Its contacts with the city were never very strong. No doubt the cathedral attracted many diverse elements, and brought some trade, to Lincoln. No doubt it attempted, and failed, to dominate the city. The links between them were never close, and though the city gilds sometimes came "uphill" to the cathedral for the processions and plays, for the most part the religious life of the citizens was entirely independent of it. Clerks from "uphill" sometimes created a disturbance in the "Street" but on the whole, city and close remained distinct from, and independent of, each other, and there is nothing to suggest either that the city existed purely to serve the cathedral or that the cathedral community was controlled at all by the city.

[17] *Med. Lin.*, pp. 120 *et seq.* and fig. 9 on p. 122.

CHAPTER IV
RELIGIOUS HOUSES: FOUNDATION, ENDOWMENT, AND ECONOMIC LIFE

WHEN the Domesday survey was made in 1086 the Lincolnshire holdings of religious persons were relatively few. It is true that the archbishop of York and the bishops of Lincoln, Durham, Salisbury, Bayeux, and Coûtances were all important tenants-in-chief in the county, and that, in addition, the abbeys of Crowland, Peterborough, Ramsey, and Westminster had important holdings there. Of these abbeys, only the great house of Crowland lay within the county boundaries for since the Danish invasions of late Saxon times all other Lincolnshire religious houses had disappeared, and there seems no reason to suppose that Spalding Priory had been founded in 1052, as its cartulary alleges. The canons of Lincoln were still, in 1086, relatively small landowners, and so were the Benedictine monks whom Remigius had established in Stow, and whom he was soon to transfer to Eynsham.[1]

Nevertheless a few signs of a coming monastic movement could already be distinguished. At Covenham the monks of St Carileph had already received a grant of church and land from King William I; Hugh Lupus, Earl of Chester, had established monks from St Séver in the church of Haugham; and an unknown founder (perhaps King William, again, or Roger of Poitou) had brought monks from St Sées to Wengale, in South Kelsey. These three small cells of Norman priories were to be the forerunners of many 'alien' houses set up by the new Norman landlords of the county; they seem to be only a further development of the process by which these men had given the tithes of their demesne, or even the rectories of small churches, to their home religious houses, perhaps as thanksgiving offerings after the Conquest. William Mustel granted to the monks of Angers two-thirds of the demesne tithes of Torrington and when, later, he gave to Bullington Priory the rectory of this parish his first grant was expressly excepted.[2]

These newly founded cells were small, and all were Benedictine, and

[1] LRS 19, *passim*.   [2] DLC, p. 105.

this was to be the pattern of foundation until after 1130. It is true that Gilbert of Gant refounded the large Benedictine abbey of Bardney about 1087, and that late in his reign King Henry I introduced Austin canons at Wellow near Grimsby, but other new foundations made after 1086 were on a very small scale. Several hospitals were set up for lepers, or almsmen, as at Grantham, Lincoln (Holy Innocents and Holy Sepulchre), Partney, and perhaps Hartsholme and Tetford, and cells were founded by larger English houses at Freiston (Crowland) and Hyrst in Axholme (Nostell) or by alien houses at Burwell (La Sauve Majeure), Cammeringham (L'Essay), and Minting (Fleury).

So far as we can tell all these foundations, small though they were, had been made either by the king, or by leading men of some consequence in the county. In so doing they acted in accordance with a custom which had been well established in their order for two centuries past, and there is no sign that they were driven by any great religious fervour. Things were soon to be different, however, for the enthusiasm produced by reforming Popes, and the beginning of crusades against the infidels, for the recovery of the Holy Land, had its natural corollary in a proliferation of new monastic orders which soon spread from Italy and France into England. Here, it may be, the twenty years of anarchy which succeeded the death of King Henry I encouraged men to attempt to secure their safety in heaven, if it could hardly be attained below. As a result, the seventy years after 1130 saw a rapid, almost feverish series of monastic foundations in Lincolnshire. Some of these were houses of Austin and Premonstratensian canons, who, though obeying a rule and sharing a common life, were not exactly monks, but more of them belonged either to the reformed Benedictine discipline of Cîteaux or else to the English canons who originated in the establishment set up by St Gilbert on his personal estate at Sempringham.[3] For the first time, it seems, women were provided for in the county, both in Cistercian nunneries and in the double houses of the Gilbertine order, where sisters and canons were both accommodated. Meanwhile a few more alien priories and cells of English Benedictine houses, like Thorney's offshoot at Deeping St James, continued to be founded, but the impetus for this 'half-way' monastic foundation was diverted, probably by crusading fervour, into the spate of gifts to the military religious orders of Templars and Hospitallers, whose first acquisitions, at Eagle and Maltby, were undoubtedly made during Stephen's reign.

Mr Colvin has pointed out that the foundation of a Cistercian, Pre-

[3] J. C. Dickinson, *The Origins of the Austin Canons and their Introduction into England*, London, 1950; H. M. Colvin, *The White Canons in England*, Oxford, 1951; R. Graham, *St Gilbert of Sempringham, and the Gilbertines*, London, 1901; L. Milis, *L'Ordre des Chanoines Réguliers d'Arrouaise*, Bruges, 1969.

monstratensian, or Gilbertine house, because of the frugality of these orders and of their liking for remote and wild situations, was infinitely cheaper and easier than that of any medium-sized or large Benedictine house. The new houses could be, and were, put into unreclaimed land on the tops of the wolds (Sixhills), in undrained fen, marsh, or river valley (Revesby, Alvingham, Catley, Haverholme) or in thick, heavy woodland (Vaudey). There, if they survived, they would serve as a focus for reclamation, cultivation, and improvement of the donors' lands, a secondary benefit scarcely likely to be overlooked by those whose first impulse towards foundation had undoubtedly been religious. The founders of such houses, too, need not have been particularly wealthy, and thus we see for the first time the mesne tenant, the honorial baron, as founder and endower of religious houses. Ansgot of Burwell is perhaps the earliest of these, a tenant-in-chief, it is true, but of a very small holding, with much of which, in the early twelfth century, he was to endow the cell of La Sauve Majeure which he had founded there.[4] Peter of Goxhill, the founder of Newhouse, was an honorial baron who held of Ranulf of Bayeux and William of Roumara; Eudo of Grainsby, who founded Greenfield Priory, was a mesne tenant of the honour of Richmond and of the fees of Arsic and Scotney; and Ralf FitzGilbert, the founder of Markby, was a baron of the honours of Roumara, Gant, and Crevequer. Miss Lees has pointed out that the Templar properties in Lincolnshire were founded by men like these, whom she calls "the county society" of the twelfth century.[5]

Founders were usually joined by their younger brothers, their younger sons, and their tenants, all of whom might make gifts to the same house, so that a mesne tenant of the fee of Gant, like Ralf son of Gilbert, might be found granting land in Steeping and the vicinity to Earl Gilbert's foundation at Bardney, in company with his "brothers" Ralf the Villein and William Grim and two of his tenants. There is no cartulary for Revesby Abbey, but a classified list of the charters of the house, drawn up in the late twelfth century, has survived to show that 'charters of barons' included many confirmations of grants made by 'knights' who were their under-tenants.[6] Thus Roger of Mowbray confirms gifts of land and wood at Gainsborough which William of Tisun had made to the abbey, and Philip of Kyme bears witness to the extent of the woodland granted to it by his man John of Mareham. There seems good reason to suppose that feudal or family links such as these were the most powerful forces in determining the way in which the Lincolnshire monasteries

[4] LRS 19, pp. 175–6.
[5] PRS new ser. 36, p. 225; B. A. Lees, *Records of the Templars in the Twelfth Century*, London, 1935.
[6] LAASRP v, pp. 19–27; BM Egerton Roll 3058.

acquired their endowments. The feudal links among Crowland's benefactors, for example, are well expressed in a drawing from the Guthlac Roll (Pl. IVa) where the donors of great estates are portrayed, each with a scroll recording his donation.[7]

Yet there is no doubt that the desire to make gifts for religious objects had a worthier and less mundane origin than mere feudal obligation. As we have seen, the European climate of opinion, to which, from the reign of Edward the Confessor onwards, England was increasingly close, had been more and more attracted by the monastic ideal; the austerities of the monks of Cîteaux, the life of regular prayer and service of the canons, and the devotion of those religious who succoured the outcasts of society, cared for the poor and aged, and fought a holy war against the infidels captured the imagination of all. Moreover, the impact made on the popular imagination by great bishops like Alexander the Magnificent, and St Hugh, and the example of their generosity and devotion intensified this impression, and set ideals of conduct to which men aspired with not inconsiderable success.

The first impulse to give undoubtedly came from a desire to aid in the monastic work, and thereby to qualify for the prayers of the monks or canons. Many of the earliest charters of grant make this abundantly clear, and none more so than a grant made by Alexander son of Osbert, and Nigel his son, to Sempringham of nine hundred and twenty acres of his demesne at Fulbeck, to make a grange, "that we may be brothers and sharers in all their prayers, and may have a burial place in their church, and as full service as one of their number."[8] At a later date, this lay share in the spiritual benefits of a monastery, this claim on its prayers, known as 'confraternity', was frequently bestowed on nobles and other leading men, and it remained to the end the monasteries' most important contribution to secular life. Even at the Dissolution a Lincolnshire man could write to Cromwell "the abbeys are now nothing pitied, the commons perceiving more conveniences to grow from their suppression, *saving that* they lose their prayers."[9] Sometimes these gifts formed part of the dower of a sister, or daughter, like the land Roger Musteile gave to Sixhills with "the two daughters whom his uncle Gilbert had received into the order of nuns," and the enclosure in Stixwold moor which William and Alan sons of Ketel gave with their two daughters to the convent there. A mill at Metheringham was given to Stixwold, along with his sister, by William son of Walter of Metheringham; and Jollan de Neville gave to the same nuns two-thirds of his demesne tithe at Rigsby, and a

---

[7] G. Warner, *The Guthlac Roll*, Roxburghe Club, 189, 1928, pp. 15-16.
[8] Sempring. Char., no. 10.
[9] Quoted by G. Baskerville, *English Monks and the Suppression of the Monasteries*, paperback edn, 1965, p. 19.

barn to house it, when his daughters, Oliva and Eustachia, were professed. Occasionally, too, a disposal of one's goods before undertaking a dangerous journey might lead to a grant: William son of Walter completed his gift to Stixwold when he halted at Deeping, on his way to Jerusalem; and Robert of Harrowby promised five acres of arable and two of meadow, in Westby, to the same house when he set out for Compostella. Even more closely linked with the Holy Land were Roger Mowbray's gift to the Templars of land in Axholme, during the second crusade, and Elias de Amundeville's foundation of a Lazar hospital at Carlton le Moorland.[10]

It has been suggested that a secondary motive in the foundation of some religious houses may well have been the expectation that the new inhabitants of heath, marsh, and fen would drain, reclaim, cultivate, and make prosperous the waste they found, and so, indirectly, add to the value of the donor's neighbouring properties. This was implicit, as we shall see, in many of the gifts to Cistercians and Gilbertines, which were intended as endowments for the large homesteads called 'granges', but it also lay behind many smaller gifts. Matthew de Praieres, giving to the monks of Bury about 1165 his whole "island" of Sailholme, included in the charter of grant a provision for them to cut turf in his own marsh to supply their fires, should they decide to build on the island. At roughly the same time Hervey the clerk, giving the nuns of Stixwold six selions in Horsington, near their sheepfold, licensed them to enclose it if they wished.[11] It was anticipated, too, that some houses would assume secular duties, such as the repair of bridges and causeways and the provision of ferries in remote areas: the small Gilbertine priory of Holland Bridge was explicitly founded for the maintenance of the causeway leading from Kesteven into mid-Holland. By the late thirteenth century some houses were neglecting their secular obligations and the Hundred Rolls contain a number of complaints on this theme. The monks of Spalding, for example, were alleged to neglect to repair Peckebridge (south of Cowbit), as they were obliged, and Revesby had failed to maintain the bridge and causeway of Northdike in Stickney, for the upkeep of which the founder, William of Roumara, had given them certain pieces of land. In 1316 the Commissioners of Sewers were told that the prior of Haverholme "ought to find a certain boat at the Bothe next to the Wathe mouth, for to carry over foot-folks, as well by night as by day."[12]

Many smaller foundations catered explicitly for poor travellers, lepers, and the aged, and their immediate practical value seems often to have outweighed remoter spiritual benefits in the minds of their founders.

[10] LRS 18, p. 17; BM Add. 46701, ff. 7, 9, 57, 78; LAASRP, 3, pp. 109–36.
[11] Douglas, *op. cit.*, p. 173.
[12] *Hundred Rolls*, pp. 276, 372; Dugdale, *op. cit.*, p. 219.

Adam Paynel and Beatrice de Amundeville each established a hospital for travellers over the Ancholme bridge, and passengers on the great road of Salteney gate, which linked the towns of South Holland with West Norfolk, were certainly served by the hospital at Winstowe, in Fleet, which later belonged to the Hospitallers of Skirbeck, and probably by the elusive Salteneya foundation, which occurs only in the Crowland records.[13]

Apart from a few small houses of canons, such as Kyme, Hagnaby, and Neubo, the flood of Lincolnshire monastic foundations was slackening by 1165; besides these only a few hospitals and alien cells were still to come. Nevertheless the established houses, like Barlings and Newhouse, continued to attract gifts of land, of greater or lesser importance, throughout the thirteenth century, and there is no real sign of a decline in the popularity of monastic houses, or of a loss of interest in them before the mid-fourteenth century. A new expression of religious enthusiasm, which began to reach England from Italy about 1230, attracted many of the most ardent of lay people, and appealed especially to the inhabitants of larger towns, whose commercial importance was now very considerable. This was the mendicant orders (chiefly Franciscans, Dominicans, Austin Friars, and Carmelites) who reached Lincolnshire in the first half of the thirteenth century in the wake of Robert Grosseteste.

At first the friars required little in the way of endowment, apart from the land on which to build their churches and convents, for they provided their buildings and maintained themselves by the alms they begged, and generally they settled in towns, where their infectious evangelical zeal attracted many penitents and much lay enthusiasm. By the end of the thirteenth century Lincoln, Boston, Stamford, Grantham, and Grimsby each had houses of some or all of the mendicant orders, which had been founded by their inhabitants. The Franciscan house at Boston is particularly notable, as having been founded by German merchants living in the town. The mendicant orders were primarily active evangelists, preachers, and ministers of God's word. Prayer and contemplation were very subordinate aims, at least in their early development, and their main field of work lay not in their own convents but in the parish and diocese, and for this reason their activities can best be considered in relation to parochial life. The last of these houses, that of the Austin friars at Stamford, was not founded until 1342, when the impetus for such things was almost spent, and the spiritual and economic disasters of the Black Death were soon to divert the energies of devout men to other things. The only later monastic foundation in Lincolnshire was a house of the austere Carthusian observance which Thomas Mowbray, Earl of Nottingham,

[13] L. B. Larking, *The Knights Hospitallers* . . . , Camden Soc., old ser. 65, 1857, p. 60; Wrest Park, f. 192*v*.

founded in Axholme in 1397-8. For the future, to secure their souls' welfare, the magnates would endow chantries, and lesser men would support gilds and fraternities, or arrange for obits. Scale and direction had changed and religious sentiment in the later Middle Ages would look increasingly for fresh outlets, in place of the 'institutionalized' religious houses.

Although large-scale gifts to monastic houses slackened by the mid-fourteenth century, pious donors continued till the end to endow obits there, which ensured the saying of special masses in the house on the anniversaries of their deaths. Such celebrations included often the distribution to all monks present of a 'pittance' (a treat) which usually took the form of extra food and drink. One such gift was made to Stixwold in 1261 by Osbert of London, rector of Silkstone, who bequeathed to the convent an annual rent of one hundred shillings, for the souls of John, Margaret, and Edmund de Lacy, and Henry of Nottingham. Of this, four marks were to be used to buy wax and oil for the convent's lights and especially for a light burning perpetually before the principal altar of the Blessed Virgin, one mark was to provide bread for distribution to the poor on Maundy Thursday, another to augment the convent's Lenten fare, and twenty shillings were to be devoted to providing a pittance for the convent on the day of the donor's death. In 1283 the abbot of Newhouse augmented, by the diversion of a rent charge of fourteen shillings, a pittance for the souls of Fredissande of Killingholme, Robert parson of Fulstow, and Gilbert of Kirmington. Dr Wood-Legh has suggested that tied gifts of this sort were common in monastic houses from the twelfth century, and were often used as foundations for perpetual chantries, and certainly this seems to have happened at Greenfield, where John of Welle in 1318 founded a chantry for two priests celebrating daily at his family burial place in the priory church. At the Dissolution two chaplains were still celebrating in this chantry and receiving £10 per annum, just as at Hagnaby a single chaplain was paid £5 to celebrate "for the safety of the soul of Robert Godefeld."[14] Occasionally monasteries were made responsible for the upkeep of a chantry elsewhere, as at Barlings, to which William of Ingleby gave a hundred and sixty marks in 1267, in return for which the abbot and convent bound themselves to build and maintain a chantry chapel at Langworth.[15] On the whole, however, the great flood of chantry foundations bypassed the monasteries, and lay piety was exercised in other fields.

[14] BM Add. 46701, f. 22; BM Harl. Ch. 46H3; K. L. Wood-Legh, *Perpetual Chantries in Britain*, Cambridge, 1968, p. 303; R. C. Dudding, *History of the Manor and Parish of Saleby*, p. 39, citing Close Roll 12E2, m. 14; *Early Lincoln Wills*, privately printed, Lincoln, 1888, p. 21; *Val. Eccl.* IV, pp. 51, 53.

[15] LRS 20, p. 24.

The 'alien priories' which were so freely founded, in Lincolnshire and elsewhere, in the century and a half after the Conquest, can rarely have had much importance in the life of the county. Few of them were intended to support more than one or two monks, and it can never have been expected that they would have a full monastic life. Indeed, it seems probable that they existed for the administration of land, the collection of tithes, and perhaps the celebration of anniversary masses for the founders' souls. It is likely that at the outset the founders may have hoped for congenial ministrations, in their own homes and churches, by monks from their birth places. Alan, son of Earl Henry of Brittany, certainly brought Premonstratensians from Beauport in Brittany to West Ravendale.[16] Gifts to Hospitallers and Templars less often included churches and were not, it seems, intended to lead to the foundation of separate religious houses. Such preceptories and commanderies as existed within the county were administrative centres for the estates, and although of great economic importance, scarcely ranked as religious establishments. Whatever the size and influence of the alien priories had originally been, they shrank to nothing during the Anglo-French wars, and after 1294 the Crown not only confiscated some of their properties, but cut off most of them from their mother houses, until in 1378 the monks were finally expelled, and their properties taken entirely into royal hands. Some, like Covenham, whose lands were sold as early as 1303 to Kirkstead, had already disappeared by then, but for the most part the Crown granted the surrendered lands to new religious foundations. The collegiate church of Tattershall (Burwell), various Carthusian houses (Minting, Haugham, Bonby, Long Bennington, and Hough), and the Cambridge college of King's (Willoughton, Wengale), all benefited in this way.[17]

When local baronial families began to apply their resources in the twelfth century to the endowment of Augustinian, Gilbertine, or Cistercian houses, it was natural that lesser men should wish to emulate them, and to share in the benefits of monastic prayers. Not all such men were ready, or able, to contribute to the endowment of larger houses, and many would wish, like the founders of alien priories, to have their own monks close at hand. This is no doubt why Ralf son of Stephen of Holland arranged with Sempringham to have two canons living at, and serving, his new chapel of St Thomas the Martyr in Holland Marsh, Walter of Gant set up his little cell of Bridlington monks at Edenham, perhaps first intending it for a hospital, and Adam Paynel installed Selby monks in the hospital for poor travellers which he founded at the

---

[16] Donald Matthew, *The Norman Monasteries and their English Possessions*, Oxford, 1962, pp. 51–65.
[17] VCH *Lincs.*, II, pp. 238–44.

Ancholme crossing.[18] In the same way many of them founded small religious houses to serve a specific local need, or in response to some personal interest of their own. Elias de Amundeville, a connection of the foundress of a hospital at Elsham, founded a small leper hospital, which subsequently was absorbed by Burton Lazars, on his lands in Carlton le Moorland, because his daughter was a leper. Others, seeing the work of the Order of St Lazarus during the second crusade, may have done similar things. Certainly an impulse of this sort probably inspired the gift to Burton Lazars of the rectories of Threekingham, Hale, and Heckington, though nothing suggests that they were a base for a hospital.[19]

Most of these small houses are described as hospitals, and many of them were conducted by communities of a few clerks observing a quasi-monastic rule, usually that of the Austin canons. They existed for a variety of charitable purposes and because much of their revenue came from the alms of the faithful they must always have been relatively cheap for the founder. The leper hospitals of the twelfth century were not all of them very small, of course, and the Malandry or Holy Innocents, which lay near the South Common at Lincoln, was a considerable establishment. In its midst lay the parish church of Holy Innocents which was its principal endowment, and around it lay the lepers' chapel, a dining hall and kitchen, and a low rectangle of individual cells. It relied very largely on the alms of the faithful, which were collected just after harvest and on three Sundays during the year when charitable sermons were specially authorized. Across the road from it lay St Katherine's, a large hospital for the sick and poor, which was administered by a house of Gilbertine canons and lay sisters, but such large foundations were on the whole unusual. St Katherine's had itself absorbed the hospital of the Holy Sepulchre which, like the Malandry, was founded by Bishop Robert de Bloet, and many other small hospitals were to fall into the hands of larger houses.[20]

When the immediate need for the small leper establishments slackened, as it did by the earlier fourteenth century, they were sometimes absorbed by local religious houses. Barlings Abbey assumed responsibility for such an establishment at Langworth. Other hospitals passed into the hands of Burton Lazars, the Leicestershire house which was the head of the order of St Lazarus in England. Burton took over Carlton-le-Moorland about 1275, and was in 1456 to acquire the property of the Malandry.[21] In the same way most of the small hospitals for the sick, the aged, the travellers,

---

[18] *Genealogist* 23, p. 76; *Cal. Pat. Rolls, 1317–21*, p. 377.
[19] LAASRP 3, p. 128; *Cal. Pat. Rolls, 1317–21*, p. 378.
[20] F. W. Brooks, 'The Hospital of Holy Innocents', AASRP XLII, *passim*; Reg. 2, f. 248v; LRS 20, p. 24.
[21] VCH *Leics.*, II, p. 36; J. Nichols, *History of Leicestershire*, II, p. 275.

perhaps because they found it impossible to survive alone, or were in an area so remote as to be of no use, disappeared within larger houses. Thus Bardney acquired the small foundations at Partney and Hartsholme, Louth Park took over the tiny establishment on Brakenholme in Farlesthorpe, the mysterious Saltney was probably absorbed by Crowland, and the Norfolk house of Creake absorbed a hospital for five poor men in Gedney fen.

The conditions imposed by the founders of this Gedney hospital when they handed it to Creake in 1256 are perhaps typical of such places: forty-seven acres of land on which were a windmill, hall, chamber, kitchen, and chapel, the whole surrounded by a moat with a drawbridge, maintained a canon and five poor people who were each to receive daily one loaf, suitable drink, and half a mess of flesh or fish, with a new tunic every second year. Not all the hospitals survived even as long as this, and most of the dependent ones had disappeared before the end of the medieval period. This was particularly true of those houses which the Hospitallers claimed, as they did with some success, to be properly their concern. Thus the Winstow hospital in Fleet completely vanished, apart from its chapel, and that of Skirbeck retained only vestigial signs of its origins. Some larger hospitals on the other hand, once the need for them was passed, were able to transform themselves into more regular religious houses and to survive until the end of the period. Thus Elsham, which was perhaps displaced as a hospital by Adam Paynel's foundation at Brigg, which was more convenient for travellers, and Newstead by Stamford, each became a regular priory.[22]

Most of these houses we have been discussing, after the initial endowment of perhaps one large manor, acquired the rest of their property in a mass of small parcels of land and portions of churches or tithes scattered over a very wide area. Sir Frank Stenton has pointed out that it was exceptional, in this part of England, for a religious house to obtain possession of an entire village, but "already, in the year 1200, there were few villages in this region in which no religious house held land." The contrast between the Lindsey Survey of 1115-18 and the returns incorporated in the Hundred Rolls demonstrate this admirably. In the wapentake of Yarborough for example, no religious house held land at the earlier date, whereas in 1276 Thornton, Elsham, Bridlington, Selby, Grimsby, Ormsby, and Newhouse were all landowners of greater or smaller importance in the vills there.[23] The spread of religious land tenure might well be determined, as we have seen, by the links of feudal tenure, and the land of a single house might lie compactly in a small area because of this, as did that of the alien priory of Ravendale, within the Soke of

---

[22] BM Cott. Vesp. E xx, ff. 57*v*, 206*v*; LRS 17, p. 145.
[23] DLC, p. liv; *Hundred Rolls*, p. 295.

Waltham, or Bourne's holdings in Helpringham, Morton, East and West Deeping, Barholme, and Stow, which were components of Baldwin Wake's honour.[24] On the other hand, it might equally be scattered throughout the county, as was Kirkstead's, with the Bek holdings, and Bardney's, with those of Gant. An otherwise compact endowment might be supplemented with one or two outlying estates: Revesby Abbey's properties on the Trent near Gainsborough, and the outlying Kesteven properties of Stixwold in Honington and Lenton, are excellent examples of this. Much of the land given was also, as we have seen, remote, unenclosed, and uncultivated, or only recently reclaimed. Kirkstead, for instance, was given an estate on the very edge of the 'high' land in Blankney, with a long strip of land reclaimed from the fen, which can still be distinguished on the two-and-a-half-inch Ordnance Survey map as "Lindwood Fen," while the site of Catley Abbey was described in the charter of grant as "the site of the grange between Walcot and the marsh, with its enclosures and ditches, and two cultures of arable land."[25]

The changes in land ownership which resulted from the religious foundations of the twelfth century had marked and far-reaching economic and social effects.[26] New and far more vigorous methods of agriculture were to be introduced by the Cistercians, Premonstratensians, Gilbertines, and Templars, and the effect of this would be seen not only in the flourishing monastic wool trade, which will be discussed later, but in the vast amount of reclamation, clearance, drainage, and enclosure, which was accomplished in the county by these monastic landlords. So much of Lincolnshire must have been moor, or fen, or dense woodland, that the opportunities were endless, and even the Benedictines, who elsewhere in England were said to have relied on the income from stable and long-cultivated estates, were, in south Lincolnshire, to launch into a large programme of drainage and reclamation. Crowland had its more conventional estates at Langtoft and Baston, but the newlands it "created" in south Holland, like Spalding Priory's seaward reclamations, were carried out by the establishment, on the margins of the newland, of a series of farms, or, as they came to be called, 'granges', staffed by one or two monks and a force of wage labourers.[27]

The system may have arisen spontaneously but it was really very similar to that which the Gilbertines, Cistercians, and Premonstratensians were to introduce during the twelfth century into the county. This

[24] F. M. Stenton, *Facsimiles of Early Charters from Northamptonshire Collections*, Northants. Rec. Soc., 4, 1930, p. iv.
[25] BM Cott. Vesp. E xviii, ff. 37v–39v; LRS 17, p. 57.
[26] Based on M. C. Knowles, *Religious Orders in England*, Cambridge, 1948, 1, pp. 64–77.
[27] H. E. Hallam, *Settlement and Society*, Cambridge, 1965, *passim*; LAOR 12, pp. 10–15.

consisted of the direct farming of the monastery's lands in ring-fence estates which lay outside the already cleared and settled agricultural areas; the labour force, directly controlled by the house itself, consisted of *conversi* or lay brethren who lived under a rule. Since almost all the houses of these orders founded in Lincolnshire were established at sites outside the regular centres of settlement, as the plan of houses in the Witham valley demonstrates (Fig. 6), their 'home' estate could become, with the monastery itself, a compact unit. Where the chosen site did not allow this the founder might arrange, as at Revesby, and perhaps at Newhouse, for the removal elsewhere of the existing inhabitants. The home 'ring fence' might cover a fairly considerable area: certainly this was true of Kirkstead's, a century after its foundation, when it was defined in an agreement about game.[28] The area, enclosed by wall, dike, hedge, or paling, with gates defended by mounds, ran along the Witham from near the mill then known as Sinker, a mile or more to the neighbourhood of the abbey and:

"from the water of Wydme eastwards straight to the dike which is between Swynehuswode and Beltesholm as that dike extends to Stokbrigg and from Stokbrigg round by Ricroft and from Ricroft by the highway as far as the stone cross which is at the end of the Causeway which comes from the gate of the abbey and thus in a line along the road which leads to Gaythusbrigg and from Gaythusbrigg eastwards round by Sinkermilneholt and Calvecroft to Sinker northwards as it is enclosed by dikes, and thus straight by the dikes to the water of Wydme."

The outlying estates which were known as granges were equally tightly enclosed, and for all practical purposes, especially among the Gilbertines, they were small religious houses, with their oratory, cloister, guest-rooms, workshops, and so on. Only lay brothers lived there, under the rule of one of their number known as a granger, and from this base they first reclaimed, and then farmed, the land. Such an estate might be created from a single grant, giving the house land to make a grange, as Count Alan of Brittany did in Gayton le Wold for the monks of Bégar, but it was equally likely to be built up from a series of small grants, like the Sempringham estate of Woodgrange, in Bulby, towards which at least eighteen small gifts of woodland and clearings contributed.[29] These granges were numerous in Lincolnshire especially in the Wolds, in the Cliff and Heath land to the north and south of Lincoln, and in the wooded highland region between Grantham and Stamford. Many survive as large farms, like Sheepwash and Grange de Lings, in the immediate neighbourhood of Lincoln, and may be discovered from the larger scale Ordnance Survey maps. It is not always wise to identify them by the

[28] LRS 17, pp. 171–2.   [29] DLC 161; Sempring. Char., *passim*.

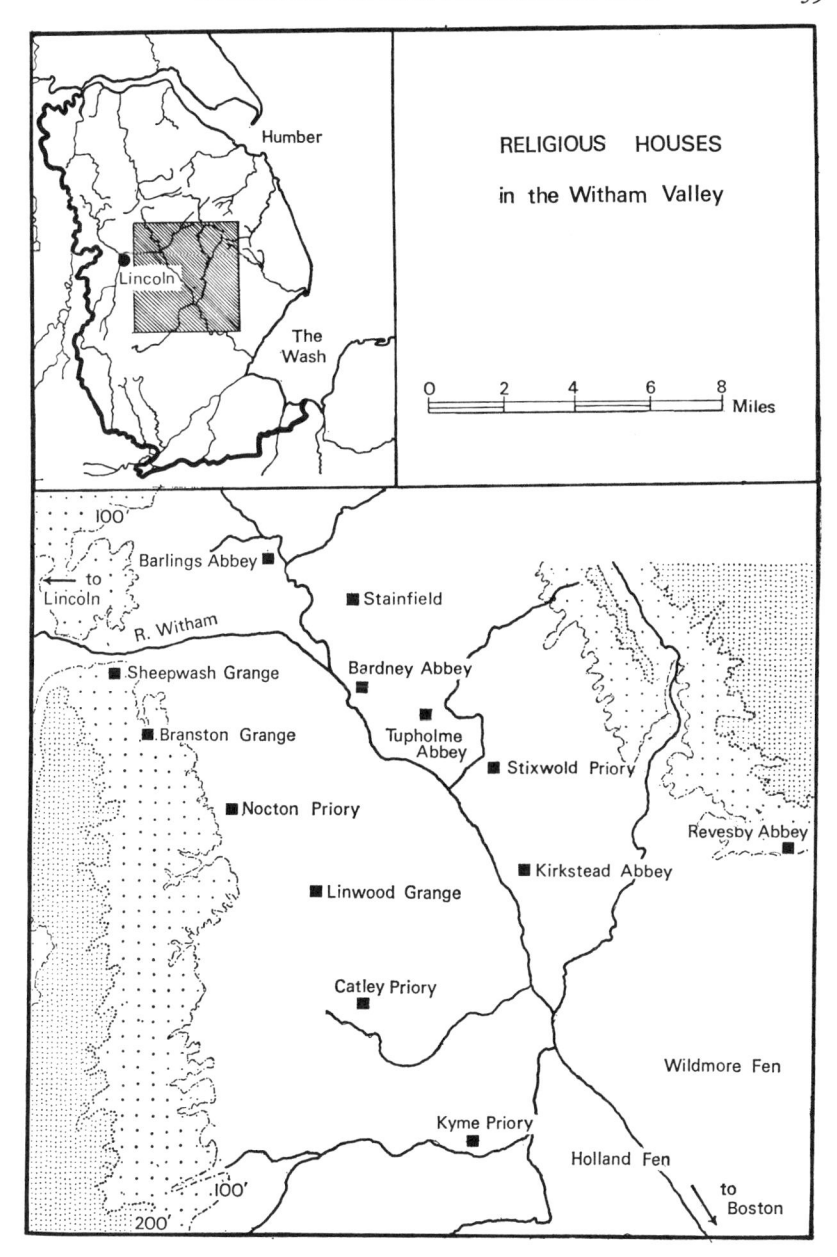

Fig. 6

modern use of the word 'grange'. 'Lost' sites have in some cases been identified by Canon Foster in his two lists of "lost vills and places," and a continuing tradition that a particular tract of land is extra-parochial, as at Bayard's Leap, Grange de Lings, Eagle Barnsdale, and Grimblethorpe, is often a useful clue to their identification.[30] The *Valor Ecclesiasticus* lists some granges, but by the sixteenth century so many had been leased to laymen, and are not included, that it is incomplete. It should also be remembered that the Benedictines (except for those of Crowland and Spalding) and the Austin canons did not often use the name 'grange' for outlying estates farmed as units, nor were such estates regarded as religious establishments, so their farms cannot be included in any list of granges.

The effect of this new unit of organization must often have been very considerable, even when it lay in an area of minimum settlement, for the edge of the reclaimable land usually marched with, and might be disputed with, the laymen of the next community, and the activities of the grange must often have interfered with their traditional practices. Bracton's Notebook includes a case arising from this sort of situation: William and Adam of Bayeux demonstrated before the royal judges their right to common on the lands of the prior of Sixhills in Legsby; this the prior refused because he had no reciprocal right of common over the Bayeux land in Linwood, which they had, they said, "because before Sixhills was founded their ancestors for forty years had it . . . because in hot dry summers the men of Legsby had easement of the water of Pitts in Linwood, and continue to have it whenever they want it." In the same way the abbot of Bardney was alleged to have set up a bank for a turbary on his land in Nocton, and so given the men of Nocton further to go with their plough oxen. The establishment of a grange, even in a marshy, unpopulated tract like the western end of Roughton, might endanger many lay rights, as Roland of Woodhall perceived: in giving to Kirkstead, about 1196–8, his demesne woodland and assarts in the parish he was careful to renounce all the claims he might have against them,

"between Theuesweng and Widma, namely the Sinker watercourse and the mill-pool, and fish-pond there, and all that is enclosed by the dikes of Sinker, as far as the course of Widme . . . and Brakene . . . and whatever their ditches enclose from the east side of the gate of Old Dufwoode as far as Mikelgate, and on the west side of the gate as far as the causeway to the moor . . . and the two selions I claimed from them in front of their sheepfold gate at Dufwode."[31]

[30] LRS 17 and 19.
[31] F. W. Maitland, *Bracton's Notebook*, no. 720; LRS 22, p. 243; DLC, 198.

The Lincolnshire granges and monastic farms were from the first used for a new and intensive type of farming, which made fuller use of all available land by draining and enclosing it, by stocking the commons as heavily as possible, and, where it was feasible, by enclosing pasture and making it 'several'. The prior of Nocton said in 1202 that since the foundation of his house fifteen hundred acres of pasture belonging to it had been converted to arable. Peterborough's grange at Twigmore, which was conveyed to Louth Park in 1216, is another excellent example of the agricultural operations and amounts of land held by such an establishment:

"Grant in free alms to the monks of Louth Park of all the land in Raventhorpe lying on the south side of *Martynwellsyke* as far as the boundary of Holme in length and the boundary of Manton in breadth; and whatever lies on the south side of *Martynwell* as far as the hill by the boundary of Manby, as it has been surveyed and divided by dykes, and so by the boundary of Manby, and of Broughton and of Scawby to the boundary of Manton again; and common pasture in Raventhorpe for 500 sheep, ten cows, their woodland [?] horses, two plough-teams of oxen with other common rights over turf and heath; and *Martynwell* furlong lying to the north, i.e. 13 acres with common pasture in Holme, and fuel from turf and heath, and water from *Martynwell*, wherever they wish to take it for their own use, and likewise in *Engcroft* on the north side of their grange at Twigmore and the crofts on the east side of their byre— all of which Gilbert son of Ralph gave them, as his charter testifies. They are also confirmed the grants of Robert de Neville in tofts and sleets in Manton, with common pasture and everything else pertaining to that fee in turf and heather, and also from the heather of that vill. They are also granted whatever they can turn into arable land and 20 acres of cultivated land in Holme, 10 acres to the west of *Suthon* and 10 on *Assedalehil*, pertaining to the assarts of Robert de Neville, and common pasture and fuel from turf and heather; and the site of their grange in Twigmore, surrounded by a ditch or moat, and three acres in the tofts of Raventhorpe, and whatever they have dyked in Manton outside their grange, and the causeway they have made before the gate of their grange, as Robert de Neville's charter testifies; and all the land which Henry son of Ralph gave them in Messingham, east of the road which runs from Holme bridge south and divides the great sleets from the little and goes on to the fields of Manton as far as the fields of Raventhorpe, every kind of land, including the common of the whole vill and the easements pertaining to his fee; and the whole furlong called 'great sleets' on the east of the vill, as Henry's charters testify; and 2 bovates with their appurtenances in the fields of Messingham, save the tofts which Tergisius held; and one bovate of land with appurtenances which was held by Lambert Suarri; and a toft formerly held by William de Rebarn [?]; and 4 other bovates of land with appurtenances which Norman priest of Raventhorpe held; and 1 selion at *Lairlondis* and 2 tofts in Messingham, formerly held by Roger of York and Stephen clerk, all of which Simon son of Henry gave them in Messingham as his charters testify. They are also confirmed common pasture in the fields of Messingham for fifty mares with three-year-old foals and the right of dyking and enclosing and turning to their own uses however they wish anything which pertains to the fee of Peterborough Abbey contained within these boundaries—i.e. as the road runs south from Holme bridge and divides the great and little sleets and so to the field of Manton, and on the east as far as the fields of Raventhorpe, in every kind of land, as Simon's charters testify."

The Templars were particularly skilful in the organization of their lands, and even at the great survey of 1182, when they had been established in the county for less than fifty years, their farms were plainly extremely prosperous.[32]

By the mid-thirteenth century there are signs that the competition of this farming was pressing hard on neighbouring lay farmers, and some agreements of the period suggest that it was necessary to stint the commons and restrain the activities of the monastic farmers. At least this seems to lie behind an agreement made in 1246 by the Templars of Bruer and Jordan son of Jordan about the commons of Ashby de la Launde:[33]

"Jordan has granted for himself and his heirs that the master, his successors and the brethren of the knights of the Temple of Solomon shall have every year pasture for 400 sheep in the common of pasture of Askeby belonging to Jordan and his heirs where formerly they only had pasture for 300 sheep in the same vill; and that they shall have every year common of pasture for 8 oxen in herbage-time in the same common of pasture; and that they shall have every year common of pasture for 100 pigs in the common of pasture in the same vill from the feast of St Peter *ad Vincula* [1 August] until the feast of St Michael when the corn has been carried. And, if it shall be necessary that the pasture shall be enclosed, it shall be enclosed in common, or the pasture shall be depastured in common by the view of the master, his successors, and the brethren and Jordan and his heirs. And it shall be lawful for the master and his successors and the brethren, when the corn has been reaped, to put the 100 pigs in their own parcels of arable land lying in the fields of Askeby without

[32] LRS 22, p. 10; C. N. L. Brooke and M. M. Postan, *Carte Nativorum*, Northants. Rec. Soc., xx, 1960, pp. 171-2; Lees, *op. cit., passim*.
[33] LRS 17, pp. 41-2.

doing damage to the corn and meadows of Jordan and his heirs and their men of Askeby for ever. And if the 100 pigs or any of them shall be found to have done damage to Jordan or his heirs or their men of Askeby, it shall be lawful for Jordan and his heirs or any of their men of Askeby to impound the pigs, without impeachment or vexation by the master and his successors and the brethren, in any place or manner until the damage to Jordan or his heirs or their men shall be fully made good; or if the pigs of Jordan or his heirs or his men shall be found to have done damage to the master and his successors and their men of Askeby, it shall be lawful for them to impound the pigs, without impeachment or vexation by Jordan or his heirs or their men of Askeby, in any place or manner until the damage shall be fully made good; provided that they be impounded within the vill of Askeby both by the master, his successors and their men, and by Jordan and his heirs and their men, for ever. And, moreover, it shall be lawful for the master and his successors and the brethren or their men and for Jordan and his heirs or their men henceforth to carry their corn and hay and food freely, as they were used, everywhere in the fields and meadows of Askeby without doing damage to the corn and hay of either party. And be it known that the master and his successors and the brethren shall not henceforth have more beasts and cattle in the said common of pasture of Askeby than the 100 pigs within the said term, and 8 oxen in time of herbage, and only 400 sheep for the whole year, without special licence from Jordan and his heirs; nor can Jordan and his heirs or any of his men henceforth claim or demand any right in the pasture between the king's highway which leads from Lincoln to Sleaford and the road which leads from Lincoln to Staunford on the west side of Askeby, for ever."

Certainly the monastic farmers dominated their localities, and it is not surprising that they were able to impose their own measures on their neighbourhood. Even in the late fifteenth century the Revesby Abbey perch of twenty feet, three and one-quarter inches was in use in East Kirkby. An interesting example of the same thing, and of the scale and extent of monastic operations, is provided by an agreement about the demesne tithe of Scampton which was reached in 1228 between Kirkstead, the owner of a grange there, and Bardney, the proprietor of the rectory. The tithe of corn, barley, and oats was to be estimated according to the stone weights of Barlings and Stixwold, and the iron rods of Tupholme and Bullington, and was then to be transported by Kirkstead's men to Sheepwash, whence the men of Bardney would convey it in their own boats.[34]

Apart from such casual references there is little direct evidence of the

[34] LAO Goulding 3/102; BM Cott. Vesp. E xx, f. 199v.

detailed working of these large monastic farms. The Louth Park chronicle mentions that Abbot Richard Dunham (1227-46) built in all the granges "halls and chambers, dormitories and dining-rooms for guests and barns, cowhouses and sheepfolds," and something is known of Crowland's manors from a few surviving central accounts. Thornton's organization can be studied in a late compilation which includes lists of the abbey's officers, with specimen accounts for each, drawn from account rolls of the late fourteenth century which have now disappeared. Cheese and grain were sent to Thornton from some or all of the farms, but stock, and the forage for it, were the principal concern of the convent's officers. The number of sheep, ewes, and hogasters passing through the stock-keeper's hands in 1315, for example, was 7,934, and the care of this flock absorbed 61 shepherds in winter, and 70 in summer.[35]

The rapid endowment of so many Cistercian and Gilbertine houses directly interested in the reclamation and exploitation of undeveloped or unoccupied land must have led to conflicts of interest among them. Not only did they compete for gifts or bequests, but they were rivals in purchases. During the thirteenth century and later there is evidence that monastic houses were buying land to round off their estates or attracting gifts of valuable estates. The monks of Louth Park seem to have been particularly fortunate or unusually adept, for not only did they acquire (by rather doubtful means, it is true) the manor of Cockerington by the will of Sir Henry Vavasour, in 1342, but forty-six years later the abbot was said to have acquired the title deeds of an estate leased to the abbey, after its owner had died.[36] Evidence of purchases by monastic houses is fragmentary but it is clear that they bought and sold as much as other landlords did. Hagnaby Abbey, for example, in 1272 sold off houses in Boston which it did not need and acquired Thoresby Wood with the proceeds; in 1291 Thornton Abbey bought the manor of Halton by Killingholme for £1,000 from the Earl of Lincoln; and as late as 1488 Markby Priory was buying land in Little Steeping.[37]

Whatever rivalry there was between religious houses in the later period, reasonable agreements and some degree of co-operation were aimed at in the first century and a half. Kirkstead, for example, was able to acquire its grange at Gayton le Wold in about 1154-5 from the alien priory which originally owned it, and Peterborough, as we have seen, transferred to Louth Park the well-developed Twigmore estate. Moreover, the Cistercians and Gilbertines, meeting solemnly in 1164 in general chapters at Kirkstead and Sempringham, agreed that thenceforth no

[35] E. Venables, *Chronicon Abbatie de Parco Lude*, p. 14; F. M. Page, *The Estates of Crowland Abbey*, Cambridge, 1934; LAOR 12, pp. 10-15; Bod. ms. Tanner 166, p. 81.
[36] Venables, *op. cit.*, pp. xxxiii-xxxiv; *Cal. Misc. Inq.* v, p. 307.
[37] BM Cott. Vesp. B xi, f. 25v; BM Campbell Ch. xxi 4; LNQ xiii, p. 55.

house of either chapter should build a grange or sheepfold within two leagues of a similar building belonging to the other order, unless a considerable river, with no bridge, ford, or ferry, lay between them, and neither order was to entice or employ wage labourers from the other. Disputes were to be settled by the Gilbertine general chapter and a committee of three Cistercian abbots; doubtless this machinery was used when in 1174 Louth Park, Alvingham, and Nun Ormsby agreed that none of them would acquire land of any kind in twenty named parishes in the wapentakes of Louthesk and Ludborough without the advice and consent of the others.[38] Other disputes between neighbouring houses might be settled by amicable composition: Bardney and Tupholme appealed to the county court to decide on the boundary between their lands, and earlier went to arbitration about their duty to scour the dike which formed the boundary between Wraggoe and Gartree. In 1155 Bishop Robert de Chesney and Archbishop Theobald negotiated an agreement between Kirkstead and the Templars about their competing interests in Nocton and Dunston.[39]

There were many disputes in parishes where two houses, one of them owning the rectorial tithes, each had interests, especially as the cultivated area increased. Belvoir Priory, which was rector of Aslackby, continued to claim from the Templars tithe of their demesne there until a compromise payment of two marks per annum was arranged after 1183; a similar pension of forty sesters of salt was paid by Bury to Stixwold (owners of Wainfleet St Mary rectory) for tithe of Sailholme; and the Bridlington Cartulary has a long section of compositions made between 1190 and 1233 concerning the tithes of Vaudey and Crowland lands in Edenham. Because of the nature of the area the most complicated and long-lasting disputes between religious houses were those about common pasture in the fen. Revesby and Kirkstead had a long series of differences about this in Wildmore until a *modus vivendi* was arrived at in 1257.[40]

The direct operation of the granges and large farms became increasingly difficult as a result of the labour troubles following the Black Death, which not only decreased the force of wage labourers, but virtually ended the recruitment of lay brothers. As early as 1230 Newhouse had found it necessary to lease the outlying grange of Rodemill to a layman, and after the mid-fourteenth century the practice became widespread.[41]

[38] DLC, p. 161; BM Add. 37022, f. 145v; Graham, *op. cit.*, p. 127.
[39] Maitland, *Bracton's Notebook*, no. 445; BM Cott. Vesp. E xx, f. 88; Lees, *op. cit.*, p. 241.
[40] HMCR *Rutland*, IV, p. 117; BM Add. 46701, p. 93; *Brid. Cart.*, pp. 364-420; VCH *Lincs.*, II, p. 136.
[41] BM Harl. Ch. 43 H42.

The evidence in the *Valor Ecclesiasticus* is difficult to interpret but demonstrates without doubt that almost all the surviving granges were by the sixteenth century in lay hands.

It seems certain that wool from Lincoln and Cotswold sheep was reaching northern Italy at the time of the Norman Conquest and that, although only one shearing house (at Stallingborough) and one flock of sheep (at Great Sturton) are mentioned in Domesday, the Lindsey marshes and wolds and the Kesteven uplands were already sheep-rearing areas. This was where, in the twelfth century, the Cistercian, Premonstratensian, and Gilbertine houses settled most thickly, and proceeded to make available yet more land for sheep-rearing, so that it is hardly surprising to find them regarded, by two Italians writing about 1300, as among the leading wool producers of the county. The trade ranged in size from the forty sacks exported yearly by Kirkstead, Revesby, and Spalding to the two sacks of Grimsby and Heynings (Fig. 7):

Kirkstead, Revesby, Spalding	40
Lincoln St Katherine	35
Louth Park, Stainfield, Crowland	30
Barlings, Sempringham	25
Vaudey	24
Newhouse	20
Bullington, Sixhills, Ormsby	18
Haverholme, Stixwold, Bardney	15
Markby	12
Alvingham, Newstead, Nuncoton, Wellow	10
Tupholme, Thornholme	8
Catley	7
Swineshead	6
Hagnaby, Humberston, Deeping, Bourne	5
Gokewell, Nocton	4
Grimsby, Heynings	2.[42]

The quantitative assessment indicated by these figures can scarcely be interpreted now, but might be a little easier if we had certain information about the size of monastic flocks. Newhouse, we know, received large grants of sheep pasture for flocks varying in size between 300 and 700; there are many similar grants to Kirkstead, and Sempringham; and Louth Park, we know, had sheepfolds in various places. The Nuncoton cartulary has a note that in 1266 Henry of Girsby, the convent's shep-

---

[42] H. C. Darby, *Domesday Geography of Eastern England*, Cambridge, 1952, p. 85; LRS 19, pp. 28, 107; E. Power, *Medieval English Wool Trade*, Oxford, 1941; Knowles, *op. cit.*, I, pp. 64–77; W. Cunningham, *Growth of English Industry and Commerce during the Early and Middle Ages*, 4th edn, Cambridge, 1905, pp. 629–40.

RELIGIOUS HOUSES: ECONOMIC LIFE 67

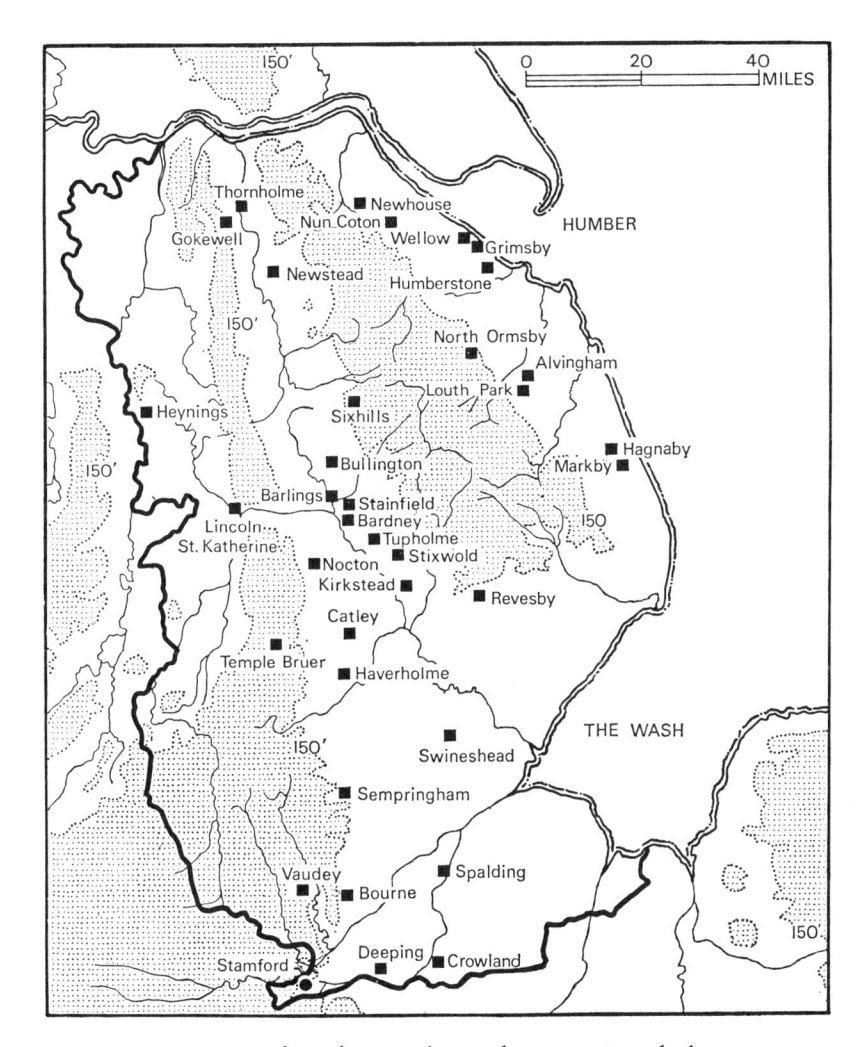

Fig. 7. *Wool-producing religious houses in Lincolnshire*

herd, received from the granger when he began office eleven score sheep and lambs. Perhaps the most detailed account we have comes from the Thornton stock-keeper's account for 1313, where the total number of sheep in the abbey's 27 farms was 7,934. The cellarer was responsible for sales of wool, and in this one year disposed of 86 sacks and 9 stones, for the sum of £490 15s. 3d., plus £200 advanced to his predecessor. The continued importance of the trade is suggested by a scribbled verse, in a fifteenth-century hand in a Spalding memorandum book, which begins:

"In a sack of wool there are as many pounds
As there are days in the year."[43]

There are indications that in the late thirteenth and early fourteenth centuries many of the Lincolnshire houses were selling wool not only to the Italians, but to Flanders, Montpellier, and the Eastlanders. This probably explains the numerous references to properties, including warehouses, owned or leased by monastic houses in Boston and, to a lesser extent, in Grimsby, Lincoln, Stamford, and Torksey during the first three centuries of their existence. Kirkstead, Revesby, Stixwold, Furness, Bridlington, Whitby, and Malton are all known to have had houses in Boston where, presumably, they stored their wool and their purchases at the fair. Barlings, on the other hand, had, or tried to have, a warehouse in Thorngate in Lincoln, for its wool and tanned hides, and Nuncoton sold its wool indifferently at Lincoln and St Ives. Some at least of the wool handled by Cistercian and Gilbertine houses was not their own, for it seems certain that they exploited their exemption from tolls to buy up wool from small producers.[44]

The wool trade was undoubtedly the principal commercial occupation of the Lincolnshire monastic houses, and the only one in which they seem deliberately to have acted as merchants. Yet they must always have sold surplus produce in good years, and perhaps regularly. Thornton undoubtedly sold ewe-milk cheese, and salt; Barlings appears to have sold tanned hides; and lay brothers at Markby were indicted as common tanners selling at an excessive profit in 1360. Quarries were worked by a few religious houses, like Thornton and Kirkstead, though no evidence suggests that it was for other than home consumption, whereas flour-mills were undoubtedly operated for profit. Finally salt-making was a specifically local occupation in which religious houses were much involved, especially in the first three centuries of their existence. It is difficult to believe that some at least of the salt manufactured in Revesby's

[43] DLC, *passim*; Sempring. Char., *passim*; BM Cott. Vesp. E xvIII, *passim*; Bod. Top. Lincs. d.1, f. 46v; Bod. Tanner 166, pp. 22, 81; G & C ms. 376, f. 169.

[44] *Hundred Rolls*, pp. 259, 317; *Cal. Misc. Inq.* II, 1628; *Med. Lin.*, p. 151; Bod. Top. Lincs. d.1, f. 48; T. A. M. Bishop, 'A Cistercian Customs Exemption', LAASRP 4, pp. 101–8.

grange at Wainfleet, or Kirkstead's at Scraine in Fishtoft, did not reach the open market.[45] The shrinking labour force of the later fourteenth century may have adversely affected the salt industry, but the wool trade had an even stronger enemy, in the shape of the royal taxation policy during the French wars. Certainly the trade shrank and it seems certain that in the last two centuries of their life the Lincolnshire religious houses can have drawn little profit from it.

There is occasional evidence that religious houses performed specific secular functions in connection with road and bridge repair, land drainage, and coast protection. The involvement of Kirkstead and Revesby in the economy of the south Lindsey fens and that of Crowland and Spalding in the low grounds of south Kesteven and Holland fill a large section of Dugdale's *Imbanking and Draining* and have recently been described in some detail by Professor Hallam. Failure to recognize their obligations, and any high-handed action against tenants, commoners, or neighbours might, especially in the disturbed conditions which began in the second half of the fourteenth century and lasted almost until the Dissolution, lead to great resentment. There had been, we have seen, friction in the early days of monastic expansion, but there was just as much trouble at the latter end. Now it was not so much rivalry in the field as "tyranny" by an established landlord which was resented. Claims to exemption from geld and from parochial dues must often have been irritating from the first, and Roger de Hanby who in the thirteenth century weakly sought to acquire freedom by submitting to the Hospitallers' protection, and putting their mark on his property in Otby, was doubtless regarded locally as a traitor. The continued conflicts between Crowland and its neighbours in the fifteenth century are well known from the narrative of the continuator of the Crowland chronicle. Some of them arise from friction concerning parish churches and will be considered later, but there seems to be nothing but secular jealousy in the dispute which came to a head in 1450 between the abbey and John Witham of Boycote Green in Baston:

"A chapel also which had been built in former times on the waste of the said vill of Baston for the convenience of wayfarers and the benefit of tenants, because there was not easy access to the parish church thereof ... he asserted to be his own separate estate. Accordingly in this same chapel, which had long ago been consecrated, he held his courts secular and for the purpose of profaning the place ... ordered a stable to be made therein for his horse."

The Hospitallers too were the target for much hostility and Bishop Trollope has printed extracts from a case in the Court of Star Chamber

[45] LRS 30, p. 62; LAASRP 9, *passim*.

brought against them by inhabitants of Ashby de la Launde which suggest some tenseness of feeling in the early sixteenth century. The farmer of the commander of Temple Bruer, Brother Babynton, "caused his chapleyn and sixteen of his servants in the Rogation days . . . to go in a riotous manner, that is to say with billys bowys arrows swords and bucklers and oder wepyns under color of a procession, about the saide Hethe of Ashby." Babynton justified himself but not perhaps very convincingly for local feeling, "He being at London his preste and v oder men persons and iii women persons went in procession in peasable and devout manner about all the Temple Hethe to pray for seasonable weder."[46]

[46] *Plac. de Q. W.*, p. 412; Riley, *op. cit.*, p. 414; E. Trollope, *Sleaford and the Wapentakes of Flaxwell and Aswardhurn*, 1872, p. 96, citing BM Add. 4936.

CHAPTER V

RELIGIOUS HOUSES:
RELIGIOUS AND DOMESTIC LIFE

So far we have looked at the monasteries as an element in the agrarian and commercial life of the county, but it is time now to turn to their religious and domestic activities. Prayer and charitable works are the dual purpose of monastic foundations, and the rules of hospitality to the stranger and traveller, and distribution of alms to the poor, were the proper duty of all. In the larger houses, such as Louth, an almoner was appointed, with funds for the support of his department, and daily distributions of broken meats and old clothes took place. In addition, either by the Founder's ordinance, or through later gifts, many houses distributed money or bread to the poor on Maundy Thursday, All Saints' Day or St Thomas's Day. At Barlings just before the Dissolution they were making a general distribution on the feasts of St Nicholas and St Thomas to all the poor who came there of one 'grey' loaf and one herring; and at Spalding forty-two shillings were given out on the five vigils of our Lady, and other smaller sums in memory of certain benefactors, besides three and a half yards of woollen cloth called 'duds' to each of thirty poor in Moulton and Aukborough, and eight quarters of 'pardon beans', to be given each year for the soul of countess Lucy, the foundress of the house. Other houses making such specific distributions were Bardney, Crowland, Freiston, Humberstone, Markby, Newstead on Ancholme, Stixwold, and the Hospitallers of Willoughton. The Willoughton entry in the *Valor* probably describes the general practice with regard to almsgiving in smaller houses where there was no almonry: "Thirteen pounds six shillings and eightpence distributed each year to the poor every day, as well within the hall of the preceptory, as before its gate, by the ancient foundation of John Were, founder of the preceptory and done thus of ancient well-established custom."[1]

Closely allied to the exercise of hospitality to all comers, and to the giving of alms to the poor, was a provision for the spiritual welfare of the beneficiaries. This was particularly necessary for the remote site of many Cistercian houses, for external persons were not admitted to the

---

[1] Venables, *op. cit.*, p. 14; *Val. Eccl.* IV, pp. 131, 98, and *passim*.

convent church and there might well be no parochial chapel or church at hand. The chapel at the gates was a marked feature of such houses and must have served not only travellers but the convent's own lay dependants. Revesby had such a chapel, dedicated to St Laurence, next its gates in 1346; Abbot Richard Dunham built a chapel of St Nicholas at the gate of Louth before 1246; and the beautiful chapel of St Leonard, at the gates of Kirkstead of the same period, still survives.[2]

Among the earliest post-Conquest grants to religious houses, tithe of demesne land, separated from the rest of the parochial tithes, was very common. As late as 1150 Hugh Malet gave to Whitby Abbey "all my demesne in Rothwell, with the chapel of my *curia*, and all the tithes of the said demesne," but by this time it was far more usual for the whole church, with undivided tithes, to be given. In a few cases, the monastery was content with the advowson (patronage) of the benefice, and perhaps received a pension from the clerk it presented, but more often the house was itself 'admitted' to the church by the bishop, or 'invested' with the parsonage. This happened at Alvingham about 1155 when Hamelin, the dean, resigned to the convent the church of St Adelwold of Alvingham. A description of the gift of Surfleet church to Spalding Priory by Jocelin son of Helpon records that Jocelin put the prior into possession "with bell ropes and church door" and then came into the chapter-house and confirmed the gift before monks, clergy, and laity then present with the knife of Huscord, steward of Pinchbeck."[3]

The monastery thus invested was entitled to farm the glebe land and to receive the entire income of the church, that is the tithes and all customary offerings, and to exploit these sources of income to the full. In many parishes the new monastic owners provided or were given a barn to house their tithe, which might well prove to be the nucleus of a group of farm buildings: Walter son of Walter of Market Rasen, for example, gave to Sixhills "the site of a barn to put their tithe in, within my own *curia*;" the monks of Castleacre were given six acres in Fleet marsh "to build a barn for their tithe." Elsham Priory, on the other hand, was permitted to build its tithe barn at the west end of the glebe house at Kingerby. The monastic rectors collected all the offerings of the parish, altarage, mortuaries, and the rest, and in return maintained the chancel of the church. Rarely (except as an act of grace) did they contribute to the building or upkeep of the nave, which by ancient custom was the business of the parishioners. As the owner of the church the convent naturally provided for the service of God in it. Not to have done so would have been, at the lowest level, to imperil the income from offerings.[4] In some

[2] Reg. 7, f. 85; Venables, *op. cit.*, p. 13; plate VI.
[3] Surtees Soc., 69, p. 50; LRS 18, p. 103; LNQ XVIII, p. 129, citing BM Add. 5844, f. 403.   [4] LRS 18, p. 21; BM Harl. 2110, f. 76; LRS 20, p. 39; BM Harl. 3658, p. 44.

cases the church was served by a stipendiary curate maintained by the monastery and housed and fed there, as at Deeping, where there were "priests who had a monk's portion and a chamber in the priory." In houses of canons the brothers of the house seem often to have served its churches, but in either case the service might well be perfunctory and unreliable.

When the church lay very close to the monastery, and particularly if it was a poor one—Markby is a good example—nothing more was done and the loose, temporary arrangement continued, but already during the twelfth century some convents had, with the bishop's approval, set aside either part of the tithes or a fixed income derived from other sources, for the maintenance in the church of a 'vicar' who was to take the rector's place, to be instituted by the bishop to his 'benefice', and to have security of tenure in it. Robert Grosseteste confirmed an ancient arrangement or 'ordination' of this sort for Humberstone, where the vicar and his deacon were each to have a monk's allowance of food, and the vicar was to receive all customary offerings on feast days, and at weddings and funerals. Almost a hundred years later Stixwold was providing its vicar every week with "fourteen gallons of ale and seven pricked loaves for his boy, twenty shillings per annum for a robe, fourteen shillings for his clerk's stipend, and for his larder eight hundred eels, two stones of cheese, one stone of butter, half a stone of soap, two hundred turves, and a suitable lodging near the parish church." Arrangements of this sort cannot always have been very satisfactory: as Richard of Coates, vicar of West Ravendale, complained in 1289, "the food supplied by the priory was wanting in meat."[5] As we have seen, Bishop Hugh of Wells, encouraged no doubt by the reforming zeal of the fourth Lateran Council, tried to persuade all monastic houses to ordain vicarages in their churches, thus securing that only priests of whom he approved would be instituted to the new benefices, and that adequate and permanent provision was made for the care of the parish.

It is difficult to say exactly how many monastic proprietors there were in the county at this point, but the *Liber Antiquus* in which Hugh's activities are recorded contains confirmations or new ordinations for 182 churches. This is by no means all the churches in monastic ownership: many more 'appropriations', by which a religious house took over all the fruits of a living apart from a portion assigned to a vicar, followed the economic difficulties and shrinking incomes of the later fourteenth century.

Omitting churches which were obviously appropriated by the dean and chapter of Lincoln, and the individual prebends, the *Valor* lists 240 churches then appropriated, and a further 107 paying pensions to

[5] LRS 11, pp. 48–9; LRS 39, pp. 54, 115.

religious houses, and probably in their gift. Since the total number of benefices in the county at this time was reckoned at about 700, it follows that by the end of the medieval period almost half of them were in some degree under monastic influence.

The ways in which this was felt varied very considerably. In general, it seems, the monasteries did not present their inhabitants to benefices, although the temptation to do so must have been very strong when the houses' resources shrank steadily from the late fourteenth century. A few monks were able to buy themselves papal licences (capacities) to acquire benefices: John Marome from Louth Park had one in 1467; but they seem to have been exceptions. The canons regular, however, were more likely to provide incumbents from among their own numbers, especially in the later period. Although Mr Dickinson has pointed out that the Augustinians had no intention of undertaking wholesale charge of their dependent churches, Bridlington Priory was already serving Edenham by one of its own canons as early as 1268, and Mrs Bowker has calculated that forty-four Lincolnshire churches in all received religious incumbents (presumably canons) in the period 1495–1520. She adds another fourteen canons-regular licensed for non-residence, because resident in their monasteries and therefore presumably using a curate or parochial chaplain to serve the cure. It must have been this sort of incumbent to whom the parishioners of Rauceby took exception when in 1500 they petitioned the bishop against William Talbot, a canon of Shelford, the patron, "because they have been used to have a secular vicar."

The hand of a conventual proprietor could lie equally heavily on a parish through the tithes and offerings which it would be reluctant to share with any other claimant, religious or secular. It is to this determination that we owe the long series of compositions regulating the status and income of manorial or religious chapels by which the religious houses defined and established their rights. As early as 1183, for example, Stixwold, as rectors of Wainfleet St Mary, forced upon Bury St Edmunds a regulation of their chapel in Sailholme:

"the monks are not by occasion of that chapel to do any injury to the parochial right of the mother church ... and especially any of them who visit or live at the chapel are to exercise no parochial function whether on sea or on land outside its old boundaries. No secular priest is to minister there on the monks' behalf without the consent of the mother-church, no *viaticum* or penance is to be administered to any except monks."[6]

Bridlington made a similar series of compositions to safeguard the

---

[6] Reg. 20, f. 86; Dickinson, *op. cit.*, pp. 231–2; LRS 20, p. 33; M. Bowker, *Secular Clergy in the Diocese of Lincoln*, Cambridge, 1968, pp. 64 *et seq.*; LAO, Dioc. Vj. 5, f. 77*v*; BM Add. 46701, f. 90; Douglas, *op. cit.*, pp. 181–2.

I. CHAPEL AT BULBY IN IRNHAM

11. THE FUNERAL OF ST HUGH

III. THE CLOSE WALL AT LINCOLN

IV. MONASTIC RECORDS

(a) Benefactors of Crowland

(b) A book from Kirkstead

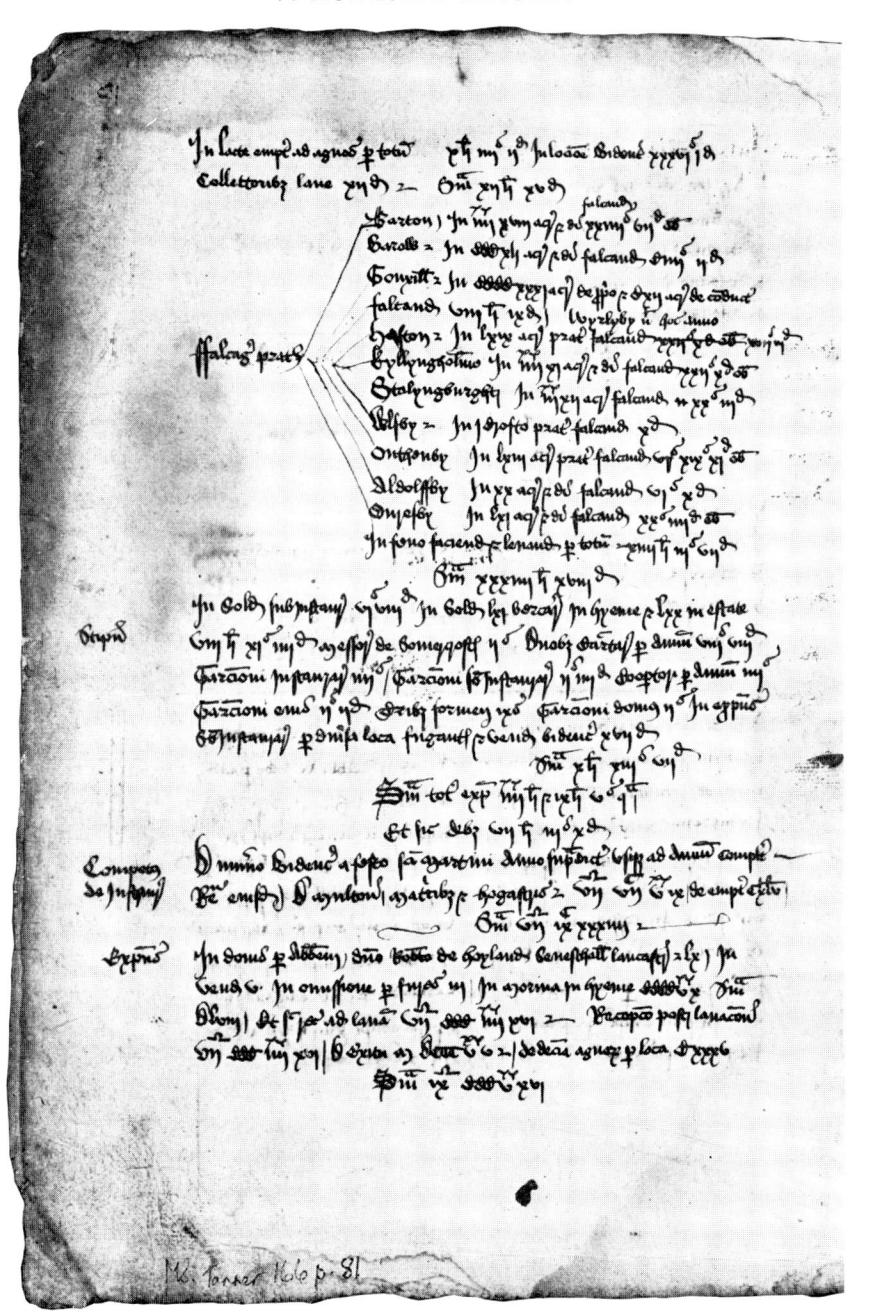

A page of the Thornton stock-keeper's account

VI. CHAPEL OF ST LEONARD OUTSIDE THE GATES OF KIRKSTEAD

A South-west View of Kirkstead Chappel in the County of Lincoln. Schnebbelie 1785.

VII. BENCH-END IN OSBOURNBY CHURCH

VIII. ROOD-LOFT AT COATES BY STOW

rights of the parish church of Edenham over the manorial chapels at Southorpe, Scottlethorpe, and Grimsthorpe, and to ensure the payment of tithe on Vaudey's and Westminster's land in the parish. Other religious houses, such as Crowland, were concerned to establish the boundaries of their tithe areas, and this explains the award of 1370 by which the boundary between Holbeach and Whaplode was defined. Monastic rectors also waged bitter wars against the 'poaching' of the friars, and at Grimsby, as we shall see in the next chapter, the bishop was called on for help against them in the early fourteenth century.[7] Rigid attention was paid to the collection of offerings such as mortuaries, which figure in many entries in the *Valor* as substantial items in monastic income, and to the proper maintenance of the land and houses of the benefice. Doubtless, as other sources of income diminished, the churches became increasingly important, and this may explain Crowland's acrimonious disputes in the late fifteenth century with the vicar of Whaplode about the provision of desks and stalls for the chancel, and the ownership of the churchyard trees. When, in addition, a house claimed to exercise the jurisdiction usually belonging to the archdeacon over the inhabitants of its parishes, discontent might well be strong: in 1246 Bardney was able to establish, and presumably maintained, its right to judge "all cases of injury done by word or deed in the parish on feast-days, non-observance of church festivals, quintain play, scot-ales, wrestling, dancing, dicing, and default in tithe-paying."[8] These are only illustrations of what monastic ownership of parish churches could do: we still await a more thorough evaluation of the evidence than has been possible here.

It is now time to turn to the monasteries themselves, and to consider the lives of prayer, contemplation, and study for which they had received their endowments. Here our sources are often misleading, since they are derived from reports of evil conduct revealed by visitations, and limited because episcopal visitation reached only the Benedictines, Austin canons, and Cistercian nuns. In the early days of monastic foundations Bishop Alexander and his immediate successors were actively involved in the endowment and support of new houses, but with the beginning of the thirteenth century and the end of the period of expansion, the bishops concerned themselves only with benediction of new heads, and the visitation of the non-exempt orders. For the benedictions an elaborate and costly ceremony was devised, as we see in the account in Repingdon's register of a choir cope covered with gold leaf which the abbot of Kirkstead wore at Sleaford in 1406.[9]

[7] Reg. 5, f. 95v; G. W. Macdonald, *Historical Notices of the Parish of Holbeach*, King's Lynn, 1891; ULC Dd. 10.28, f. 84v.
[8] BM Add. 5845, f. 103; Riley, *op. cit.*, p. 403; AASRP XXXII, pp. 35-96.
[9] LRS 57, p. 89.

The machinery of episcopal visitation which was elaborated by Hugh of Wells and his successors, in obedience to a papal mandate of 1232, enabled the bishops to censure and punish irregularities of conduct, to enforce the observation of the law, and to make sure that the goods of the house were not dissipated. It was the bishops' practice to instruct the brethren of a house by means of a visitation sermon, to ask a series of detailed questions about the temporal and spiritual welfare of the house which were answered by each of the brethren in turn, often on oath, and to frame orders or injunctions designed to correct the faults they discovered.[10]

There is little precise information about the organization and size of Lincolnshire religious houses at any period except 1376-7, when a return of numbers was made for a clerical subsidy; nor is it always easy to find out what officials there were, and how the finances were administered. It seems to be generally true that all but the smallest houses had, by the mid-thirteenth century, set aside separate endowments for their head, and for the refectory, infirmary, clothing, and so on. We can see this happening in the endorsements on Vaudey charters, which show that the abbey had separate funds for the abbacy, the convent (that is, the monks), the fabric, the gate-house, the wool-house, and the mill and tannery.[11] Each fund was separately administered and accounted for by a brother assigned to the task, and in larger houses there were in addition departments for the infirmary, sacristy, building work, almonry, pittances, and so on, each with its head or 'obedientiary'. Each department was subject to a central annual account by a committee of senior monks; at this time, in the Cistercian houses, the grangers submitted their detailed accounts. The Thornton Abbey chronicle includes separate accounts from a cellarer, sub-cellarer, bursar, chamberlain, almoner, fabric master, sacrist, refectorian, infirmarian, gate-keeper, cheese-keeper, and stock-keeper. Most of the accounts date from the early fourteenth century, though the context of the chronicle suggests that the officers were still functioning a century later. Crowland had an even more elaborate arrangement which was set down during a vacancy in the abbacy in 1328, and which portrays admirably the complexities of the great household. There were forty-one monks, five chaplains living in the convent as corrodians (pensioners), ten other chaplains receiving the monk's daily allowance of one loaf, one and a half gallons of ale, and two dishes of meat or fish, a chaplain to serve the corrodians, and thirty-five lay servants, one for the church, two for sick monks in the infirmary, one each for the refectory, hostelry, and common hall or entrance of the abbey, two cooks

---

[10] Based on C. R. Cheney, *Episcopal Visitation of Monasteries in the Thirteenth Century*, Manchester, 1931, and A. H. Thompson in LRS 7, 14, 21.

[11] LAOR 5, pp. 39-40.

for the convent and one for the infirmary, a buyer of flesh, fish, and other food, two men in the cellar, two bakers, two brewers, two kiln men, a maltster, two millers (one for the horse mill and one for the windmill), a janitor, tailor, cobbler, laundryman, carpenter, mason, plumber, roofer, smith, carter, and four stablemen. In addition there was a marshal, a watchman, and a wood-keeper.[12]

As to the numbers of religious, no information is really complete and it would be unwise to draw any firm conclusions. As the figures of 1376–7 stand (and excluding Crowland, for which there is no return), no house of male monks or canons was nearly so large as the largest of the double houses of the Gilbertines (Sempringham, Bullington, Sixhills, Nun Ormsby, and Alvingham), and the largest houses of monks, those of Kirkstead and Revesby, rank only with the nuns of Stixwold of the same order.[13] If the figures given by the Louth Park chronicle of sixty-six monks and one hundred and fifty *conversi* in that house in the first half of the thirteenth century may be relied on, it seems that the Cistercians had suffered a very marked decline, especially in the numbers of *conversi*, and doubtless the numbers of Benedictines, Augustinians, and Premonstratensians had shrunk correspondingly. The principal reasons for the losses were probably the epidemics of the mid-fourteenth century, which presumably were the more severe because of the closeness of community life, and the subsequent scarcity of labour. But something must also be attributed to the changing climate of religious opinion, which had already, as we shall see, turned the minds of many potential monks to the evangelical work of the friars, and now was seeking expression in the more secular foundation of gilds, chantries, and the like. It seems probable that some houses, at least, recovered their numbers somewhat during the next century, but here again the evidence is by no means complete.

Reference was made in the Crowland return, quoted above, to corrodians, and something must be said about this feature of monastic life. It appears, in a simple form, at an early stage in monastic history, in arrangements such as one made by Alvingham Priory in 1218, by which it gave five loaves each Sunday of her life to Alice of Portmore in return for a resignation to the house of her right of dower in a carucate and bovate of land in Cockerington.[14] Similar grants of daily food or of small daily 'wages' when the monks themselves began to receive them, and even of chambers in the house, were made to recompense old servants, reimburse benefactors, or pay parochial chaplains for their services. In many cases it was regarded as a provision for old age. Provided the numbers

[12] Bod. Tanner 166, *passim*; BM Add. 5845, f. 32v.
[13] PRO E179/7/35, quoted from a Foster Library copy in LAO. For full returns see Appendix 2.
[14] W. O. Massingberd, *Abstracts of Final Concords*, Lincoln, 1896, p. 116.

were reasonable, and the burden on the houses not too great, there was nothing inherently wrong with the system, although visiting bishops were probably wise to be suspicious of the continuous presence of too many laymen in the cloister, and of the beginnings of a virtual hotel industry in the nunneries. When, as a financial expedient, houses sold corrodies for ready money the situation became dangerous, and the Crown, the 'founders' (that is, their descendants or representatives), and even some bishops made things no easier by quartering their own nominees on the houses. Most houses probably kept the numbers of their lay parasites within bounds, but for the small house of Wellow in 1372, excessive grants of corrodies were obviously an important factor in the serious dilapidation of the house. Five corrodies are described, including one for Joan de Routhe and William her son (aged four) for their lives in survivorship and this Joan, alias "fetys Jonet," obviously wasted the abbey's goods, and made it a place of ill-fame. At Humberstone in 1440 the sale of a corrody to a harper called John Hardene was equally obnoxious; and at Bardney a young monk complained to the visitor that "a young layman who dwells with the abbot did most foully browbeat and scold this deponent, and it is notorious that this youth Taylboys is upheld by the abbot against the young monks."[15]

Few details are known about the domestic life of the monastery even with the help of visitation records except in the larger houses such as Crowland. We can imagine the abbot's or prior's household, and those of the obedientiaries in the larger houses; we know something of the infirmary, the refectory, and the guest house. From the fifteenth-century visitations we see the occasional breaks in the monotonous undeviating life. Visitors came to see even the young monks at Bardney, but usually the monotony of the life was little broken. The daily wage was paid, for clothes and other necessaries, the daily chapter met, meals were taken in the refectory, and there were regular small treats or pittances of almonds, fruits, and spices on feast days, besides the blood-letting, to recover from which the sufferers were sent away to a 'holiday home'. The monks of Bardney went regularly to Southrey, to their "seyney house" after the blood-lettings.

Then, too, we must remember that though the monks were 'conventual', and obliged to remain within their monastery for the greater part of their time, they were by no means isolated or enclosed from the world. Even if the house had no lay corrody holders the monks must have seen other laymen. Besides, many houses had doors opening into the towns or villages near which they lay, and many monks must have had to ride off to superintend outlying farms, or granges, or churches. It was obviously very easy for John Gedney, the sacrist of Humberstone,

[15] *Cal. Misc. Inq.* I, no. 850; LRS 14, *passim.*

to slip out in secular dress and go wildfowling, once he had rung the bell for matins, and friendships with laymen in the neighbourhood seem to have been common in the late fifteenth century.[16] The business men among the monks and nuns, those who managed the building work, the tannery, and the various workshops, and above all those who made the financial decisions were plainly men and women of practical ability; even if decisions of principle were taken by the whole community in the chapter meeting, the implementation was left in their hands. Variations in their abilities, as much as the pressure of external conditions, must have affected the worldly fortunes of the houses. Those houses which were able to lend money to crusaders in the mid-thirteenth century, as Nuncoton did, might find themselves, with Sempringham, Bardney, and Crowland, at various points in the following three centuries, seeking loans for themselves from the Italian financiers.[17]

For the smaller houses we know little apart from the visitations.[18] The convents, it seems, went on tranquilly enough, drawing their nuns from purely local families, taking in local children and widows as boarders, and muddling their accounts by granting pensions or corrodies to members of influential local families. Fosse, for example, was being used in 1440 by Sir John Pygot of Doddington as a dower house for his widowed mother, who had a hall and chamber there. In the same year the bishop told the nuns of Gokewell, who were much distracted by lay company, to take in as boarders only girls under ten and boys under eight. Similarly in the monasteries gentlemen's sons were boarded at the prior's table, often without charge. The visitations leave a general impression that rules of strictness and simplicity were everywhere relaxed. At Gokewell again the nuns were said not to live on the regular food enjoined by the rule, nor to eat it together, but to mess together in households of two or three, drawing only bread and beer from the house, and adding to it such private dainties as they fancied. At Thornholme, too, eating and reading in the refectory were altogether neglected, the stated hours of silence were not observed, and the night hours not said at all.

In the daily conventual life, and particularly in that of the Benedictines, there was a decided place for books and learning. After the learned Gilbert of Hoyland, the friend of St Bernard, who was an early abbot of Swineshead, there was no particularly distinguished monastic scholar or writer in the county except Robert Mannyng, canon first at Sempringham and then at Bourne (fl. 1288–1338), whose *Handlyng Synne* and *Chronicle of England* are of some literary importance. There was, nevertheless, a sound tradition of book-making and of chronicle writing in a

[16] LRS 14, p. 141; LRS 10, p. 50.
[17] Bod. Top. Linc. d.1, f. 28*v*; R. Graham, *op. cit.*, p. 137; VCH *Lincoln*, II, *passim*.
[18] LRS 14, *passim*.

number of houses. In this Crowland, with its long history and its large resources, was easily the leader; it produced not only the misleading and deliberately falsified history, compiled in the later middle ages, which goes under the name of Ingulph, but also a fifteenth-century continuation which is of great merit as a historical source. Louth Park, Spalding, Hagnaby, Barlings, and Thornton each produced chronicles of some merit, but all covered relatively limited periods. The Hagnaby compiler gives vivid pictures of the destruction wreaked by the great storms of 1284, 1286, and 1288: "in 1284 on the Monday night after the Assumption there was continuous rain and floods, so that all the hay near the Trent went uncut or was destroyed in the winrows... All the convent's beasts perished... In 1288 on St. Aschetin's day another flood came in as far as Maltby field . . . ."

At Thornton there was in the early sixteenth century another historically minded compiler to whose activities we owe the partial preservation of the monastery's accounts, but, this apart, no other writers of history seem to have been produced within the county.[19] Some books were undoubtedly written in Lincolnshire houses, and a few of them survive, like the thirteenth-century *Excepciones monachi Croylandie* (which is now Sidney Sussex MS. 73), and the Book of John Welle, canon of Hagnaby (Gonville and Caius MS. 190). There is ample evidence, too, that there were books, and even large libraries, in a few houses, and even a small cell like Deeping owned twenty-three books in the mid-fourteenth century.[20]

Although Leland, visiting Lincolnshire houses just before the Dissolution, reported only printed books at such small houses as Kyme, Haverholme, Nocton, Elsham, Ormsby, Humberstone, Thornholme, and Newstead, Mr Ker lists surviving manuscripts from Axholme, Bardney, Barlings, Boston Dominicans, Crowland, Deeping, Freiston, Grantham and Grimsby Franciscans, Hagnaby, Humberstone, Kirkstead, Kyme, Lincoln, St Katherine, Franciscans, Dominicans, and Carmelites, Louth Park, Markby, Newhouse, Newstead by Stamford, Nocton, Revesby, Sempringham, Stamford, St Leonard, Franciscans and Carmelites, Swineshead, Thornholme, Thornton, Tupholme, and Vaudey. It is interesting to know that so far as Mr Ker can tell, many of these books were the personal property of individual monks or canons before passing into the library of the house. One Bardney manuscript, for example, had belonged to a monk of the house who acquired it while he was *prior*

---

[19] VCH *Lincs.*, II, pp. 105–17; Venables, *op. cit.*; BM Cott. Vesp. B XI, ff. 1–60 (Hagnaby); BM Campbell Ch. xxi 4 (Thornton); G & C 376 (Spalding); Oxf. Magd. 199 (Barlings).

[20] *Mon. Ang.* IV, p. 167; EHR 54, 1939, pp. 88–95; N. R. Ker, *Medieval Libraries of Great Britain*, 2nd edn, 1964.

studencium at Cambridge; several Crowland books retain the names of their monk-owners; and the Wisbech town library contains a fine copy of the 1501 edition of the *Provinciale* of William Lyndwood, with the name of Robert Streyl, canon of Kyme, and many annotations in his hand.[21]

Closely associated with the library were the monastic scribes and here we know almost nothing about the Lincolnshire houses. Mr Bishop thinks he has identified a scribe working in Kirkstead and Revesby in the twelfth century, and some of the Vaudey, Revesby, and Newhouse scribes of the same period can be recognized fairly easily, but we have very little solid fact about the writing and illuminating of books for the monastery's own use in church and outside it. Oldfield mentions, without quoting his authority, a rector of Addlethorpe, Ralph de Folceby, who was "illuminator and librarian to the priory of Spalding;" and canon John Welle of Hagnaby copied in 1440 the manuscript belonging to his house (now Gonville and Caius MS. 190).[22]

Study and contemplation were an essential part of the monastic life, and the early instruction of the young monk to fit him for this and for the priesthood were undoubtedly carried on in the house. Besides this teaching Thornton had a school for fourteen boys in the almonry, to provide servers at masses, and probably to encourage the supply of novices. Presumably Crowland and Bardney had similar establishments, evidence of which has not survived. A little is known of convent schools, from mentions like that in a will of about 1520: "I will that Helyn and Agnes my daughters be put into an abbey to lerne and eyther of theym to be there the space of half a year." Canons of the Gilbertine order could complete their training in theology after 1300 in a house of studies in Stamford and there was similar provision for Benedictines from Durham, Cistercians from Vaudey, and for Carmelite friars. The town was also the scene, in 1334–5, of a short-lived attempt by some discontented Oxford masters to set up a "third foundation."[23] Increasingly, however, the Benedictines sent their student monks to Oxford or Cambridge, sometimes devoting the profits of an entire manor for the purpose, as Crowland did with its manor of Oakington, housing them in Buckingham College (on the site of Magdalene) at Cambridge, which Crowland founded, and in Gloucester and Durham Colleges at Oxford. Canons of all three orders and a few Cistercians were also students in both universities.[24]

[21] *Ibid.*, appendix, *owners*.   [22] LAASRP 4, pp. 101–8; E. Oldfield, *op. cit.*, p. 109.
[23] VCH *Lincs.*, II, p. 164; LRS 10, p. 148; VCH *Lincs.*, II, pp. 468–74; Surtees Soc., 76, pp. 324 *et seq.*
[24] Queens' Coll. Oakington rolls, now in ULC; A. B. Emden, *Biographical . . . Oxford*, Oxford; *Idem, Biographical . . . Cambridge*.

All these activities were subordinated to the true *raison d'être* of the monastic house, the life of prayer and the service of God, around which the monks' day revolved, with its observance of the canonical hours and its daily masses. Into this context of regular worship the secular work of the house had to fit itself. It is true that the sacrist of Humberstone might ring the bell for matins and then slip back to his warm bed, but for most monks and nuns the church services, and the daily chapter meeting enjoined by their rules, must have been the central fact of their lives. It was in the church itself that all the greatest treasures of the house were displayed, and it was the church and its furnishings which in the later centuries attracted most gifts from the outside world. In 1377 Gilbert of Umfreville, Earl of Angus and lord of Kyme, gave to Kyme Priory, for use on the greater festivals, a magnificent set of vestments embroidered with his arms, and similar gifts must often have been made by pious laymen. Only Crowland, Bardney, and Sempringham were fortunate enough to possess saintly relics which attracted pilgrims, and even they seem to have been mostly local in their importance; for the rest, the monastic churches were probably of importance only to their own communities. We hear of them equipped with organs, made beautiful with glass, adorned by glorious plate and vestments. Even the austere Cistercians at Louth adorned their churches with pictures: "1309 New work was done about the high altar and it was painted by Master Everard. And two pictures at the altar of St. Mary Magdalene and a picture at the altar of St. Stephen were painted by brothers John of Brantyngham and R of Welton." At Crowland there was much gilding and glazing, and provision was made of gilded reredoses and screens, elaborate vestments, and fine plate by Abbot John Litlington (1427–70).[25]

The buildings to house these multifarious activities, once the primitive simplicity of foundation was over, conformed to set patterns so that, although nothing except a few stones remain at Vaudey, we know very well that it must have been surrounded by a perimeter wall with a gate in it, and have had a *capella ad portas* close by, and that the western range of the cloister would have been devoted to the *conversi*, for whom also there would have been a second choir in the church. In the same way the buildings of Bardney and Crowland conformed to the regular Benedictine plan of a cloister on the south wall of the nave, with a chapter house on its eastern range and the dorter above it, a frater on the southern range, a separate infirmary block to the south-east, and, on the west side of the western range of the cloister, the great court where were the workshops, the almonry, guest house, and so on.

As for the churches, they varied in size and magnificence with the

[25] LAO D & C Dii/62/iii/12; R. Foreville, *Le Livre de Saint Gilbert de Sempringham*, Rennes, 1943, p. 72; Venables, *op. cit.*, p. 20; Riley, *op. cit.*, pp. 30–3.

wealth and importance of the house, but it seems that a number of them were rebuilt or extended in the thirteenth century (Thornton, for example), and that bell towers were added in the thirteenth and fourteenth centuries. The tower at Hagnaby was evidently under construction in 1247 when a youth who fell from its stone parapet had a miraculous escape from death. The fifteenth century saw the addition of coloured-glass windows at Hagnaby in 1467, and at Wellow in 1462 (with a crucifix in the middle and donors to right and left): doubtless there were many others. It may be noted in passing that the 'Guthlac Roll' may have been designed during the twelfth century as a series of cartoons for windows to be put into the conventual church at Crowland which was then extensively remodelled.[26]

The undertaking of such elaborate structures as these, the servicing, drainage, and water supply, and the arrangements for maintenance required considerable skill. Quarries of stone, as we have seen, provided the initial building material, but in 1438–9 Revesby, Bardney, and Kirkstead were all receiving bricks from the kilns set up for Tattershall Castle, and no doubt many other houses were doing likewise. Certainly the great gate of Thornton, built in brick at the end of the fourteenth century, apparently to serve as an abbot's lodging, suggests that it was already a desirable material. The detailed work was usually in the hands of a monk 'master of the works' and something of his duties may be guessed by a chapter order agreed at Crowland in 1327, concerning the duties of this obedientiary. He was no longer to be responsible for *all* buildings but was to maintain

"the walls, roof, windows, doors, and gutters of the conventual church, of the revestry above and below with its glass windows and outer door, the sacrist's chamber above the vestry, the cloister above and below, the dormitory above and below and all contiguous buildings, all houses, buildings, chapels and appurtenances in the Infirmary and Hostelry, the door of the monks' parlour and the two doors of the cellarer's parlour, the kitchen with its gutter on the east side towards the hostelry and the building called Le Dresser."

Few significant remains survive from any of the Lincolnshire houses except Thornton. The late Colonel King Fane put together notes on the sites as they were known in 1929 and these, with suitable revisions, have been incorporated in the list of monasteries in Appendix 3.[27]

[26] PCC 41, 39; I owe the Wellow reference to my friend Mr E. Gillett; Warner, *op. cit.*; M. C. Knowles and J. St Joseph, *Monastic Sites from the Air*, Cambridge, 1952, pp. xi–xxv.
[27] LRS 55, pp. 57, 73; BM Add. 5845, f. 44*v*; W. King-Fane, *A Summary of Lincolnshire Monasteries. Commanderies & Preceptories*, Lincoln, 1929.

CHAPTER VI
THE MENDICANTS

THE late twelfth century was a time of crisis for the Latin church: on the one hand, the faith was attacked in the south of France by heretical movements usually known as Albigensian; on the other, Christendom itself was threatened once more by a renewed Turkish attack. To combat this double danger the faith must be strengthened and defended and Christian armies must be somehow raised and financed. True Christianity must be taught, better and more widely, by missionaries trained and armed for the purpose, and the crusade must be preached incessantly by the most skilful of propagandists. These needs were met by the spontaneous generation of an entirely new religious phenomenon, the friar, whose explicit aim was to preach the Christian faith, who had little of the corporate life and liturgical preoccupation of the ordinary monastery, who had no property to manage, but depended for his living on charitable gifts, and who had few local roots, but moved from house to house at frequent intervals. The friars' typical activities were regular sermons preached to popular congregations in the churches of their own convents, and 'preaching tours' during which they delivered sermons on Sundays and feast days, either in parish churches or in the open air.[1]

The followers of St Dominic and St Francis were the first of these groups, soon to be followed by Carmelite and Austin friars, Sack and Crutched friars, all of whom established themselves in England during the first half of the thirteenth century. The period was remarkable for the great series of reforming bishops, all of whom were engaged in the task of teaching the Christian faith to their flocks and who saw in the friars powerful allies who would at once invigorate, strengthen, and supplement the existing servants of the church, and be unaffected by the local ties and proprietary considerations which continually impeded the local churches.[2]

Robert Grosseteste was among the first to welcome and invite the friars to England; long before he was bishop he was the patron and protector of the Dominicans and Franciscans in Oxford, and it was no doubt

---
[1] M. C. Knowles, *Religious Orders*, I, pp. 113–252; J. R. H. Moorman, *A History of the Franciscan Order* . . . , Oxford, 1968.
[2] M. Gibbs and J. Lang, *The Bishops and Reform, 1215–72*, Oxford, 1934, *passim*.

through his infectious enthusiasm that so many university-trained clerks and distinguished monks left their secular cures or their comfortable monasteries, to preach the word of Christ with the mendicant friars. This recruitment of scholars and close association with universities were to give a peculiarly scholastic flavour to all the English friaries, and nowhere was this so marked as in Lincolnshire. Here before 1300 each of the five centres of population, Lincoln, Stamford, Boston, Grantham, and Grimsby, had at least one friary, founded for the most part not by great feudal landowners but by individuals or groups of merchants. The founders must often have been concerned, as some founders of monasteries had been, to augment the forces of the church in their own locality and to provide for their own religious needs. From the first the friars were popular and highly successful not only as preachers, but even more as confessors and religious directors, and it seems to have been particularly in this capacity that the townsmen wanted them. The foundation of the Boston Franciscan friary, with its many German friars, by the Easterling community of that town is a particularly good example of the importance of the friars in the towns. It is equally important, perhaps, that no more was needed for a friary than a small piece of land, a simple building, congregations to hear sermons, and charitable Christians to give small regular doles, all of which could be easily supplied in the Lincolnshire towns. It is not therefore surprising that while the only rural friary in the county of which we know, that of the Crutched friars at Whaplode, survived for a very short time, most of those in the towns were soon confirmed in their positions, added to their strength, and remained as important elements in local life until the Dissolution.

Lincoln, Boston, and Stamford each had houses of the four major groups of friars, Austin, Carmelite (White), Dominican (Black), and Franciscan (Grey); Grimsby had Austins and Franciscans; and Grantham Franciscans only. Little survives today to demonstrate to us the size and importance of these houses, many of them served by conduits bringing water in from the countryside (at Boston the Dominicans' water supply came from Bolingbroke). The nave of the Franciscan church at Lincoln houses the City and County Museum; part of what seems to have been the Dominicans' guest house lies on the east side of Shodfriars Lane in Boston; but there is little else. The early poverty and simplicity of these mendicant houses disappeared as the thirteenth century progressed, and certainly these surviving fragments are sufficiently imposing. It seems from the Huntingfield episode recounted below that the Dominican church at Boston was of some size and importance: "two parallelograms divided by a walking space giving access to the street, and bridged by the belfry or tower," and this was presumably intended to accommodate large urban congregations during Lenten sermons. Such large buildings near the centre of the town were inevitably of importance to local life, if only as places of sanctuary for criminals. This seems to have been particularly true at Grantham, where twice in the fourteenth century murderers fled to the Franciscan church, which lay to the north of the present market place. They might also be used for more secular purposes, as at Boston where eleven tuns of wine stored in the Franciscan convent were stolen in 1268. Two centuries later this same church at Boston is said by Pishey Thompson, the nineteenth-century historian of the town, to have been celebrated for the Corpus Christi plays performed there, and certainly this activity accords with the part played by the friars in popular urban religion.

We have only slight knowledge of the routine of life in these mendicant houses or of their physical layout. What is certain is that the friars moved from house to house, sometimes taking away with them books from the libraries. As young recruits they had received instruction in theology in their friaries or had gone, if they were Carmelites, to the house of study at Stamford, or if Dominicans at Lincoln. At a later stage they proceeded to a *studium generale* (a university). Much time and ingenuity have been spent in estimating the average population of the friaries, from the payments of alms to the friars made on a *per capita* basis out of the Wardrobe. The information is irregularly spaced and rather unconvincing but appears to demonstrate for the Dominicans, as might have been expected, that no Lincolnshire friary could compare in numbers with those at Bristol or in the university towns. Dr Keith Egan's fuller figures show how much the numbers of friars fluctuated: the Lincoln Carmelites seem to have numbered 40 in 1315, 32 in 1316, and 22 and 32 at different points in 1317. The figures are available from 1285 to 1335; the largest population of any Lincoln friary was 63 Franciscans in 1301, and no house during the period fell below 20 in number. The Dominican and Franciscan friaries in all the towns seem to have been more populous than those of the other two orders of friars.[3]

The work of the friars was financed in a way completely different from that of the regular monastic houses. It is true that after the very earliest days all the friaries were willing to receive property (as distinct from alms) and came to depend, to some extent, on income from house rents. At the same time the major part of their living continued to come from the gifts of the faithful, collected by specially deputed *questors* or *limitors* who went their rounds within the area of their houses. One such, a Carmelite, John of Lincoln, was robbed of five shillings at South Gay-

---

[3] *Grantham Journal*, 5 Jan. 1935; *Abbrev. Plac.*, I, p. 176; Ker, *op. cit.*; W. A. Hinnebusch, *The Early English Friar Preachers*, Rome, 1951, pp. 274, 340; W. Harrod, *The Antiquities of Stamford*, London, 1785, I, p. 24; K. Egan, 'The Establishment and Early Development of the Carmelite Order in England', Cambridge Ph.D. thesis, 1965.

ton on a Sunday night in Lent, in 1380. No doubt the questors made regular calls where alms were habitually bestowed; the payment made to the Carmelites of Lincoln in 1467–8 and recorded in a household account for Little Cawthorpe was presumably collected in this way.[4] At the same time the many bequests to the 'four orders of friars' which are common in Lincolnshire wills not only of townsmen, in the fifteenth and early sixteenth centuries, must have been collected by the questors. It seems probable that they also engaged during the last century of the friaries' existence in the negotiations by which lay people, for an appropriate consideration, were accepted into the confraternity of the friary and shared the benefits of its prayers. Stukeley has recorded a letter of confraternity, a blank form, which was presumably printed: "Mr. Weston minister of Empingham sent me a deed under seal of John Tenell prior of the friar preachers' convent at Stamford, being a grant to a man and his wife [blank] of the benefit of all their prayers, preachings, fastings, alms etc. living or dying. Dated 1511."

One further source of income which seems to have been particularly profitable in the two centuries before the Dissolution was the regular celebration of the friary churches of anniversary masses for the souls of dead benefactors. Edward Brown of Lincoln, for example, in 1504 ordered that the four orders of friars in the city should say "*placebo* and *dirige* in my house where my body lieth and do their messes at home in their owne place." The custom was well established, for as early as 1307 the Austin friars of Grimsby were forced by the rector of Grimsby St James to refrain from tempting the parishioners to arrange annuals and trentals in their church rather than in the parish church. This custom, as well as the diversion from the parish churches of a variety of other offerings, was deeply resented in the thirteenth century, but doubtless continued, as did the offerings, to provide an important source of income.[5]

Preaching was, as we have seen, the primary purpose of the friars' existence and at all periods after their appearance in Lincolnshire the friars were actively preaching. It seems that in their earlier years much of their preaching was done out of doors in an unsystematic and unconventional manner. At Lincoln before 1270 they preached on ground near the Castle, "le Batailplace," where games were also played, and in Grimsby the Austin Friars were known "to preach the word of God in streets and open places, in their oratory and in the parish churchyard" in the late thirteenth century. As time went on, however, the sermons were, it seems, more frequently preached in the friary churches, especially during Lent, in cathedral and collegiate churches (friars are recorded as

[4] LRS 56, p. 22; LAO M.M. 1/3/26.
[5] Surtees Soc., 76, p. 338; LRS 5, p. 24; ULC Dd.10.28, f. 34*v*.

preaching in the cathedral at Lincoln in 1306, perhaps for the first time), and, where incumbents agreed, in the parish churches. The fourteenth and fifteenth centuries saw increasing attention to, and provision for, the preaching of sermons everywhere in Lincolnshire and especially in the large, rebuilt parish churches of the towns and large villages of the prosperous marsh and fen areas, and many of the sermons enjoyed in these churches on Sundays and festivals were preached by friars.[6] At times the friars must have ridden out from their houses and returned at night, as Friar Baudellzinus did from Stamford, in a story recounted by Professor Owst, although the more distant churches can have been reached only in the course of a preaching tour. We have no evidence of conflict between the orders about these tours, but it is clear from the cartulary of the Carmelite house at King's Lynn that a demarcation of the spheres of influence of different houses of the same order might sometimes be necessary. Here in 1346 the Carmelites of Lynn were ordered to confine their preaching to the area of Fleet and Gedney, while Tydd and its neighbourhood were to be left to the Cambridge friars.[7]

It has not proved possible to identify with certainty any sermons preached by mendicants in Lincolnshire, but Friar Baudellzinus' story may well have been used as an illustrative anecdote to point a moral in a sermon and is worth quoting. He told his brethren how he was due to preach on Sunday in a Lincolnshire church six miles from Stamford, and a kinswoman of his who lived in the parish asked her husband to come and hear the sermon. He refused, preferring to spend Sunday with his bow and arrows in the open. On entering a wood to enjoy the chase he saw the devil in the form of an immense hare. He shot, the devil vanished, but the arrow, rebounding, pierced his clothes. How well-deserved a shock for the impious vavassor Robert! Certainly the sermons were practical homilies, addressed to the layman in terms he would understand, and teaching the same simple and fundamental lessons of doctrine and ethics as Robert Mannyng of Bourne treated in his poems. There is in the cathedral library at Lincoln a volume of fifteenth-century sermons for all possible occasions in the church's year, and while there is no certainty that they were composed by or even collected by a friar, their tone seems so much to be that of the popular preacher that they may well illustrate the mendicants' techniques. The sermon for Christmas Day contains this telling bit of observation:

"The property of a yong childe is that he cannot be maliciously disposyd ne ber no rancour ne wrathe to the that bete hym never so sore as

[6] *Hundred Rolls*, p. 312; LAO D & C A./2/22, ff. 3v, 4; G. R. Owst, *Preaching in Medieval England*, Cambridge, 1926, p. 63.
[7] PRO E135/2/50, f. 13. I owe this reference to the kindness of Mr Michael Borrie.

yt fallythe for a childe to have dew chastisyng, but a none aftyr as ye hast bette hym then schewe to hym a feyre flowre or ellys a feyre redde appull then hathe he forgotten all that was done to hym before and then he wyll come to ye rynnynge with his clyppynge armys for to plese ye and to kysse ye."[8]

There were times, however, when the friars abused their authority as popular preachers, and Stamford, near enough to the Great North Road to catch the sounds of religious and political heresy, was the scene of two such episodes, which may well have been paralleled in countless unknown cases. It was reported that about 1424 a Franciscan called William Russell while preaching in Stamford denounced tithes as contrary to the law of God, and said that it was lawful for a religious and monastic person to have carnal commerce with a woman and that there was no sin in it. Thirty years later a Dominican friar, William Lilford of Deeping, was accused by the Crown of fomenting treason in Stamford.[9]

The mendicants did not, however, preach solely to the layman, or in the vulgar tongue. The bishops often employed them to preach to the clergy at synods and visitations and to proclaim crusades. Indeed, they soon had a special place in the diocesan administration as penitentiaries and suffragan bishops, and two Franciscans and one Dominican are known to have served in that capacity during the fourteenth and fifteenth centuries.

After their sermons, however, the chief role of the mendicants was, undoubtedly, as religious directors and confessors. Before the end of the thirteenth century so many laymen flocked to them everywhere that not only the parish priests, some of whose functions they were thus usurping, but also the diocesan authorities became very hostile to them. So universal was the problem that the Pope attempted to deal with it by a constitution *Super cathedram* which enacted that all friars seeking to act as confessors must be licensed by the diocesan bishop. In Lincoln the hostility of the parochial clergy towards friar-confessors was strong enough, as early as 1298, to call forth a severe rebuke from Bishop Sutton, and after the publication of the papal constitution Bishop Dalderby at first showed a decided tendency to limit severely the numbers of licences which he granted. Even much later there was a marked lack of cordiality between mendicants and the diocesan authorities, of which the unfortunate incidents accompanying the burial of the last Lord Huntingfield in the Dominican church at Boston were a distasteful symptom. Nevertheless it was at parochial level that the hostility was strongest.[10]

[8] Owst, *loc. cit.*; Lincoln Cathedral ms. 50, f. 27.
[9] Harrod, *op. cit.*, 28; PRO C47/67/9/373; KB 9/65; C67/40, m.6. I owe this PRO reference to the kindness of Dr R. L. Storey.
[10] Hinnebusch, *op. cit.*, p. 329.

The success of the friars as religious directors naturally made their houses, their preaching, and their churches more attractive to their penitents, so that many townsmen who would in normal circumstances have attended, and been buried in, their parish churches tended to take themselves and, what must have seemed more important to the parish priests, their customary offerings to the friaries. It was this which so much roused the wrath not only of incumbents but also of the monastic houses who were rectors of parish churches. Probably with good reason they suspected the friars of deliberate encouragement of the desertion, and at Grimsby and Boston the disputes became acrimonious enough to require intervention by the bishop. At Boston in 1293 an agreement between the Carmelites and the rector of St Botolph exacted from the friars one-third of the offerings made on behalf of those parishioners who chose burial in the friary cemetery, and the whole of the offerings made in the conventual church on feast days by parishioners. The friars were forbidden to admit outsiders to communion on the feasts of Easter, Christmas, Pentecost, and St Botolph and required to promise that they would impress on parishioners the duty of paying tithe.[11] The Grimsby agreement, reached in 1307 between the Austin friars and the abbot and convent of Wellow as rectors of Grimsby St James, illustrates very clearly the extent to which the friars had infiltrated parochial life, and the means by which it was suspected that they were encroaching on rectorial privileges. Here the friars were forced to bind themselves not to administer confession and absolution to any parishioner of St James, and to let no parishioner hide or be cherished in their house, knowing him to be in error. They agreed not to manufacture or openly distribute blessed bread (*pain bénit*) after mass, nor to administer any sacrament, either openly or in secret, to any parishioner. No one was to be encouraged either to choose burial in the friars' cemetery or to alter wills in their favour and if someone "spontaneously" chose to be buried by the friars the parish was to have all his offerings, except those made at the second mass, and the trental and anniversary masses were to be held in the parish church. The friars were to accept no personal tithes or offerings from parishioners, and were themselves to pay over all tithes and parochial dues like wax-scot for plots or gardens they acquired in the parish. They agreed not to fix their own hours of celebration to coincide with the parochial high mass nor to admit parishioners to matins and vespers on Sundays and festivals, and they undertook to preach no sermons either in their own church or in streets and open spaces at times when high mass was celebrated. Finally they were to refrain from reading the gospels, distributing holy water and *pain bénit*, and administering the last rites of the church to sailors coming into the harbour of Grimsby.[12]

[11] LRS 52, pp. 127–8.   [12] ULC Dd. 10.28, f. 84v.

Much later than this there are enough bequests to mendicants, and requests for burial in their churches, to suggest that the parochial claims can never have been fully met, and that the mendicants continued to be very popular. It seems likely that they were able to provide a greater degree of pastoral care, and to offer a sort of supervision, which was more attractive to the urban layman, because it was more personal than that of the parochial clergy. Much of the attraction must have lain in the frequent, lively sermons, providing the sort of drama and colour which would also be furnished by the plays and gild ceremonies. It is not at all surprising to find that in Grantham, at least, the Franciscans went in front of the Corpus Christi procession organized by the gild of that name.[13]

It seems difficult, at this distance of time, to distinguish among the various orders of friars, but there is no doubt that the Dominicans, in some places and at certain times, were the least popular of the four. They were combative and provocative, and in Stamford in the early fifteenth century attacks were made on them and their property which suggest that they were much disliked by the townspeople. The extent of their claims and the way in which they enforced them are well illustrated by the disagreeable incidents which marked the Huntingfield funeral.[14] William, the last Lord Huntingfield, who died in 1376, had signified his wish for burial in the Dominican church at Boston, and the bishop, John Buckingham, was prepared to conduct the obsequies of so distinguished a subject. The Dominicans, seeing his action as an invasion of their privileges, and fearing the loss of the funeral offerings, resisted his entry to their church with swords and bows and when on the next day he made a second attempt to enter, rolled down huge stones from the central tower on all who tried to reach the choir of the church. Buckingham thought the Dominican threat to episcopal privileges sufficiently big to seek redress from a council of the English church, and it is scarcely surprising that others felt equally hostile. Three years later "unknown persons scaled with ladders the walls of the house of the Friar Preachers in Boston, broke their doors and windows, and assaulted the prior Roger Dymmok, and his friars in their beds, so that they were obliged to ring their bells to raise the commonalty of the town to come to their aid, and to cry fire for rescue."[15]

---

[13] H. F. Westlake, *The Parish Gilds of Medieval England*, London, 1919, cert. 109.
[14] *Cal. Misc. Inq. 1399–1422*, no. 535, 1416.
[15] Reg. 12, f. 144; John Lydford's Book (Exeter diocesan records), p. 30: *Cal. Pat. Rolls, 1377–81*, p. 421.

CHAPTER VII

CHANTRIES AND COLLEGIATE FOUNDATIONS

As we have seen, the giving of endowments to the church, in the hope and expectation of receiving in return the prayers of the recipients, was a well-established practice in England, of which the religious houses we have been discussing are a visible proof. Not only the leading men and women who founded them, but many lesser men, shared in these gifts and in the prayers of the house. Side by side with monastic endowment, however, and eventually taking its place as a vehicle of religious benefaction, and as a means of assuring the donor of the benefit of perpetual personal prayers, there grew up a multitude of smaller foundations, known somewhat loosely as chantries. The donors of these chantries set aside funds to provide daily masses and annual commemorations at specially equipped altars in parish, monastic, or cathedral churches, sometimes for a term of years, but more often in perpetuity.

The earliest of these endowments were of a simple nature: before 1200, for example, Henry of Longchamp endowed the altar of the Blessed Virgin in the church of Burton Pedwardine, and the vicar already serving there, with three acres of arable in Burton, in return for which the vicar was to say a weekly mass for him and his heirs and to provide a half-pound wax candle for his altar at every festival. Others maintained lamps for the altars, the rood, or the blessed sacrament, in return for prayers, and this remained a favourite form of benefaction to the very end of the Middle Ages. The *Valor* records that Stixwold Priory's outgoings included "ten shillings for oil and wax for burning perpetually before the crucifix for the soul of Margery Gulburn on whose account we have our lands in Hagnaby" and William Wolhede of Marston whose will was proved in 1533, left "to the rode light xxd."[1]

Such gifts were intended to be perpetual, but obits, or arrangements for the saying of masses on the anniversary of a donor's death, were usually for such limited periods as twenty years. When Joan Kay, whose daughter was prioress of Stixwold, died in 1527, she provided for an obit to be kept in St Peter at Arches in Lincoln for the twenty years after her

[1] BM Add. 32101, f. 12*v*.

death "with *Placebo Dirige* and Commendation with nine lessons, at which said obit I would there be six prests and the parish clerke and messe of requiem and every priest to have fourpence and the clerk fourpence." On the other hand the more elaborate chantry foundations, such as those of Edwinstow and Flemming in the cathedral, often included provision for perpetual obits on the anniversaries of their founders' death.[2]

As the area of occupied and settled land increased within the county, we have seen that the small new communities, or outlying manor houses, often sought to provide themselves with residential chaplains, whose services, in small chapels or oratories, might supplement those of the distant parish church. Such foundations were usually described as chantries, and where they were founded by a manorial lord, or the men of a vill, for the perpetual commemoration of themselves and their successors, or where they were endowed with property for the regular maintenance of a chaplain, they might with justice be so regarded. A number of such foundations was included with the returns of chantries made to the Crown in 1548. Thus, Burton Chantry in Burton Stather: "The foundation is unknown, but so far as can be understood from the relation of the parishioners there, it was founded with the intent that two chaplains perpetually should celebrate divine service for the souls of the founder and others; to wit one of them in the chapel of Stather and the other in the chapel at Normanby."

In this case Stather was an outlying community, and Normanby a demesne chapel. The Dogdike chantry is an even better example: it was founded in 1343 by Gilbert de Umfreville, Earl of Angus and lord of Kyme, for the souls of himself, his wife, his predecessors, heirs, and all faithful departed, and in 1548: "the inhabitants of certen housholds to the noumbre of eighteen scituate nighe and aboute the saide chauntrie and likewise distant from the said parische church of Billinghay have used, tyme out of mynde, to here ther dyvine service within the chapell of the said chauntrie."

Long after the Reformation men living in Edenham described the priest who served the outlying chapel of Scottlethorpe as "the chantry priest."

"Arnold Healey of the age of lx yeres and above affirmeth that he did know Sir John Bucke, many yeres the chauntrie preist at Edenham and saieth morever that he hath holpen Sr John Bucke to say masse many tymes in the chauntrie chappell at Scottlethorpe oftentymes and how that Sr John Bucke used to ryde uppon a litle white nagg which he had and when hee came theare he putt his nagg alwaies into the chauntrie close at Scottlethorp the which close is called by the name of the chauntrie

[2] LNQ VIII, p. 73; Chantry Cert., no. 7, e & f.

close at this day. And further he saieth that Sir John Bucke had alwaies the rentes of the chauntrie lande duryng his tyme wholy to himself never accountable to any other person for the same and how that the rent was then but vli.viiid. by the yeare which he used to receave by xiid and a grote at once sometymes as his necessitie required and that so he continued untill his death and died the chauntrie preist."[3]

In general, although not always, the provision for services like this in an outlying chapel was made by a grant of endowments in perpetuity to the chantry, which then became a benefice. The founder and his descendants or successors were patrons, who presented clerks to the bishop for institution to it, and its incumbent for the time being had the same sort of security as any other incumbent in any other benefice. On occasion, however, the chantry priest was no more than a stipendiary, appointed and dismissed by trustees who held the endowments and were responsible for them. The Dalderby cantarists, in the church of St Benedict at Lincoln, were maintained at the total cost of ten silver pounds by the prior and convent of Thurgarton, on the foundation of Robert Dalderby, citizen of Lincoln; the dean and chapter were trustees of a chantry founded in Harrington church by Mr John of Harrington, canon and prebendary of Spaldwick; and, by agreement with Roger de Wolsthorp and Richard de Saltby, Vaudey Abbey maintained the three secular chaplains who served a large and important chantry at Grantham.[4]

Foundations of this order, unless, as we shall see, they created grandiose collegiate churches, were decidedly less expensive than even the smallest monastic houses, and allowed men and women who were relatively much poorer than those who had founded monasteries in the twelfth century to provide for their souls' welfare in a way that was both satisfying and moderately inexpensive. Although some chantries, especially those in the towns, were well provided with land and house property, few of them were worth as much as £10 per annum by 1548. Churchmen, from bishops down to parish priests, were among the earliest of Lincolnshire chantry makers, with a few country knights like Sir Thomas Cumberworth, and a great many citizens and merchants. Many of the Lincoln citizens' foundations had been made before 1300, while the city's prosperity was at its height, but the turn of the smaller towns came only in the second half of the fourteenth century and after. It is then that the Sleaford and Grantham chantries were founded, and this too was the great age of foundations in Holland, where, as Professor Hamilton Thompson has pointed out, a remarkable number of chantries was founded during the last decade of the century. It is difficult to say

[3] Chantry Cert., nos. 30, 112; LAO Anc. 3/3/173.
[4] Ibid., nos. 2, 58; Cal. Pat. Rolls, 1348–50, p. 414.

what class was most active in these later foundations; certainly the more prominent of the Holland foundations, such as the Littlebury and Bellers chantries founded in 1392 in Kirton, were the work of one or more leading local residents.[5] Such 'group' foundations were a sort of half-way stage to the many chantries founded and maintained by parochial gilds. There will be more to say of the gilds and their activities at a later stage, but for our present purposes it is important to remember that those who could not otherwise hope to endow a chantry of their own might gain great satisfaction from participation in a joint enterprise, such as that of the Great Gild at Lincoln, the members of which from time out of mind had maintained a chaplain celebrating in the church of St Andrew in Wigford for the souls of all the brethren and sisters of the gild. The five Boston gilds among them supported nineteen chaplains who celebrated in the parish church of St Botolph; and Louth and Stamford each had three chaplains maintained by their gilds.[6]

Like other foundations many chantries as they aged suffered from insufficient or shrinking endowments, shifts of population, and local neglect, and the enthusiastic chantry founders of the later fourteenth century in many cases refounded or augmented these decayed or lapsed institutions. It was reported in 1365 that the chapel founded at Eagle, with three chaplains to celebrate for the welfare of King Stephen's soul, had had no chaplains for the last thirty years; and a chantry chapel of St Laurence in Horncastle, where the prior and convent of Wilsford were supposed to maintain a chaplain celebrating three days in the week, had been allowed to lapse just as completely. The chantry of St Mary and St Katherine founded in Epworth by Lord Mowbray in 1344 was modified by the bishop in 1365 as "owing to the unhappy course of the present times and the exility of the fruits of the chantry, the number of chaplains and clerks required by the ordination cannot be maintained. . ." The Ravenser chantry at Waltham was endowed in 1374 with the revenue of a lapsed chantry in Belleau church, and a chantry in the parish church of Frampton seems to have absorbed the endowments of an earlier chantry founded in the chapel of St James in Moulton manor in Frampton.[7]

As early as 1279 some of the larger and more elaborate chantries had received from their founders detailed regulations not only for the religious duties to be performed by the cantarists, but also for the security of the property of the chantry and for the lives of the priests. The Fitzmartin chantry in the cathedral was regulated by an ordinance drawn up by Oliver Sutton when he was dean:[8]

"Now the chaplain shall every day before the said mass of the blessed

[5] Chantry Cert., nos. 4, 63.   [6] Ibid., no. 5.
[7] Cal. Misc. Inq. III, p. 571; ibid. IV, p. 287; Chantry Cert., nos. 17, 37, 59.
[8] Chantry Cert., no. 7.

Virgin say Commendation specially for Simon's soul, and in the mass itself after the first collect of the blessed Virgin he shall say another collect to wit, *Adiuua nos, domine Deus noster, et beatissime Dei genitricis Marie precibus exoratus, animam famuli tui sacerdotis,* etc., for Simon's soul; and in the canon of the mass where there is a memorial for the dead, he shall make a special memorial of him first; and after the mass, when he has finished, he shall say *Placebo* and *Dirige* with nine psalms and nine lessons, except at Easter-tide, when he shall say them with three psalms and three lessons, as the use of the church is. On double feasts, however, when a canon celebrates mass, in place of it the chaplain shall celebrate the mass of the dead specially for the soul of Simon, his relations, and benefactors, in which mass he shall use these three collects: *Inclina domine, Miserere,* and *Fidelium.* Further, on the day of Simon's anniversary, the said priest shall procure another priest to celebrate the mass of the blessed Virgin; before which mass, he himself shall celebrate the mass of the dead for Simon's soul at the same altar with musical notation (*cum nota*), and shall provide that sixteen clerks of the choir shall take part to each one of whom he shall give a halfpenny directly mass is ended. Also on the same day he shall feed thirteen poor people at his table for Simon's soul with bread, beer, pottage, and one mess of flesh or fish (etc.). Moreover, the chaplain shall perform the services due and accustomed to the chief lords of the fee according to the tenor of the charters of feoffment. And every year during the month preceding the day of Simon's anniversary, he shall pay to the clerk of the common of the canons of the church of Lincoln 23s. 4d. to be distributed on the day of the anniversary, to wit, to the canons residing and able and willing to take part in Simon's obsequies 5s. 4d., the canon who celebrates mass on the day of the anniversary in chapter having 4d. more than the other canons; to the vicars who take part in the obsequies in the choir and mass in chapter, 5s. by equal portions; to the poor clerks on the same condition, 12d.; to the children on the same condition, 12d.; to the servants ringing the bells both at mass and at *Placebo* and *Dirige,* 6d.; to 200 poor people, 10s., namely one halfpenny each; to the clerk of the common who shall make all these distributions, 6d. Further, with Simon's consent, we ordain that the priest for the time being shall maintain the tenements and buildings in a good state of cultivation and in good condition; and when he departs or dies, or otherwise is removed on account of any misdeed, he shall leave to his successor four sufficient oxen and two horses each of the value of 10s. at least, to till the land which is at Welleton."

Although the earlier chantries seem to have been celebrated at altars in the body of the cathedral or parish church, the elaborately ordered later chantries almost always had an additional chapel specially built, like those of Burgh and Thonnock at Gainsborough, on the north or south sides of the church, or a specially rebuilt aisle, as at Beckingham or East Kirkby. Indeed, a careful examination of the fabric of surviving medieval churches in the county will reveal a large number of aisles rebuilt or refenestrated between 1360 and 1530, which can almost certainly be associated with chantry foundations. Such chantry chapels or aisles had their own books and ornaments, often carefully enumerated in the foundation deed, and governed by detailed regulations even of such matters as the resewing of the service books. The chantry of John of Harrington in Harrington church (in an "oratory built at my cost on the south side of the parish church") received from the founder

"two chalices, one of the price of fifteen shillings and the other of the price of twelve shillings, two vestments, one for feasts, of the price of twenty shillings and the other for weekdays, of the price of ten shillings, one missal of the price of twenty shillings, one portas of the price of forty shillings, one good chest for the keeping of the ornaments of the price of five shillings, and two cruets."

There was much music in these daily celebrations: at Epworth, for example, careful regard was had for the standard of the singing: "And there shall be four clerks in the chapel, ... of whom one shall know sufficiently how to sing tenor, and another the middle part, and the other two the third part." Such foundations must have brought much light, colour, and beauty to the parish churches of the county.[9]

The usual stipend of the priests who served the chantries seems, by the end of the fifteenth century, to have been in the region of five or six pounds per annum; few of the Lincolnshire foundations were outstandingly wealthy or desirable, and there are signs before 1400 that endowments were shrinking in value, so that the founders' regulations could not be maintained. Thus at Epworth in 1365 the original ordination was modified by the bishop.[10]

"Lately, most beloved son, in our presence you explained that, owing to the unhappy course of the present times and the exility of the fruits of the chantry, the number of chaplains and clerks required by the ordination of the chantry could not be maintained in these days, nor so moderate a salary as, for instance, 30s. for you the master and 20s. a year for each of the chaplains besides raiment and victuals be found; adding moreover that whereas long and close surcoats [*supertunice*] are most fitting in these days not for simple priests but for doctors and for men pre-eminent in dignity, the chaplains by such close tunics [*tunice*] being, like pharisees, conspicuous among the ignorant from other secular

[9] Chantry Cert., nos. 15, 16, 58. [10] *Ibid.*, no. 17.

chaplains, are often held in ridicule, and that such a habit leads rather to their disparagement than to the praise or honour of God; touching which things you humbly prayed us to find a fitting remedy. We, therefore, with the consent of Sir John Mowbray, lord of the Isle of Axholme, and patron of the said chantry, and with your consent as master, have thought well to ordain that during the badness of the times and for the other abovesaid inconveniences, the number of clerks contained in the said ordination shall be diminished by two, and that you the warden shall receive 50s. and each of the two clerks 30s. by the year besides victuals and raiment. We grant also that you and the chaplains shall use garments [*vestibus*] befitting the order and state of priests, provided that they be of becoming length and fulness. And that, when the aforesaid hindrances shall cease, and when by the grace of God the number of priests and clerks has so increased that they may be had for the salaries of old accustomed, and the fruits of the chantry have returned to the accustomed or a greater measure of wealth, the present change of the ordination shall entirely cease, etc. In witness whereof our seal is appended to the presents. Dated at Lidyngton, 5 kal. July [27 June], 1365."

The chantry priests came, as we shall see, to act as additional parochial chaplains, schoolmasters, and parochial men-of-all-work, and were immensely important elements in parish life, without whom the daily round of worship could hardly have been maintained. Nevertheless, it is difficult to avoid the conclusion that the existence of the chantries as sources of employment encouraged larger numbers than ever to seek ordination, in the hope of finding a livelihood. A single fairly small parish like Great Hale might have as many as four chantries; and the populous wealthy villages of the deanery of Holland, counting the staff of the parish church, the parochial and private chaplains, and the cantarists, had most of them between eight and thirteen resident clerks paying subsidy, besides their incumbents, in 1376. The 1526 subsidy shows that these figures were being well maintained 150 years later, and, as Professor Hamilton Thompson has pointed out, the number of choir stalls of fifteenth-century construction which survive in large town churches, like St Botolph at Boston, are an index of the number of clerks for whom provision was then required. It is perhaps just as much an indication of excessive provision, as of the shrinking value of the endowment, that at the Reformation not only were some of the chantries vacant, but that one at least, in Holbeach St Nicholas, was used for the exhibition of a scholar at the university. No doubt the episcopal dispensations for study might reveal other similar cases.[11]

Many of the larger chantries, and particularly those founded by the

[11] Appendix 1; Chantry Cert., no. 85.

nobility, were clearly associated with and sited very close to the burial places of the founder and his family. The family aisles still surviving in parish churches—there is an excellent example at Irnham—were very often chantries. Sometimes, as at Spilsby, such chantries were the basis of an elaborate collegiate foundation, where a master and a group of cantarists lived a common life under elaborate regulations laid down by the founder. The founder of Tattershall college, Ralph Lord Cromwell, Lord Treasurer of England, rebuilt the church side by side with his new castle in 1440; an almshouse completed the foundation soon after, and the final form of the statutes, laid down about 1460, provided that there should be seven chaplains (of whom one was to be warden), six secular clerks, and six choristers, in the parish church of Tattershall, to pray for King Henry VI, Ralph Lord Cromwell, and Maud Cromwell late lady of Tattershall, and all the faithful departed, together with an almshouse of thirteen poor people of either sex.[12] The accounts of this college in the brief century of its existence show the elaboration of its life. There was a choristers' school; and an organist, washerwoman, gate-keepers, gardeners, bakers, brewers, and swan-keepers were employed. Money was spent on music copying, and some of this was secular, for a song called 'The Cry of Caleys' is mentioned. As late as 1482 the famous glass windows depicting the history of the Holy Cross, the Magnificat, St Clare, and the Seven Sacraments were still being installed, and in that year over £104 was spent on beautifying the church, which even now, in its noble proportions and the richness of its brasses, gives an impressive idea of the richness, colour, and variety which were added to the churches of the county by the founders of chantries. Indeed, it seems certain that where wealthy benefactors of the fourteenth and fifteenth centuries were able to rebuild entire churches or large portions of them, as at East Kirkby and Burton Pedwardine, they often looked on the rebuilt fabric as an appropriate site for a chantry and associated such a foundation with it.

The conventional motive for the foundation of chantries, after the prayers for the souls of the founders, their benefactors, and friends, was the desire to increase divine worship. And the mere increase in the numbers of priests available to say mass within a parish after the foundation would ensure that this would be achieved. Yet, in addition to this, some chantries were specifically founded to provide service where none had existed. This was particularly true of the chapels founded for the solace of inhabitants in outlying hamlets or fen settlements, like Kinnard's Ferry and Amcotts in Owston, the latter of which was founded by Geoffrey Crowle and William Amcotts in the mid-fifteenth century to save the inhabitants of the hamlet from the winter floods on the way to the parish church. Similarly St Katherine of Saltfleethaven was founded

[12] HMCR *De l'Isle*, I, *passim*.

in 1411 by William Lord Willoughby to provide and endow regular services in a chapel built by a hermit eighty years earlier in the sea marshes of Skidbrook. A cantarist in a parish church might also be specifically instructed by the founder to provide occasional services in an outlying chapel, as Walter Awnesby arranged for his chantry at Aunsby, the priest of which was also to celebrate twice a week in the chapel at Crofton.[13]

Assistance within the parish service was also anticipated by the founders of chantries. At Sleaford, Thomas Blount and other merchants provided that their chaplain "when he is present ought to take part with the parochial chaplain in the canonical hours and gratuitously to assist him in his office whenever there is need." The Harrington and Hale chaplains were to "attend on double feasts and Sundays at lauds vespers and mass to give their help if they are needed, in the psalmody." The cantarist of Roger Bellers in Kirton Holland was to deputize in the parochial chaplain's absence; at Edenham the cantarist had similar duties and was specifically called a secondary; at Grantham there was endowment for a deacon to "chant and read daily the most holy Gospel at high mass in the said church." At Louth the chantry of St Mary's gild provided for lay clerks called 'singingmen' in the church, and at Boston the St Mary's gild maintained choirmen and an organist within its chantry chapel. Indeed, the regular mention in the chantry and gild foundation deeds of masses, especially those said in honour of the Blessed Virgin, *cum nota*, with music, suggests the possibility that much of the church music which characterized the last two centuries of the pre-Reformation church may well have been provided and sustained out of the funds of the chantries.[14] William Newton, who had once been a canon of Bourne, in 1551 "was the town clerke of Ednam many yeres, and was hired to play uppon the organes ther, and contynewed organ player in Sir John Buckes tyme many yeres, and when he left off his clerkship theare he left Sir John still the chauntrie preiste." The maintenance of choirs of boys, as in the cathedral and at Tattershall, presupposed their instruction, at least in elementary grammar and singing. So at Tattershall the Master "shall hire a clerk or priest to teach grammar to the choristers and to all sons of tenants of the lordship of Tattershall and of the College without charge" and the Burghersh chantry in the cathedral included provision for the teaching, maintenance, and clothing of six boys, whose life was carefully regulated in the foundation deed.

Some chantries, and especially those in the towns, came to provide teaching for others besides the choir boys. The Sleaford chantry of St Mary actually allowed for a payment of twenty shillings per annum for

[13] Chantry Cert., nos. 21, 26, 42.
[14] *Ibid.*, nos. 105, 114, 58, 98, 64, 12, 97, 45, 121.

a scholar's exhibition at the university; the Curteys chantry at Grantham was said in 1487 to have provided for one of its two chaplains to keep a school in a house by the church and to instruct boys "as well in good manners as in the art of grammar;" and Stamford St Mary had a similar foundation in 1532, on the very eve of the Reformation.[15] The gilds were even more alive to the need for educational provision in their chantries; the Holy Trinity gild at Louth maintained on the staff of its chantry one chaplain "sufficiently learned in the art of grammar to instruct the boys of the said town and of the country adjacent, as well in good manners as in polite letters," and St Mary's gild at Boston had similar responsibilities.[16]

It can scarcely be maintained that the dissolution of the chantries involved the destruction of a universal school system within Lincolnshire: even if every chantry priest had been also a schoolmaster, and there is no proof of this, the distribution of chantries was too haphazard to have benefited every parish. In the same way, although some larger chantries, especially early ones, included provision for the distribution of alms, and some later ones for the maintenance of almshouses, there is no reason to suppose that all chantry foundations supported innumerable poor men. We have seen that an almshouse formed part of the Tattershall collegiate arrangements; and the Burgh chantry at Gainsborough, founded in 1498, provided for maintenance of five bedesmen each receiving sevenpence a week. The Louth and Boston gilds had their dependent almsmen too, but there is no evidence of systematic and large-scale almsgiving by other chantries, nor does it seem that many founders of chantries envisaged almshouses as part of their schemes.

[15] LAO Anc. 3/3/73; HMCR *De l'Isle*, I, p. 182; Chantry Cert., nos. 7a, 97; *Val. Eccl.* IV, p. 119.
[16] Chantry Cert., nos. 119, 44, 131, 15, 44, 45, 124, 125, 130.

CHAPTER VIII

THE CHURCH AND THE LAITY

THE services of the parish priest touched the lives of his parishioners at every point, from the earliest possible time in a child's life, when he was received by the church at his baptism, to his death, when he was accompanied to the grave with the solemn sequence of *Placebo, Dirige,* and *Requiem.* It is hardly necessary to indulge in the nostalgia for the 'good old times' which informs much of Cardinal Gasquet's work to be able to imagine how important the parish church, and the manifold activities which centred on it, must have been to the laymen of the parish.[1] No Lincolnshire source states categorically what was to be done in the parish churches and chapels, but it is certain from the many descriptions of services to be provided in chapels that at least one daily mass was said and heard by many parishioners in all churches and many chapels. In addition, where there were chantries or other special endowments, there was an early 'morrow mass' and many other masses at subsidiary altars. At Louth about 1500 there seem to have been daily matins and evensong, with "Our Lady Masse," "and olde custome was that Tisday and Thoresday masse was songe in the hey quere with plansong."[2]

In the great churches, such as the cathedral itself or at Tattershall, the full daily office was always said, and matins, mass, vespers, and compline with music, prime, and the third, sixth, and ninth hours without. The first bell for matins at Tattershall rang at 6 a.m., the second half an hour later, the last at 7 a.m. After matins solemn mass with organ and choral music was sung in the chapel of the Virgin and at the high altar a mass was also said. The first bell for vespers rang at 3 p.m., the second at 3.30 p.m., when the choristers said vespers and the compline of the Blessed Virgin; at 4 p.m. vespers for the day were to begin.[3] In the parishes such elaborate usage was only for Sunday and feast days. On Sundays, too, before high mass there, the celebrant blessed the holy water for the coming week's use and after mass was over blessed and distributed to all present as a symbol of fraternal love loaves of bread known as 'kirk-loaves' or 'singing bread'. The important role played in

---

[1] F. A. Gasquet, *Medieval Parish Life*, Antiquary's Books, 1909.
[2] LAASRP x, p. 136. [3] HMCR, *De l'Isle*, I, pp. 180-1.

the lives of ordinary parishioners by this weekly mass and its two associated ceremonies is demonstrated by Grosseteste's careful provision, in Robert D'Oyry's chapel in Whaplode Marsh which had no sacraments except mass, that holy bread and water should be available, and there was a similar arrangement much later at West Halton and Gunness.[4] It was usually the business of the churchwardens to 'find' the kirk loaf, as the Sutterton accounts show, though at least one will bequeathed an endowment for it at Quadring Eaudike.[5] The administration of all sacraments was very firmly in the hands of the parish church, and the obligation of all Christians to receive them gave it still greater importance.

Baptism, it seems, was administered wherever possible on the day of birth, and there is an interesting example of this practice which emerges in an inquiry about the age of an heir John de Welle who was born at Bonthorpe on the eve of the feast of St Bartholomew (i.e. 23 August), a Tuesday, in the eighth year of King Edward III (1334), and baptized on the same day at Willoughby in the church of St Helen.

"John Musters knight, aged forty-five years said that he came on the said Tuesday to do fealty to Sir John de Wilughby, knight, for his lands in Somercotes, and saw the god-mother of the said John, Margaret, prioress of Greenfield, carrying him from the said church wrapped in swaddling clothes. Robert de Alford agrees, and says that on the said Tuesday an agreement was made between him and John Jolyf of Willoughby in the said church touching divers trespasses, when the said John son of Adam came there to be baptised."[6]

The purification or churching of the mother after childbirth followed in due season, and so did confirmation of the child, which took place at an early age.

Penance (confession) was obligatory on all Christians at the beginning of Lent and often, it seems, also preceded the great festivals of Christmas, Easter, and Pentecost. At the point of death there was the visitation of the sick, in which the sacrament was carried to the sick parishioner and he was anointed with holy oil. These were sacraments to be shared by all parishioners at some point in their lives. For most, if not all of them, there was also the sacrament of marriage, which, after the triple proclamation of banns, was celebrated first at the church door (for the promises) and then before the altar. Finally, for all, there were the solemnities which ushered the dead to the grave. These began with vespers (*Placebo*) the night before burial; on the day of burial there were matins (*Dirige*) and mass for the dead (*Requiem*); thirty days after the burial vespers were repeated (a *trental*). For such ceremonies as this some testators provided

[4] LRS 11, p. 25; Reg. 20, f. 9.   [5] *Arch. J.* xxxix, pp. 53–63; LRS 5, p. 141.
[6] *Cal. Misc. Inq.* IV, no. 264.

in their will for suitable attendance to be recompensed with gifts of food or money, and in one case at least a wealthy testator, dying in 1451, ordered the church at Somerby by Brigg where his obsequies were to be celebrated to be put into mourning: "the preistes araye the autairs and overe sepultures with blak auter-clothes and the coverlid of Blak and the clothis of gold ordaned therto."[7]

These constituted the official bonds between the parishioner and his parish church, but in the close-knit life of a small community, as we shall see, a mass of other customs, habits, and observances, by no means entirely religious, was inevitably focused on it. Many of these were connected with burial ceremonies, and were elaborated by the growth of commercial wealth in the later centuries of the Middle Ages; others, like the bede-roll, or list of persons to be remembered in prayer on the anniversaries of their deaths, were of honourable antiquity. More will be said later of these elaborations of ceremony and additions to the liturgical round, but it is meanwhile important to remember that at all times some secular, and even military, events were conducted within the walls of the church. We have already seen many examples where laymen announced their gifts to churches and monasteries by laying their charters and knives on the altar of the church, and it is not surprising to learn that it was customary for the belt of knighthood to be conferred in a parish church in the time of Robert Grosseteste. In the widely scattered parishes of Holland, such as Sutton and Holbeach, the parish church was an essential meeting place. It is said that anti-enclosure rioters met in Holbeach church in 1189, and in 1361 secular courts were being held, to the dismay of the bishop, in all the chapels of Sutton. Then, too, churches were frequently used to store valuables, like the "evidences in a red box" stored at Louth in 1388 by Alice de la Lake. Perhaps the best statement of the community use of the parish church, however, appears in the depositions of a witness in a Star Chamber case:

"out of time of remembraunce of many their within the said parishe hathe been accustomed that whensoever any thing or act was to be entreated or concluded for the benefitt as well of the church of Holbeach aforesaid or for the amendement of the sea dykes and bankes within the same towns or for any other cause or matter concerning the wealthe of the saide towne it hathe been used by them all the saide tyme because the paryshe ther ys gret and the parishioners also dwellyng wyde a sondre that a bell within the saide church hathe beene used to be knolled or rungen to the entent that the said parish heryng the said bell should resort thither to comon and to entreat of and uppon such cause..."[8]

[7] EETS 56, p. 56.
[8] LRS 11, p. 25; Macdonald, *op. cit.*, pp. 19–20; *Cal. Misc. Inq.* v, p. 307; FNQ I, pp. 154–6; Reg. 7, f. 60.

If the church provided the only large building in a parish, the churchyard must often, in densely cultivated country or fenland, have offered the only open-air meeting place in some parishes. This, no doubt, is one reason why markets were sometimes held there: the practice was condemned by Grosseteste about 1239, but was still going on at Stainfield, and doubtless elsewhere, in 1392. Churchyards were equally tempting for the playing of games and the holding of feasts. Grosseteste forbade the mounting of a quintain on a wheel and other games, and the drinking feasts called scot-ales, or church-ales on ecclesiastical premises, but such practices were evidently well entrenched, for in 1306 Bishop Dalderby repeated the prohibition during his visitation of the deanery of Grimsby.

Services such as have been described above required considerable numbers of clerical staff, and Bishop Grosseteste's statutes had laid down that "in every church, where it is possible, there ought to be (that is, besides the priest) a deacon and a sub-deacon, but, failing this, at least a suitable and honourable clerk to serve the priest during the divine offices."[9] It is improbable, if the 1376 subsidy may be trusted, that every parish had its full complement of clerical staff. Many fifteenth-century wills provide for payments to a 'secondary' or to a deacon in the testator's parish church. As late as 1515, for example, John Porter founded a 'deaconship' at Bolingbroke. Parish clerks, doubtless a cheaper and easier alternative, are much more often found than deacons and sub-deacons, and a Lincoln citizen's will of 1407 could assume that each church in the city was provided with one. Matthew the chaplain, Walter the clerk, and the whole parish of Habrough had witnessed a grant of land made to the parish church in the late twelfth century, and during the succeeding centuries there are enough references to parish clerks to suggest that they were a regular feature of the parochial scene. Nevertheless the 1376 subsidy for the not particularly prosperous deanery of Beltisloe in south-west Kesteven shows clerks in only five of the twenty parishes. They were, presumably, local men in minor orders and their duties were by no means entirely clerical. A passing reference about 1290, in the Thornton Abbey chronicle, suggests that the clerk then usually dug the graves and acted as sexton, but by the time that wills became more numerous, bell-ringing appears to have been his primary duty.[10] One of the clearest statements of what the clerk generally did appears in the will of William Hill, a London mercer, who in 1480 left money to maintain one or two parish clerks at Moulton: "to helpe to synge or saye divine service and also to go with the priest when he shall be called to housel folkes in the saide parishe . . . to ringe belles and take charge of suche goodes as belongen to the saide cherche and keepe the keys

[9] *Counc. & Syn.* I, pp. 273–4; Reg. 12, f. 392; Reg. 3, f. 108; *Counc. & Syn.* I, p. 273.
[10] LRS 5, p. 69; LRS 57, p. 109; DLC, p. 203; BM Campbell Ch. xxi, 40.

of the same by the discretion of the thrifty men of the same parishe."

It is scarcely clear who normally paid for the services of the parish clerk, and whether they existed solely on the bequests of those whose funerals they assisted, but they must have benefited enormously from the regular celebrations of obits and funerals which the greater and wealthier gilds were to foster. Thus, in St Mary's gild at Louth, the parish clerks received 4d. each, as the custom of the town was, for ringing the bells on the night preceding the anniversaries celebrated by the gild. The clerks also shared in the distributions made by the gild of the Blessed Virgin at Boston during obits, and it seems likely that from such sources, from the bell-ringing fees at funerals and from various local perquisites of which wax probably formed an important part, they did very well. About 1300 a series of small outbreaks of anticlericalism in towns such as Grantham and Grimsby and in Holland were directed against the ancient funeral customs by which the corpse candles fixed around the bier at a funeral were appropriated "to the users of the church or of its servants" and this perhaps indicates one source of the clerk's livelihood. Clearly the priest or chaplain had little to do with his maintenance: he was already a parochial officer. The Moulton bequest provided that the clerks were to be under the supervision of the leading men of the parish, and about 1500 a memorandum of clerks' duties at Louth was laid down by "the hole body and most honest men of the Parish." These duties consisted of regular bell-pulling, care of the church keys, books, vestments, and holy water stoups, and searching and watching of the church at night.[11]

At Louth, it seems, the clerks performed the duties of holy-water carriers, but a separate clerk was often appointed by the incumbent to this office and sometimes allowed or expected to keep school in his spare time, and instruct the boys of the parish in the rudiments of the Christian faith. The vicar of Haxey, after a dispute with his parishioners in 1290 about the right of appointing this functionary, was allowed by the bishop to nominate his own candidate. In most small rural parishes, however, a single clerk must have performed all the offices of the church for which an ordained priest was not required and it was only in the towns that there was any large body of lay servants of the church, and many of them were employed by the gilds rather than the parish. Louth had a functionary known to the gild accounts as a *polinctor* (a species of undertaker's assistant) who acted as bellman and lamplighter. Boston had bellmen, cross-bearers, and light-bearers, but these were obviously unusual luxuries.

The Louth clerks were ordered, "at half owre to VII of the cloke—of

[11] AASRP XLII, p. 187; LAO Mon 7/1; BM Egerton 2886; LRS 64, pp. 78, 88; LAASRP X, pp. 133–7.

Wensday and Friday to kneyll to the procession . . . ," and the solemn processions thus summoned were regular features of all church life at every level. On Sundays and feasts, for example, it was customary for the whole cathedral foundation to go from the choir to the last pillar of the nave and so back again to the choir, singing an antiphon. The *Liber Niger* explains how these processions were to be formed:

"There will first be three clerks carrying three crosses preceded by a lesser clerk bearing the holy water and sprinkling it. In the second row will be two candle-bearers carrying candles alight upon a stand. Thirdly two incense bearers with thuribles in their hands. Fourthly three little [lesser] clerks bearing relics. In the fifth place goes a subdeacon bearing before his breast the text of the Gospels its binding silvered or gilded and having the crucifix and Mary and John. Sixthly the deacon bearing the silver or gilt cross before him and in the seventh place goes the celebrant with his two servers."

No such elaborate processions can have graced the parish churches, yet on Sundays all the available clerks of the church seem to have made a solemn circuit, with cross and incense and holy water, singing as they went, and on such feast days as Palm Sunday and at a later time Corpus Christi they were joined and followed by the congregation in a solemn procession of witness customary since the earliest days of the Christian church. The Palm Sunday procession, in particular, seems to have visited the churchyard and listened to a sermon at the cross there.[12] Annual parish processions to the cathedral during Whitsuntide seem to have been an extension of this custom, already well established in the diocese, and reinforced by the authority of St Hugh. Their purpose was to bear to the cathedral on the Wednesday in the octave of Pentecost the offerings of the parish, known as pentecostals or smoke farthings, and to take part in the Pentecostal processions. Each parish sent its priest and his clerk and a small number of laity: they bore a banner with them, and at times skirmishes took place between parishes, in which the banners were used as offensive weapons. The rectors and parish priests were ordered by Grosseteste to prevent this for the future "because fights and even death have resulted from the practice." It was still going on, nevertheless, in 1356, when banners were said to lead to disturbances, and, indeed, any procession outside the church's precincts might well be a provocation to the next parish.[13] Intermittently processions of intercession for favourable weather, the success of the nation's arms, the tranquillity of the realm, or pardon for rebellion were asked for by the king or the archbishop and the bishop duly transmitted the request to rural deans and so

[12] LRS 48, p. 104; LCS I (Black Book), pp. 374–5; Owst, *op. cit.*, p. 20.
[13] RA I, pp. 258–9; RA III, p. 278; *Counc. & Syn.* I, p. 274; Reg. 7, f. 84v.

to parishes. A curious example of such 'political' processions took place in 1298, when the vill of Anwick bribed a royal official with sixpence to avoid taking part in a procession of protest against the levy of procurations by two papal legates. In the previous year processions were arranged to pray for the good success of the king in the war in Gascony, and during the next century there are a number of similar examples.

There remained one annual procession in Rogation, or Cross week (Ascensiontide), which was both religious and secular in intention. This was the 'bound beating', or progress, by as much of the parish as could be brought in, over the processional way along the parish boundaries. This seems to have evolved from the ancient custom of singing the litany in procession, and always retained its element of intercession. Dr Owst prints, from a manuscript at Lincoln, a sermon preached during Rogation which explains this:

"In these processions the clergye of holy chirche prayethe in theyre latynes for the helppe of all seyntis; and so scholde all other pepyll do that follow the procession, for many dyverse skyllis. ffirste that God scholde withestonde the batell of owre enmyes bothe bodyly and gostly. ffor in that tyme of the ȝere the devylls and other wickyd spyritis are moste besy a bowte for to drawe a man in to synne and wrechednes. Also holy chyrche prayethe that criste scholde kepe the tender frutis that be done on the erthe to mans helppe, and so scholde al cristen pray for the same. . .

"Also in these processions baners and crossis ben borne and bellis rong that the spyritis that flye above in the eyer as thyke as motis in the sonne scholde flee a wey frome us, when they see baners and crossis on lofte, and heryng the bellis ryng. for lyke as a kyng hathe in his oste baners and trompettis and claryons to the drede of his enmyes, ryȝte so in lyke wyse almyȝtti god that is kyng of all kyngis hathe bellis for his clarions and for his tromppis, and a cros reysed for hys banere. ffor lyke as a tarrant scholde be a drede if he herde a nother lordis clarion, and see a nother lordis banere in his londe, ryzte so in lyke wyse the devyllis and the spyritis that flyethe on lofte in the eyer dredythe moche more cristis clarions and his tromppytt is that ben the bellis, and cristis baners that ben the crossis a reysed . . .

"Wherefore ye schall come to the chirche these iii dayes, as I have tolde yow, that ye may go devowtely in yowre procession praying to all the seyntis in heven to pray for yow to criste that he wolde have mercy and pite on yow as he bowyte yow on the roode, . . . etc. Amen, etc."[14]

The Rogation week was often marked by a sermon of particular

[14] LRS 36, p. 104; LRS 64, pp. 21-3; Owst, *op. cit.*, pp. 201-2.

solemnity, like that endowed at Friskney, to be preached at the cross there on the Wednesday of the week, and on occasion it might be used for special intercessions. At Ashby de la Launde, as we have seen, the Hospitallers' men and their priest "went in procession in peasable and devout manner, about all the Temple Hethe, to pray for seasonable wedder." The fact that this particular procession seemed riotous to the neighbours is not entirely surprising: such demonstrations were often the occasion of horseplay and roughness, such as survived the Reformation. Another Rogation-tide sermon, from the same Lincoln collection, warned its hearers: "not to come and go in processyon talkyng of nyse talys and japis by the wey, or by the feldes as ye walke ... but ye scholde come mekely and lowly with a good devocion and follow yowre crosse and yowre bells."[15] Refreshments were usually provided for participants; at Careby in 1528 a bequest was made to ensure the provision of bread and ale "in the dayes of Rogacions called Crosse weke" and by various observances the marks of the parish bounds were impressed on the minds of the young. At Scopwick, it is said, small boys were put head first into holes on the boundaries, and at Grimsby St Mary hand-bells were rung around the fields. Whatever the observances, it seems probable that by the early sixteenth century the need for the custom was passing; at Bourne and Harrington in 1519 the vicars were neglecting the circuit, and at Clee enclosures were making it impossible.[16]

There seems to have been little place in the parochial life of the twelfth century for the regular preaching of sermons and it was only gradually that they became usual adjuncts of the church's year, outside the cathedrals and other great churches. Grosseteste had insisted in his statutes that all parish priests were to know and to expound frequently to their people the elements of the faith, and to explain the gospels after the divine office was finished, but it seems probable that many of the parish priests of his time were incapable of such exposition. It was not until the friars were firmly established in the country that the sermon as a vehicle for the instruction of the laymen became an established part of the life of the parish church. Even then it was not the weekly affair with which we have become familiar, but associated only with the greater festivals, with Rogation processions, and with special occasions of fund-raising for crusades, for the cathedral building, or for the repair of Northdike causeway in Stickney.[17] Palm Sunday sermons, and perhaps others, were preached out of doors on the steps of the churchyard cross, and it was not until the fifteenth century that efforts were made to cater for sermon

---

[15] *Val. Eccl.* IV; Trollope, *loc. cit.*; Owst, *op. cit.*, p. 215.
[16] LRS 10, p. 75; Gomme, *Manners*, Gents. Mag. Lib., 1883, p. 36; LAASRP VI, p. 29; LRS 33, pp. 57, 67, 87.
[17] *Coun. & Syn.* I, pp. 268–9; Neilson, *op. cit.*, pp. 154–5.

audiences within the church. There is a whole group of churches in the Lindsey marsh, Theddlethorpe All Saints, Addlethorpe, Croft, Wainfleet St Mary, Ingoldmells, and North and South Somercotes, which was rebuilt or remodelled during the period, allowing ample space in the great naves and their aisles for the preacher and his congregation. It is hardly accidental that most of the surviving medieval benches in the county, like the example illustrated in Plate VII from Osbournby, belong to this period, and the earliest surviving pulpits, at Boston, Claypole, Coates-by-Stow, Partney, and Tattershall, were installed at much the same time. The preachers seem often to have come from outside the parish: they might be monks or friars from the vicinity, like the Stamford Dominican going six miles from his house to preach a Sunday sermon, or collectors licensed by the bishops to preach what we should now call 'charity sermons'. The sermons, like those previously quoted, were of course in the vernacular, and full of the lively stories and homely illustrations which would appeal to a simple audience. The many surviving sermon collections suggest that such sermons were frequently repeated.

At all times the ecclesiastical authorities were concerned to see that Sundays and festivals were marked by the cessation of secular labour and by due observances in church. Every episcopal visitation, from Grosseteste's time onwards, seems to have uncovered fresh Sunday markets, despite the fact that the preaching of Eustace de Flaye directed against them in 1201 had taken deep root in the county. Gatherings of the population at church time had always provided excellent opportunities for trade. There had been Sunday markets at Burton Stather, Fleet, and Edenham before the beginning of John's reign. In 1303 Ingoldmells and Grimsby each had one and in 1423 Sempringham, Holbeach, and Marshchapel.[18] None the less, the custom gradually declined and observance of the Sunday holiday was fairly complete. It was even extended to Saturday, and as Robert Mannyng recounted in the mid-fourteenth century:

> "Sum tyme hyt was wont to be dowun
> To halewe the Saturday at the noun,
> Namlyche yn Inglonde..."

and there are signs that, in the general upheavals which followed the Black Death, Saturday too was regarded as a festival, for in 1360 Bishop Gynwell found it necessary to forbid the custom.[19]

The number of days to be treated as festivals varied considerably, and it is not easy to discover what observances were likely in the parishes.

[18] *Abbrev. Plac.*, p. 70; Reg. 3, f. 52v; Reg. 16, f. 225.
[19] *Handlyng Synne*, Roxburghe Club, 84, ll. 845-7; Reg. 7, f. 149.

On the whole it cannot have varied very much from the list of feasts observed by the cathedral workmen, which included thirty-seven throughout the year, besides five days after Christmas, four days at Easter, and three at Pentecost.[20] To these would have been added the commemoration of the dedication of the church, which sometimes, as at Grantham, was celebrated by a fair, and which seems to have become immensely important in the fourteenth century when many parishes were at pains to alter the day of its celebration so that it did not clash with harvest or vintage, or some other great feast.[21]

The dedication and other feast days were often marked by special services and processions, observances such as the Palm Sunday and Corpus Christi processions, and the bringing in of observant candles at the Purification. The gilds were often, as we shall see, to intensify the interest and devotion of these, and their importance in the parishioners' eyes is reflected in the complaint of the men of Friesthorpe in 1348 that the rector there on the day after Candlemas maliciously and against the will of the parishioners took down and carried off all the candles from the image of the Blessed Virgin, which had been offered there for devotion and penance. Some of the local observances at festivals were more secular in spirit. They ranged from pretty customs like rush-strewing at Dorrington and Clee and well-dressing on Ascension Day in Louth to gifts of eggs to the celebrant on Easter Day at Clee, the young men's Wessell at Hagworthingham, bacon and eggs consumed after the Easter mass at Nettleham, a church-ale at Pentecost, and a "lord and lady dancing" at Grimsby. None of them was so persistent, so deeply rooted in the pagan past, as the Fool-feast, usually held on the feast of the Circumcision, which Grosseteste condemned as an "execrable custom" but which persisted in the cathedral as late as 1384, at least, when "the vicars and clerks of the church, putting on lay garments, seriously impede the divine office by their shouting, chatter, tricks and games."[22]

Celebrations akin to this must often have shocked the more serious-minded and devout, and no doubt Robert Mannyng, in condemning "carolling in churchyards, miracle plays, and the worship of unworthy saints," was reflecting much serious opinion of his time. Nevertheless, they continued, and were to some extent absorbed in the great dramatic activity which distinguished the last two centuries of the medieval English church.

This activity seems to have been twofold in origin: on the one hand there was the drama created by the liturgy itself, especially at such times as Holy Week and Easter, when the solemn extinction of all lights during

[20] LCS III, pp. 545–7. [21] Reg. 12, ff. 239, 428–9, 439.
[22] LAO D & C, A/2/24, f. 76v; Trollope, *op. cit.*, p. 10; White 1872, *passim*; *County Folk Lore*, v, pp. 6, 194; Gomme, *Manners*, p. 3; Reg. 12, f. 450; D & C A/2/28, f. 23v.

Tenebrae, the adoration of the Cross on Good Friday, and the revelation of the Easter sepulchre were all striking attempts to 'act out' with 'audience participation' the events of the Gospel story, and on the other the masking or 'mumming' customary at pre-Christian winter feasts and undoubtedly represented in the Fool-feast, and in the dancing and horseplay known as 'carols'. Both strands were fused in the miracle plays which were acted, sometimes by clerks but more often by associations of laymen, and which presented dramatizations of bible stories and the lives of saints either in the church or out of doors, in the static 'pageants' on waggons or stages which were common in Lincoln, Louth, Sleaford, and Boston. These were, for obvious reasons, mostly summer festivals, associated with the feasts of Corpus Christi and the Assumption, although there are traces of plays acted at Christmas, Candlemas, and St Matthew in Addlethorpe and Thorpe St Peter.[23] The more elaborate town cycles were the affair of the gilds or the cathedral. On 7 July 1483, the dean and his brethren:

"stood before the West door of the choir, and after discussing the procession of St Anne to be made on the next feast day by the citizens of Lincoln, decreed that the play or ceremony of the Assumption of the Blessed Virgin should be performed in that procession in the cathedral nave, according to custom, the costs to be borne, after voluntary contributions had been made, equally by the Common and Fabric funds."[24]

It has recently been suggested that some of the Lincoln plays have been preserved in the well-known 'Coventry' cycle.

The larger villages had their own companies of players (the young men, perhaps) whose costumes were provided by the parish, and who took their play, whatever it was, round the neighbouring parishes. In the early sixteenth century Sutterton welcomed, and paid for, players from Frampton, Kirton, Whaplode, Swineshead, and Donington, and, it seems, took up a collection during the performance: "1524, increments for the play played on the day of the Assumption of Our Lady, nine shillings and sixpence received." The churchwardens of Holbeach in 1543 disposed of some of the properties of their play: "Harod's coat and all the Apostyls coats and other rags," for 18s. 8d.[25]

The building in which the activities we have been discussing took place must have altered and developed continually in the course of the four and a half centuries after 1100. Even if the body of the church itself belongs to a single period, and was built within a single fairly short span of years, new windows were inserted later, a porch or a spire added,

[23] E. K. Chambers, *The Medieval Stage*, 1927, *passim*; H. Craig, 'Mystery Plays at Lincoln', LH II, no. 11; Oldfield, *op. cit.*, appendix, p. 7; LNQ XVIII, p. 112.
[24] LAO D & C A/2/38, f. 22. [25] *Arch. J.* XXXIX, pp. 53–63; FNQ I, p. 9.

a chantry chapel enclosed from an aisle or plastered on to the exterior, or new altars erected. It is generally only in the fourteenth and fifteenth centuries, when the episcopal registers record many consecrations of new or reconstructed buildings, that there is much documentary proof of the dates of this activity, but there is excellent detailed evidence about Louth and its steeple, about the rebuilding of Wyberton after the thirteenth-century church had collapsed, and about the reconsecration of Sutterton after extensive repairs in 1490.[26]

Some of the church buildings of the twelfth century were evidently put up hastily and cheaply. The wooden church of Sutton in Holland was, as we have seen, removed to a new site before 1180 and rebuilt in stone, but Whaplode Drove chapel is said to have been of wood until its destruction in 1820, and a wooden chapel, stone fronted, survived in Toft in Kesteven until Stukeley's time.[27] Even the stone buildings were not entirely durable, especially if the details of upkeep were neglected. During the twelfth and thirteenth centuries responsibility for the church fabric came to be divided between the rector, who was to look after his own portion (the chancel), and the parishioners, who maintained the rest of the building and the churchyard. The weak point in the fabric was often the chancel, which could easily be neglected by a non-resident rector or an impropriating religious house or corporation. The sad tale of what could happen is illustrated by the complaints made by the parishioners of Scredington in 1336 about the dean and chapter of Lincoln, who were rectors of their parish: "it rains upon the high altar in such a manner that when it is raining and there is also a wind the chaplain cannot celebrate at the altar, or sit in the desks or even in his place for matins." Many chancels, like Heckington or Surfleet, were nobly repaired by their rectors, but even sequestration of the fruits of the benefice, as at Withern in 1454, did not always constrain others to do their duty and there is a sad tale of ruinous chancels in the 1521 visitations.[28]

The parishioners' responsibilities in maintaining the nave might not always be observed, particularly if much money were involved. Grosseteste's statutes had included a general injunction that the church and its dependent houses were to be suitably built and equipped, but by Sutton's time there are many signs that some parishes were neglecting their duties. Moulton's church and belfry were in disrepair in 1298, so were those of Kirton Holland in 1303; at Hagworthingham, Burton Stather, and Stapleford the belfries were being slowly and reluctantly rebuilt in the same period in the face of 'rebels' who refused to contribute to or actively

[26] J. E. Swaby, *History of Louth*, Lincoln, 1954, *passim*; R. C. Dudding, *Churchwardens' Accounts*, *passim*; LNQ XIV, pp. 226–35; Sutterton accounts, *loc cit*.
[27] BM Harl. 2110, f. 70; White 1872, p. 786; CCCC ms. 618, p. 3.
[28] LAO D & C A/2/24, f. 4v; Reg. 20, f. 80; LRS 35, *passim*.

interfered with the work.[29] If neglect went on too long, total collapse of the fabric might easily result, as at Wyberton. There are few examples of such disasters, however, especially after the mid-fourteenth century, when gilds and wealthy individuals began to assume responsibility for repair and rebuilding, and when also the parishioners themselves may have been better organized. Indeed, the years after 1350 seem to have seen an immense growth of pious activity in the Lincolnshire parish churches, which was part of the general growth of popular religious activity which these years witnessed. It was marked by appeals for national support in the form of indulgences granted by the bishop to those who aided the rebuilding. As early as 1301 there was one of forty days for St Paul in the Bail, Lincoln, but the fifteenth century saw many more. One granted in 1454 for the rebuilding or extensive repair of Boultham mentions a fact which must often have provided an incentive for rebuilding: there was in the church an image of St Petronella which was an object of pilgrimage.

More often than not, rebuildings and extensions must have been begun, apart from cases of sheer necessity, out of local or individual pride, to display the wealth and importance of the builder (Tattershall and Great Ponton offer excellent displays of their builders' wealth), or to beautify the donor's native parish. This latter reason must particularly have affected the gilds in towns such as Louth, and even in smaller places such as Hogsthorpe where the gild of St Mary built the porch, or Owersby and Kirkby cum Osgodby where the north windows were the work of a gild, or Gosberton where the gild of St John the Baptist inserted the south-westernmost window of the south aisle.

Sometimes the foundation of a chantry would involve a virtual rebuilding of a large part of the church as at East Kirkby and Burton Pedwardine, though in most cases they were founded in rebuilt or beautified individual chapels, like those in Gainsborough or Stoke Rochford. Where for reasons of space, and to provide for preaching and processions, the church was enlarged, individual parishioners might pay for, or bequeath money for, the building of an aisle, an extra bay (as at Gosberton where John Whytebrede in 1440 left a bequest to enlarge the church by one bay), a single pillar, or a window. Grimsby St James in 1365 and Ropsley in 1380 each received gifts of pillars, and an aisle was given to North Kelsey by John Wyga in 1372. What does seem certain is that monastic houses and other corporate bodies rarely undertook the work of rebuilding even the chancels which belonged to them: Holles records the gift of a window in the chancel at Wrangle by the abbot of Waltham who was rector of the church; it is certain that Bardney church

[29] *Counc. & Syn.* I, 272; LRS 64, p. 112; Reg. 3, f. 53v; LRS 48, pp. 25, 113, 153; Reg. 3, f. 24v.

was rebuilt on a new site by the abbot and convent there; but little remains to suggest that other religious houses were in any way active and, as we shall see, Crowland spent much energy in defeating efforts to enforce its rectorial obligations.[30]

As for the builders and their materials, we have only slight indications. In Wyberton and Surfleet in 1420 there was a master mason Roger Denys who, although perhaps local in origin, settled in London and died there, and with whom the representatives of Wyberton parish and the rector of Surfleet had made detailed written agreements. The Surfleet agreement is particularly interesting. Roger agreed with Mr Adlard Welby, rector there, to take down the choir or chancel and rebuild it on the foundations of the old, having first satisfied himself that they were sufficient and suitable. It was to have seven windows, three on the south side and three on the north of three lights each, and one in the east wall with five lights. Each light was to have a figure and text and be of English glass. The other materials were to be cement, lead, chalk, dressed stone, timber, and iron. The editor of the *Louth Churchwardens' Accounts*, Mr R. C. Dudding, thought that John Spencer, the bishop's steward in the town, was probably the designer of part at least of the last great rebuilding at Louth, but the accounts make it clear that the churchwardens themselves were supervisors of the building work. They were buying their stone, timber, and ironwork from a wide area, and others must have done the same.[31] A local church might of course benefit from the tithe paid by a neighbouring quarry owner or kiln burner: Edlington, for example, received five thousand large bricks for its rebuilding programme in 1445 from the Tattershall Castle kilns. Other building materials, and luxuries such as glass, came from further afield, especially in the larger churches. In 1482 Tattershall bought worked stone from Ancaster and Wilsford, wainscot boards from Lynn, and glass from Burton on Trent, Stamford, and Peterborough.[32]

At a time when church fabrics were ageing noticeably, after two or three centuries of patching, responsibility for the maintenance of the larger part of them fell squarely upon the parishioners. Money had to be accumulated to meet these responsibilities, and a fabric fund became a normal part of parochial organization. These funds were administered by officers who began to appear in the later thirteenth century. A 'proctor' who collected tithe was known at Wyberton in 1276; he may well have been also the clerk, and at Grimsby St Mary a chaplain accounted for the fabric fund.[33] The officials were variously known as

[30] Reg. 3, f. 34; Reg. 20, f. 40v, LRS 1 (Holles), *passim*.
[31] LNQ XI, p. 162; XIV, p. 228; XVII, p. 110; Dudding, *op. cit.*, pp. xiv, *et seq*.
[32] LRS 55, p. 77; HMCR *De l'Isle*, I, p. 199.
[33] *Hundred Rolls*, p. 308; LAASRP VI, p. 29.

proctors, kirkmasters, church greeves, fabric masters, and keepers or wardens of the fabric. They were soon to be indistinguishable from the churchwardens of the sixteenth and seventeenth centuries. They acted as trustees of houses and land given or bequeathed to provide income for the fabric. They often received the burial fees and 'wytwords' or small bequests, and had often to invoke the help of the bishop or archdeacon during visitations, and even the secular court, to obtain their money or compel their predecessors to hand over funds. Detailed bequests are mentioned at Barrowby in 1340 and Mumby in 1357; in 1336 the peculiar court of the dean and chapter was told that Agnes, widow of Roger Eudon, owed 3s. 4d. to the fabric of Strubby for her husband's burial, and in 1322, in the court of Crowland Abbey held at Langtoft, a case was brought for recovery from a former keeper of the church fabric of 10s. which he had omitted to transmit to his successor.

Each parish might have, in addition, its own individual sources of income, either regular or intermittent, for the upkeep of the church. At Sutterton much of the regular income seems to have come from the sale of candles to the devout, with an occasional receipt from the plays; at Kirton Lindsey the members of two parochial gilds each contributed 2d. every year. In Louth the Trinity gild made loans to the fabric fund in 1500 and 1501 during the building of the choir, but there is no sign of other regular contributions. At Hagworthingham the church masters had the rent of the guildhall or common house, and collections from the dancers and from "the young men called the Wessell" who may have been a plough gild which processed with a vessel cup or small image of the Christ child at Epiphany.[34] The ancient custom of the church seems also to have allowed the parishioners and their representatives to use timber growing in churchyards for church repairs, although the claim was often successfully disputed by rectors. At Aylesby, for example, the parishioners alleged in 1295 that they had used the churchyard trees whenever there was need to repair the fabric of the church, and the parishioners of Whaplode were involved in a similar dispute with the abbot and convent of Crowland in 1482, but in each case the rector's case was sufficiently strong to end in a compromise.[35]

Since the kirkmasters could be, and were, held to account for the administration of the funds with which they were entrusted, some form of accounting was desirable, though who wrote and kept the accounts is never very certain. A few pre-Reformation Lincolnshire accounts, all of the fifteenth century, have survived, but only in the earliest, that from Grimsby, is it clear that the accountant was a clerk. Fifty years before

[34] Reg. 5, f. 587; Reg. 7, f. 82; D & C A/2/24, f. 2v; LAO 6 Anc/1/20; *Arch. J.* xxxix; Kirton Lindsey parish, *passim*; LAO Mon 7/1; LNQ I, p. 7; *County Folk Lore*, v, p. 214.
[35] LRS 60, pp. 55–6; BM Add. 5845, f. 103.

this time, in 1376, a 'proctor' was named among the clerical staff at Moulton, and doubtless in many cases chantry priests, parish clerks, and holy-water carriers may also have acted in this capacity, and must certainly have written the accounts. By the late fifteenth century, however, the accountants seem to have been laymen employing clerks to write for them, and by this time too they are responsible for much more than the simple upkeep of the fabric. As early as 1291 the parishioners of Haxey were claiming, unsuccessfully it is true, that they, and not the vicar, should appoint a holy-water carrier, and thirty years later those of Crowle were hiring a priest to celebrate in their church.[36] On the whole, however, the kirkmasters were concerned with the safety and good state of the various church furnishings, plate, books, and vestments, which made up what is sometimes called the kirk stock, with the provision of necessaries (the elements and the kirk loaf, candles, and incense) for the conduct of services, and with meeting such expenses as fees for dedications. The Leverton churchwardens, whose accounts begin in 1493, provided for bell-ringing, the binding of books, and the thatching of the church; they bought a new Lenten veil to cut off the sanctuary, they installed an alabaster table and seventeen alabaster images in the roodloft, they provided a painted cloth to hang before the high altar, they rode to Tattershall to buy wood for the church, they marked the church linen in black silk, and they paved the "Lady floor" with stone from Folkingham, in the years before 1530. Their income was drawn from specific bequests, obligatory 'wytwords', income from obit funds, and weekly "gadderings in the kirk." Considerable expertise must have been necessary to account clearly for the multifarious endowments of altars, crucifix, and lights. What is notable, however, is the way in which their functions included the secular. Just as the church building was used for every sort of parish occasion, so the churchwardens acted for their fellow inhabitants in secular business; and it is not surprising to find them paying for the writing of the "sedyke book" in which the rates allotted for sea-defence were recorded. Like the wardens of other parishes they rewarded the players, this time from Swineshead.[37]

Since in 1237 the legate Otto had enjoined on archdeacons the duty of "overseeing the holy vessels and vestments" in the parishes, and archbishops Winchelsey and Reynolds had laid down that the parishioners must provide them, the latter's responsibility was quite clear. Very soon it was to be the churchwardens who acted for them in this context. The Deeping cartulary includes a copy of the archiepiscopal decree, which states explicitly what was to be provided and repaired by the parishioners:

[36] PRO E179/7/35; LRS 48, p. 104; LAO Crowle Manor 1/9, m. 6.
[37] LRS 56, p. 84; P. Thompson, *op. cit.*, pp. 561-7.

"a legenda, antiphoner, grail, psalter, troper, ordinal, missal, and manual; a chalice, a principal vestment of chasuble, dalmatic, and tunic; a choir cope; a frontal for the high altar, three towels, three surplices, a rochet, a processional cross, a cross for the dead, an incense vessel, a lantern, a bell to carry before the sacrament when it is taken to the sick; a pyx, a Lenten veil; a banner for Rogation processions; bells with ropes; a bier; a holy water vat; a pax; a holder for the Easter candle, a font with a lock; statues in the church; a principal statue in the chancel, the churchyard wall."[38]

Clearly the quality and quantity of equipment varied with the generosity and wealth of incumbents, patrons, and parishioners. Few parish churches could have had vestments of blue velvet wrought with the arms of the earls of Angus, such as Gilbert, Earl of Angus, gave to Kyme Priory in 1377, or the red cope wrought with gold peacocks and beasts and with green branches, which went from Crowland to the cathedral in 1470. But a parish such as Coleby might benefit very handsomely from the gift of a rector. In 1315 John of Fleet, rector of the parish, gave to the use of the high altar in his church a set of silver vessels, an ordinal of the use of Sarum, a silk cope with fleur de lys, another with gold leopards, a chasuble of Lucca weave, powdered with gold leopards, and many other things. In 1323 the 'ornaments' of the church of Bishop Norton were carefully recorded at the institution of a vicar, as a:

"festal vestment with tunic and dalmatic, a Sunday vestment lacking the stole and girdle, a daily vestment, complete but old; one new corporal and two old ones, an offertory of silk to use as a paten; two festal towels and two poor daily ones, one new and one old choir cope; three new surplices and three old ones; a silver gilt chalice, two new cruets and one old one; a copper incense vessel; three portable crosses with shafts; two ivory pyxes, a pax, a vat for holy water, a chrismatory; a lenten veil; an old missal; a portifory of the Sarum use; a psalter with hymns, capitulars and collects; a platter alone; an old antiphonary with psalter etc; another antiphonary in poor condition; a manual; an old legendary; a poor book of saints; a grail with troper; two old grails; an old troper. There is no processionary."

Many churches benefited by bequests, especially of plate, but also sometimes of books, bells, and even altar cloths. Richard Welby esquire of Moulton in 1487 arranged in his will for an altar cloth and frontal of damask to be given to his parish church. Books were often bequeathed, but wear and tear was obviously heavy, and renewal and repair seem frequently to have been needed. The kirkmasters of Hagworthingham

[38] BM Harl. 3658, f. 9v.

bought two antiphoners at Stourbridge fair in 1531, and the Leverton books required attention almost every year from a bookbinder who sometimes spent as long as a fortnight in the parish in each year.[39]

The 'ornaments', plate, vestments, and books were the essentials of church furniture which were inquired into at visitations. The font and bells, providing the former was properly locked and the latter not cracked, almost escaped comment. It is true that the occasional will provided for a new bell, as did that of John Haldin of Burgh in 1504: "to the bying of a new bell in the same chyrche of Borowe for to be tenor to the odder iii belles xl.*li.*" Or a will made a bequest for the upkeep of the sanctus bell, as did that of Elizabeth Chittok, the widow of a London draper, at South Kelsey St Mary in 1482. The churchwardens provided new ropes and bell-frames, and paid the clerk for ringing the daily bells from early morning until curfew. We have already mentioned the Holbeach bells calling the scattered parishioners to a secular meeting, and the bells must often have been used to give warning of disasters, especially where floods were likely. The 'lantern lights' at Moulton and Whaplode churches, for which bequests were made in 1514 and 1526, were undoubtedly intended for the same practical purpose.[40]

Endowments for altars and altar lights were already common in the twelfth century although the lights were then probably few in number, but the elaborations of the fourteenth and fifteenth centuries seem to have multiplied the lights and places to hang them, especially in the larger churches. Thus Henry Chambers of Horncastle in 1524 made bequests to lights, many of them hanging before crucifixes or statues of "Our Lady of the high quere, St Loy, Holy Rood in Jesus quere, St Trinion, St Saviour, St Anthony, St Laurence, Our Lady of Pity, Our Lady of Grace." At Long Sutton bequests were made soon after this to the "rood light, plugh light, yomans light, maydens light, light of St Anne's gild, St Jamys light, St Catherine light, St Christopher light, Holy Ghost light, Our Lady of Grace light," and it is clear that some lights had been installed by, or were the special care of, gilds and other groups in the population. The ploughmen and their light are often mentioned in the fifteenth century, and so is the young men's Wessell, Weslid, or Wesdayle light which appears in Thimbleby and Authorpe.[41] Besides these lights, which were presumably oil lamps or cressets, the churchwardens were responsible for providing wax, or candles, for the candelabra or corona which hung before the rood loft, and for the special Paschal candle.

---

[39] LAO D & C Dij/62/iii/12; *ibid.* D & C A/2/36, f. 99*v*; LNQ VII, p. 131; Reg. 4, f. 14*v* (for this reference I am grateful to Mr C. M. Lloyd); AASRP XLI, p. 38; LNQ I, p. 8.

[40] LNQ XXII, p. 114; AASRP XLI, p. 17; LRS 5, pp. 63, 152.

[41] LRS 10, pp. 15, 115; LRS 5, p. 132; LRS 10, p. 178.

If they also sold candles to parishioners for Candlemas, or for funerals, they must have handled considerable quantities of wax, and presumably conducted a thriving business. It is hardly surprising that chests were needed to house not only the church plate and vestments, but also the churchwarden's funds.

For the most part we have been dealing with the 'essentials' of worship and devotion, but it must not be forgotten that as the fourteenth and fifteenth centuries went by the trappings of the church were elaborated, often, it seems, by the generosity of private donors wishing to provide the latest and most fashionable device. This, no doubt, was how bequests for organs or organ players began in the wealthy marsh and fen villages, Gosberton, Marshchapel, Fleet, and Quadring, for example, in the early sixteenth century, and why walls were painted with scriptural and legendary scenes or heraldic devices, from the fourteenth century onwards. Some of the perpendicular fonts which are common in the county must have been presented from similar motives, but only Burwell and South Ormsby can be clearly assigned to a donor. Alabaster tables, screens, and reredoses, like those provided at Leverton, were perhaps fairly widespread, since they were manufactured in nearby Nottinghamshire. De la Pryme recorded that in 1670 a number of alabaster and brass figures were found at Scotter, "three or four score pretty images in alabaster and brass, fished out of a pond at Scotter twenty years ago;" and in 1844 a variety of angels, saints, martyrs, etc., more than fifty in number, were dug up at Epworth. Elaborate timber screens were often part of the fittings of a chantry, as at East Kirkby, and benches, as we have seen, were introduced for congregational sermons. But the rood lofts which spanned the chancel arch, and the Easter sepulchres inserted into the north walls of chancels, had their liturgical importance, and existed, in some simple form perhaps, everywhere in the later Middle Ages.[42]

The laymen of a parish were liable, in the person of their churchwardens, to answer to the bishop or archdeacon for the security and good state of the church and its furnishings, but they were equally liable to answer for their own misdeeds and excesses. After Bishop Grosseteste had published his constitutions the nature of the faults inquired into were fairly wide: Sabbath and festival breaking, the frequenting of quintains and other shows, wrestling and dancing, attendance at church-ales, and playing at dice were among the crimes investigated in the parish of Bardney in 1246. The archdeacon's visitations continued to be concerned principally with the fabric and furniture of the church: for those of the bishop, with their emphasis on the delinquencies of clergy and

[42] LRS 5, p. 169; LRS 10, pp. 146, 185; Pevsner, *op. cit.*, p. 209, W. O. Massingberd, *A History of Ormsby*, p. 332; Surtees Soc., 54, p. 85; Gomme, *Top. Hist.*, p. 121; J. C. Cox and A. Harvey, *English Church Furniture*, Antiquary's Books, 1907, *passim*.

people, we have little evidence except for reports of occasional cases (like the churchyard trees at Aylesby), submitted to the bishop's decision during the visitation, and for the formal summons of the clergy and four or six worthy men from each parish, according to size, to meet the Visitor at centres for the deanery. In 1321 Lawres deanery went to Scampton on the Wednesday after Saints Fabian and Sebastian (21 Jan.). Aslacoe went on the following Friday to Spridlington. Corringham attended on the Tuesday after the Conversion of St Paul (27 Jan.) at Grayingham, and Manlake on the Tuesday after Candlemas (3 Feb.) at Aukborough.

Records of the faults presented at these early visitations have survived only for the parishes belonging to the jurisdiction of the dean and chapter, but these allow us to see how the laity were disciplined and what their characteristic faults and those of the clergy were in the fifteen years or so before 1349. There are presentments for adultery and fornication, of course, for failures to pay the burial fee and to execute the provisions of a will, for harvest working on Sundays (those presented at Hainton being all women); there were also two sorcerers, one of whom, a Stow man, was able to prove his innocence. The vicar of Wellingore was accused of carelessly leaving an unguarded light on the altar at Pentecost and the rector of Friesthorpe had, as we have seen, interfered with the observance of Candlemas. The penances imposed varied from pilgrimages to Canterbury to twelve beatings round the church.[43]

It seems probable that this was the regular pattern of lay faults throughout the period. A few more cases of sorcery have been recorded: one was a clerk in the Lincoln neighbourhood in 1378, whose penance is described in awesome detail in the episcopal register; another was John Lamkyn, a Holbeach schoolmaster of the early sixteenth century, who invoked the help of a wise man, one Nasche, to tell him where the stolen church goods had been taken. The ancient privilege of taking sanctuary in consecrated buildings led laymen into trouble with the church, for it must often have been hard for injured men to see a thief slip through their fingers in this way, and breaches of sanctuary were certainly not unknown. From the late thirteenth century these were punished with some severity. At Gainsborough, in 1298, a man who had sought sanctuary in the churchyard was "borne out, though he embraced the cross erected there, and clung to the chapel door." At Irnham in 1361 certain parishioners were absolved for laying violent hands on Henry Halpeny who had taken refuge in the church, and were enjoined each to walk round the church for penance on the following Sunday bearing in his hand a half-pound wax candle which he must afterwards offer at the altar during high mass naked except for vest and hose. Violence and bloodshed in churchyards

[43] AASRP XXXII, pp. 35–96; Reg. 5, f. 271; LAO D & C A/2/24, *passim*.

were endemic and might well be directed against the clerks or servants of the church, for, as we shall see, anticlericalism was also endemic. One such case at Grantham in 1469 was punished by the penance of reading aloud a confession when the market was fullest:

"All Cristen people here assembled and gadred shall understond that Thomas Wortley tanner, here present, doth this his penaunce inioyned him by the Reverend Fader in God John by the grace of God Bishop of Lincoln in this cause. Forasmuch as the said T.W. in the nyghte tyme smote violently oon Edward Syngar a minister of the churche of Grantham and drewe blood of him within the Churcheyerd of G. whereby the said churcheyerd was poluted and of administration of all sacramentes and sacramentalles suspendyd, to the grete displeasure of God, contempt to oure moder Holy Churche and grete noyanse and offense to all this paryshe by occasion whereof he stode accused."[44]

Elsewhere in the diocese many heretics were discovered after the condemnation of Lollard doctrines, but there is little evidence that such doctrines had much hold in Lincolnshire. John Bagworth, rector of Wilsford, and William Smith, parochial chaplain of Corby, were imprisoned after proceedings taken against them as heretics in the episcopal visitation of 1416. John Potter of Asgarby confessed in 1458 to absenting himself from church, refusing to use holy water, to adore the cross at Trinity, and to take discipline from his curate at the Passion. Three cases, at Wainfleet, Sausthorp, and Baumber, figure in the Alnwick court book of 1447, and Mrs Bowker mentions a Whaplode man who in 1500 said "he had as lever to see the sacreng of a podyng, as to see the sacreng of a masse." Two persons at Brumby in 1517 and at Harrington in 1519 are the only heretics mentioned in Atwater's visitation. There appear to have been no such persistent Lollard groups as survived in Leicester and Buckingham, yet so much evidence has been destroyed that generalization from the surviving data would be unwise and Professor Dickens has shown us that in the north of the county at least, on the eve of the Reformation, heresy might well be hidden, but was certainly not unknown.[45]

We have already seen how the religious feeling of individual laymen sought expression at different times in the foundation of religious houses or perpetual chantries, and the endowment of obits. Such acts were feasible only for relatively wealthy men. Lesser folk would bequeath small sums to have their names inserted in the Sunday bede-roll,

---

[44] Reg. 12, f. 161; FNQ v, p. 31; *English Clergy*, pp. 220–1; LRS 64, p. 20; Reg. 8, f. 133; Reg. 20, f. 90v.

[45] LRS 57, pp. xxxv–xxxvi; *Cal. Pat. Rolls, 1413–16*, pp. 261–2, 272; *English Clergy*, p. 228; LRS 35, *passim*; LRS 61, p. 33; A. G. Dickens, *Lollards and Protestants in the Diocese of York, 1509–1558*, Hull, 1959, pp. 17, 25.

like two Sapperton men who died in 1517. They also treasured and passed on to their heirs their psalters and primers, their crosses with relics, and their prayer beads of gold or of coral (with fastenings and gauds of silver), amber, or jet. The livery servants of Sir Thomas Cumberworth in 1451 received as bequests from their master "bedes of pecok fedyrs or of bone or tree from the stock," and an amber rosary and psalter are among the objects stolen from houses in Skirbeck and Wrangle in 1395.[46]

The treasuring of religious books and prayer beads shows the degree to which laymen participated in the prayers of the church, but there were more active and direct means, short of ordination or entry into a religious order, by which religious feeling sought its expression. A widow might take a vow of perpetual chastity, such as that taken in 1329 by Joan, the widow of Gilbert of Totheby, in the presence of the bishop; she might even seek to be enclosed as an anchoress, which would provide her with a living and a certain amount of religious esteem. Such enclosures were made occasions of some ceremony. The abbot of Crowland and the prior of Peterborough acted as the bishop's commissioners in 1435, when Emma Tong was enclosed in a house butting up to the church of St Paul at Stamford, and bequests were sometimes made to such women in return for their prayers. In one such will, a "vowess," Joan Harby widow, of St Peter at Arches, Lincoln, bequeathed 3s. 4d. to the "Ankeres" there.[47]

Long before the outset of our period the more enterprising and active of English laymen had left their homes to visit holy places in England and abroad. For many men in the twelfth and thirteenth centuries this signified a journey to Jerusalem and even participation in a crusade. There were three main periods of crusading activity. During the third crusade Elias de Amundeville was in the Holy Land, meeting and receiving great favours from the brethren of St Lazarus, and returning home to found a hospital of their order at Carlton le Moorland. Many others must have participated in some degree in the early crusading enthusiasm, for the mid-twelfth century saw an immense number of Lincolnshire gifts to the crusading orders of Templars and Hospitallers. It was not, however, until the enthusiasm generated by the third crusade that any large numbers again left the county, this time during the last decade of the century, in the wake of King Richard I. In 1189 the crusaders gathered in Stamford about the time of the mid-Lent fair and made it an excuse for robbing and pillaging Jewish merchants. One of the companions of the king was Guy de Craon, whose estates lay in North Holland, and who

---

[46] LRS 10, p. 32; *Early English Wills*, pp. 83, 85, 89, 91, 119; A. Clark, *Lincoln Diocese Documents*, E.E.T.S., 149, pp. 45–57.

[47] Reg. 5, f. 412; R. M. Clay, *Hermits and Anchorites*, Antiquary's Books, 1914, passim; Reg. 17, f. 187v; AASRP XLI, p. 209; LRS 5, p. 44.

died in the Holy Land.[48] Many others in Holland took the cross, and an interesting list of them survives—presumably as a report to Archbishop Hubert—among the records of the dean and chapter of Canterbury. The names and descriptions of the men, and comments on them, indicate some of the difficulties of those taking the cross:

"*Skirbeck:* Robert son of Bruman took the cross and set off but has returned without accomplishing his journey. He is married with one son and scarcely able to make the journey. Lambert son of Eltruth is in the same state as Robert; he earns his bread by the labour of his hands.

"*Boston:* the following have gone: Benedict of Sibsey, Gerard son of Gudred, William the skinner, Robert the potter, Robert the butcher, William of Kirkby.

"*Wyberton:* John Buchart went for Jerusalem at the time when William king of Apulia stopped the Mediterranean crossing, and so has returned, and now has a papal indult freeing him from his vow until the way is easier. He is married with several children, very poor, and of middle age.

"*Kirton:* John le Borne, young, married, with children, scarcely fit for the journey; Walter the smith, has married since he took the cross but is ready and able to go.

"*Algarkirk:* Richard son of Thurstan, married, with five children and very poor but asserts he has been to Jerusalem, though there is no proof.

"*Sutterton:* William son of Swift makes the same claim.

"*Wigtoft:* Thomas of Holflet married after taking the cross and now has five children and cannot make the journey.

"*Swineshead:* Hugh son of Gimer is in the same state as Thomas.

"*Bicker:* Elyas son of Hervey is almost a beggar.

"*Gosberton:* Andrew the clerk, married and with two children made the journey but returned when Jerusalem was laid waste.

"*Surfleet:* Hubert son of Guy took the cross five years ago but came back from Lombardy.

"*Pinchbeck:* Hugh son of Guy took the cross ten years ago, is married with children and too old and poor to make the journey.

"*Spalding:* Alexander the vintner, married with two children and very poor, though still a young man; William Cuping married with four children, very poor, and middle-aged.

"*Moulton:* Roger Stoile a young man, is able to go.

"*Holbeach:* William the diker, a young man and unmarried, but very poor.

---

[48] LAASRP 3, p. 128; W. Harrod, *op. cit.*; *Abbrev. Plac.*, p. 32; R. C. Dudding, *Saleby*, p. 4.

"*Gedney*: William the baker, married, with two children, old, and almost a beggar."[49]

Many who went to the Holy Land were away for many years, or were presumed to have died there: three cases where this had happened are reported in the Assize Roll of 1202, from Theddlethorpe, Wellingore, and Leadenham, and four others, from Grimsby, Toynton, Croxby, and Hacconby, in the 1219 assize. There was evidently still much activity during 1218–19, for six men who had taken the cross and were actually in transit at the time of the assize are also named in the record of that year. There were two further bursts of activity during the thirteenth century, the first in 1240–5 when William son of Umfrid of Stallingborough went off, leasing his land to Nuncoton priory for four years in return for the money to make the journey, and Ralph Bolebec sold his Fulstow marshland to Malton Priory for forty marks and a horse worth three marks, in order to go upon a crusade. The end of the century saw a further period of activity with William, Lord Willoughby, setting off immediately after the feast of St John the Baptist in 1282, Thomas son of Lambert of Moulton pledging land to Castleacre Priory, and Bishop Sutton in 1291 instituting a series of inquiries about crusading vows and finances, which intensify the impression created by the Canterbury reports that lack of financial aid prevented many men from performing their vows.[50]

From this time on only genuine pilgrims, well able to finance themselves, went so far afield as Palestine: two of these, from South Ormsby, set off for Venice in 1407, armed with letters of exchange drawn on the Albertini Company. Another pilgrim was Arthur Ormsby esquire of North Ormsby who made his will in 1467, "while on his way to visit the holy city of Jerusalem and also other places to the same adjoining."[51]

The Jerusalem journey was an arduous and expensive affair, and for the middling wealthy it was never within reach, and it was they who patronized the shrine of St James of Compostella. At the very outset of the twelfth century Ansgot of Burwell returned from a pilgrimage to Saint James via La Sauve Majeure, and it seems possible that the many small chapels, manorial and otherwise, dedicated to Saint James during this century are reminiscent of similar journeys made by small landowners. The chapel of St James at Rodemill between Stapleford and Norton Disney may well recall a journey made by its founder, just as the gild of St James in Burgh le Marsh was founded by five men of the parish

[49] HMCR *Var. Coll.* I, 1901, pp. 235–6; C. R. Cheney, *Hubert Walter*, 1967, pp. 131–2.
[50] LRS 22, pp. 31, 49, 166; Selden Soc., 53, *passim*; Bod. ms. Top. Linc. d.i, f. 28*v*; BM Cott. Claud. D XI, f. 19*v*; BM Cott. Vesp. B XI, f. 28*v*; BM Harl. 2110, f. 76*v*; LRS 48, pp. 157–9.
[51] LAO MM 1/3/9; AASRP XLI, p. 47.

who had been to Compostella. Pilgrimages to St James continued throughout the medieval period: the steward of Tattershall College was absent for the purpose in 1479; and as late as 1516 the founder of an obit at Croft provided for his priests to "go pilgrimage to Rome, to seynt James, or any other pilgramage."[52]

For most Lincolnshire people, however, an English journey was as much as they could accomplish. Many must have gone to Canterbury, to the tomb of Becket, and it has been suggested that at least one pilgrim gave land to the cathedral priory there during his visit. Others went to Walsingham in Norfolk, like Richard Shavelock of Boston and Jone his wife, who thought the fact worthy of record on their tomb. Men from Bourne went to visit the holy blood at Hayles Abbey in Gloucestershire about 1440, and on their way through Warwick recognized an apostate canon from home. Then there were Lincolnshire's own shrines, at Crowland, Sempringham, and in the cathedral, all of which attracted multitudes, especially during the feasts of the saints honoured there. The shrine of St Hugh's head retained its attraction until the Dissolution and so, it seems, did the tombs of Bishops Grosseteste and Dalderby. Antiphons, especially composed for use on the festal day of "Saint" John Dalderby (neither he nor Grosseteste achieved canonization), recount the miracles performed during his life and after on a man vexed with a devil, Rutland men who could only bark like dogs, a litigious monk, a woman with a diseased breast, a child drowned in the sea, and a cleric afflicted by gall stones. "Happy is the church which rejoices in the tomb which contains that spotless body."[53]

In the fourteenth and fifteenth centuries a series of minor cults, originating in miracle-working crucifixes and statues, seems to have usurped much popular favour, at least for brief periods. There was, for example, the image of St Edmund in the ruinous chapel of the saint at Sailholme, which in the years 1374–5 worked miracles for many local people within a circuit of ten miles or so, and even saved the lives of sailors in difficulties on Rabwater deep in the fen, and so materially aided the repair of the building. The parish priest and men of Rippingale alleged that miracles had been worked by a certain statue popularly known as Jurdon Cros, which stood out in the fields. Sermons were preached at the cross, bells rung, and public processions held. But the bishop, believing that this all was done for gain, and that the allegations were nonsense, forbade the practices in 1387, only to find that an appeal was made to the Pope, who in 1390 granted a licence to the rector

"to found and build a chapel of Holy Cross and have mass and other

[52] J. H. Round, *Calendar of Documents, France*, no. 448; H. F. Westlake, *The Parochial Gilds of Medieval England*, London, 1919, p. 158; HMCR *De l'Isle* I, 193; LRS 5, p. 71.
[53] AASRP XLI, pp. 39–45; LRS I, p. 154; LRS 14, p. 37 and note; AASRP XXXIII.

divine offices celebrated therein upon the spot in certain fields within the parish bounds near the high road in which stood and stands still a certain wooden cross whither by reason of the miracles wrought there, great multitudes with offerings resort from the said diocese and other parts of England."

The chapel survived as a hermitage into the next century, without mention of further miracles. The statue of St Petronella at Boultham was enjoying similar popularity in 1454, and seems to have survived until the Reformation; and the Good Rood or Holy Rood at Boston, with the chapel there called the *Scala Coeli*, was very much visited throughout the fifteenth century. Pilgrims visiting shrines of this type did so partly in the spirit of later tourists, and expected to buy souvenirs to display to all where they had been. Knives had been distributed to all comers at Crowland on St Bartholomew's day, in memory of his flaying, until about 1476, and many must have brought back cockleshell tokens from Compostella, but smaller metal badges are known to have been bought by pilgrims at the shrines they visited. None has so far emerged in Lincolnshire except one illustrated by Pishey Thompson and reproduced in Fig. 8, but many must have been made and bought.[54]

Devotion to the church could be expressed with almost equal satisfaction and considerably more cheaply by membership of one of the many parochial gilds or societies, which seem to have been in existence in a rudimentary form throughout the medieval period, but which multiplied in the fourteenth and fifteenth centuries, especially in the more prosperous marsh and fen areas of the county. The gild members were mostly inhabitants or natives of the parish, who wished for, and enjoyed, the corporate activities of the gild. The sole exception to this seems to have been the Corpus Christi gild at Boston, the members of which included bishops and archdeacons, abbots and peers, and which continued to attract large numbers of members to its very last days. Indeed, bequests to gilds continued without ceasing to the Dissolution, and they were clearly a valued and important element in parochial life. In the towns and larger villages, such as Lincoln, Grimsby, Horncastle, or Holbeach, the gilds are for the most part the religious counterparts of the craft associations of fullers, tanners, cobblers, tilers, ship men, shepherds, minstrels, or parish clerks. In their secular capacity these associations often survived the Reformation. A good example is the mariners' gild at Grimsby, which before the Reformation had been called the Holy Trinity gild, and which kept a votive ship before an altar in St Mary's church. Its members had taken the ship in procession through the town

[54] C. Horstmann, *op. cit.*, II, p. 677; LNQ XIV, p. 61; *Cal. Pap. Reg.* IV, p. 101; Reg. 12, f. 331*v*; BM Harl. 773, f. 36*v* (I owe this reference to Dr Alan Rogers); Reg. 20, f. 8*v*; Pishey Thompson, *op. cit.*, pp. 134, 300; FNQ I, p. 94; Riley, *op. cit.*, p. 476.

on Plough Monday and had afterwards supped together. It survived to the late sixteenth century to regulate conditions of employment, its members supping together on plough night.

In the country parishes the one or more gilds were rarely vocational. They arose spontaneously, it seems, from a desire to maintain an unendowed light or altar or chapel or a derelict chantry, to offer special devotion to a particular saint with whom its members were associated (as did the Compostella pilgrims at Burgh le Marsh who founded the gild of St James there), or to honour a new and overwhelmingly popular cult such as that of Corpus Christi. They may have combined to light the church at special times such as the three days before Easter called *'Tenebrae'* (shadows), to provide furnishings for the church, to help to maintain its fabric, or to "increase divine service" by hiring priests to sing morrow masses. Some of the larger and richer gilds were, in fact, corporate chantries with priests who celebrated daily for the souls of dead members.[55]

The earliest gilds must have existed solely on the contributions of members: there is a reference in 1230 or so to the collection of *"fraternites"* in Frampton; 'soul-scot', paid annually, financed the Holy Trinity gild at Sleaford; and wytwords, or small bequests from members, seem to have provided most of the funds of the Corpus Christi gild at Deeping.[56] Many gilds, however, came to own property in houses and lands, by bequest or purchase, and were considerable landowners, especially in the larger towns, so that in Boston and Louth, for example, these provided substantial endowments for the post-Reformation corporations. All gilds, whatever their wealth and size, seem to have shared certain common features: they performed specified ceremonies at burials, and had special obits for former members; they attended church together on the feast of their patron saint, often bringing a "great candle" to his altar or statue, and they afterwards ate a meal together. This communal feast usually took place in a house or hall belonging to the gild or the parish, and may perhaps have evolved from or replaced the obnoxious 'church-ales'. The arrangements of the Corpus Christi gild at Grantham, which were set forth in the return made in 1386 to a royal inquiry, suffice to illustrate many similar celebrations:

"Before the time of procession on Corpus Christi Day they assemble at the church, the two priests in the sacred vestments carry the Body of the Lord attended by two boys in albs carrying the gild candles, followed by the brethren and sisters with candles. At the mass each offers as he pleases. After the mass the two candles are carried to the high altar by the

---

[55] Westlake, *op. cit., passim*; LH 2, no. 2, pp. 27-30.
[56] LAO, MCD23 (KM's notes on Magd. Coll. Oxford).

boys and remain there. Of the other candles, two burn daily at the high altar and one at the Corpus Christi altar during mass. After the [Corpus Christi] mass they eat together and each couple—i.e., husband and wife, gives food to a poor man. To the friars minor who go in front of the procession they give fourteen loaves, a sheep, half a calf, etc."[57]

To provide for these solemnities the gilds often accumulated table linen and silver cutlery and kitchen equipment, bought considerable quantities of food, and caused special equipment to be made. A garland used in the solemnities of the Corpus Christi gild at Lincoln is mentioned in the will of a canon of Lincoln who was a member of it, and this same gild displayed its banner over the houses of dead members. A model ship appears in the Grimsby sailors' procession, and at Pentecost and Corpus Christi the Boston gild of the Blessed Virgin carried about a "little ship called Vodschip."

Funeral services and obits (*rode diriges* at Boston) were affairs of great solemnity in the greater gilds: the obit of John Nuttyng, brother of the Boston Corpus Christi gild, was kept on the morrow of the feast of the Nativity of the Blessed Virgin.

"First on the Saturday previously the bellman of the town of Boston shall announce it throughout the town, as is usual with other obits, and it is to be kept with full solemnity of wax and cloth. The gild chaplains, two or more shall say the office of the dead on that Saturday, in the gild chapel, and mass for the dead on the following Sunday, and on the obit day all the gild chaplains shall make special prayers in the course of their mass. All this is to be done without music."[58]

For all this activity, and for the regular saying of mass in the way of a chantry, many small gilds maintained an altar with its own furnishings of plate, books, and vestments and hired one or more priests. At the time of the gild returns of 1389, 55 chaplains are mentioned in the returns of 115 Lincolnshire gilds and this number probably increased considerably during the next century and a half, especially in the greater gilds at Louth and Boston. In Louth the two gilds of St Mary and the Trinity each had two chaplains, a sexton, and a number of junior clerks and choir boys. Thomas Cawode, who eventually became the leading priest of St Mary's gild, in 1477 received an appointment as server, to officiate at the organ and in song, and to obey the curates and other priests of the church. He received a stipend of 13s. 4d. and a chamber lying next the parish church, butting south on the common way. At Boston, St Mary's gild had a staff of ten chaplains at the end of the fifteenth century, with a choir and other junior staff, and Corpus Christi had nine chaplains. There is no

[57] BM Add. 28533; Westlake, *op. cit.*, p. 162.
[58] *Early Linc. Wills*, p. 96; BM Egerton 2886; BM Harl. 4795, f. 3*v*.

doubt that the daily gild masses in these places were far more elaborate and ornate than the parochial masses which were side by side with them. It is not easy to say how many of these gild chaplains survived until the Reformation: certainly at Boston there was an array of eleven stipendiary chaplains in addition to the cantarists in 1526; and the larger parishes of the deanery of Holland each had groups of four or five stipendiaries. Louth had eight stipendiaries, Horncastle two, Grimsby three, Barton on Humber six, Deeping St James four, Grantham eight, and Sleaford two. How many of these were supported by gilds, it is hard to say: the *Valor Ecclesiasticus* includes only one instance (at Swineshead) of a beneficed gild chaplain. On the other hand, the chantry certificates of 1548 show that eleven gilds were supporting one or more chaplains, although the four Stamford gilds had allowed their appointments to lapse.[59]

The celebration of obits sometimes involved a distribution, in money or kind, to poor members and this often extended itself until these larger gilds were acting as benevolent friendly societies distributing coal as at Louth, making loans to members as at Kirton Lindsey, or maintaining bede houses as at Boston St Mary. Many even of the smaller gilds had declared that mutual aid, especially in carrying out pilgrimages and in burial expenses, was among their objects. It might well be that charitable donations were made to the widows and orphans of members. Moreover, at both Louth and Boston school was kept for the choir boys, and was to provide a nucleus for the post-Reformation grammar school there: in 1515 a new school building went up at Boston after "le ravyng" of the old school.

There is no doubt about the social functions performed by the ceremonies and solemnities, and by the feasts and charities of the larger gilds. They provided entertainment too, in their way, generally it seems in connection with the solemnities of Corpus Christi. At Boston, St Mary's gild made annual payments to actors and mimes and one of the Corpus Christi chaplains was called "Master of the Plaies." At Sleaford the gild of Holy Trinity paid for minstrels on Corpus Christi Day in 1478 and in 1480: "Paid for the Rygynall of the playn for the ascension and the wrytyngs of spechys and payntyng of a garment for God, 3s. 8d."

The lesser gilds of the small country parishes also had their important social functions of self-help and entertainment, and this must have been particularly true of the Wessell and Plough gilds, with their lights in the church and their 'dancing gear' and plough dinners. It is difficult to avoid the conclusion that the Plough or Mumming plays of the post-Reformation village had their origin in the partly ceremonial horseplay of the "young men." The Hagworthingham church book with its "gatherings" from the dancers and the "yong men called the Wessell," its pay-

[59] LAO, Mon. 7/1 and 2; H. E. Salter, *op. cit.*, pp. 66-7.

ments for "painting the dancing gear," and the malt given to the plough dinner must have been typical of many such parochial arrangements. Those gilds which had endowments of land or money of any quantity were soon to evolve an office-bearing hierarchy to administer them, which, like the churchwardens, changed annually. Even those gilds which had no income but their members' contributions needed a collector, while the great Boston gilds had clerks to collect the rents and keep the accounts, and sacrists and jewel-keepers to safeguard the property of the gild. Thus side by side with the churchwardens there were in the greater churches an alderman and two chamberlains of each gild; and the members seem to have progressed through a variety of ranks— it is difficult to avoid comparison with the nineteenth-century friendly society's 'chairs'—until they had served all offices. In the smaller parishes where the gild property and that belonging to endowments of lights or altars were equally small and often difficult to distinguish, it seems certain that the churchwardens must have acted for the gild. Certainly at Leverton the churchwarden was lending out the funds of the plough light, and the Kirton Lindsey gild accounts are included in those of the churchwardens. Conversely, gild funds were often used in support of those of the parish: at Deeping, for example, church repairs, surplices, bridge repairs, and journeys to London for the town's business were all paid for by the "occupiers of the gild" and frequent large loans were made by the gilds to the kirkmasters during the building of Louth steeple. The inscriptions recorded by Gervase Holles show that gilds contributed windows to many churches, such as that in the south aisle at Horncastle, which bore a legend which can be translated as: "Pray for the benefactors of the cobblers' gild who caused this window to be made with St Ninian with lock and chain and SS. Crispin and Crispinianus, with the tools of their trade," or the north window at Kirkby cum Osgodby which showed "a man holding a Cup on each hand of him divers kneeling, under him this motto: Gilda de Ouresbi me fecit (the gild of Owersby made me)."[60]

[60] Kirton Lindsey par. f. 13, s.a. 1485; LNQ 1, p. 1; LRS 1, *passim*.

CHAPTER IX

THE PAROCHIAL CLERGY

THE priest and his clerk were the essential minimum of clerical staff in Grosseteste's time, but the most usual complement of staff, in all but the smallest parishes for most of the medieval period, was an incumbent, resident or otherwise, a parochial chaplain who was a priest, and occasionally a deacon or subdeacon. The incumbent provided all this staff, often reluctantly, except in the few parochial chapels where the vill hired its own chaplain. Bishop Gravesend found it necessary, in 1276 and 1277, to order the vicars of Louth and Corringham to pay the stipends of their deacons, and the incumbent of Denton attempted in 1358 to lay the burden on his parishioners. Occasionally a chantry might be established, as at Edenham, to provide additional pastoral help, and chantries and gilds employed priests who might help in emergencies. But the actual burden of the cure of souls fell upon the incumbent and his substitute or representative, the parochial chaplain.[1]

The duties of the deacon, according to the incumbent of Sedgebrook in 1500, were to read the gospel at high mass and to ring the bells at the canonical hours, but it seems improbable that many parishes could find men to fill such places, at least after the Black Death. The duties of the parochial chaplain, curate, or priest on the other hand, as set out in a lawsuit about Stragglethorpe, were "to reside continually, to serve the chapel and its inhabitants, to administer to them all due sacraments and sacramentals."[2] Those filling such an office, who might be termed the great clerical proletariat, were for the most part no more than literate local men, ordained in the diocese, and spending all their lives within twenty miles of their birth places. There is only one complaint, from Wrawby in the 1519 visitation, of lack of learning in a parochial chaplain, but their accomplishments were undoubtedly slender enough. In the 1526 subsidy there were two foreign chaplains, an Irishman at Fulstow and a Scot at Croxby, but they were very much the exception. In the Stragglethorpe case already quoted a witness of over seventy told how in his youth he knew a priest called great Sir William who remained as chaplain for sixteen years, staying and sleeping there continually, and afterwards three others, the first of whom was also there for sixteen

[1] LRS 20, pp. 70, 95–6; Reg. 7, f. 145v.   [2] LAO Vj/5, f. 71; LRS 61, p. 38.

years. These Stragglethorpe priests had a house provided by the parishioners of the chapelry, and stayed there throughout the year, but the Rigsby chaplains provided from Alford were expected to sleep at Rigsby only in the summer (from May Day to Michaelmas). Most parochial chaplains functioning in parish churches seem to have been expected to live in a room in the benefice house and were presented at the bishop's visitation when they did not do so. A case of theft heard by the justices in Quarter Sessions in 1370, in which a former servant of the rector of Sudbrooke broke into the chamber of John of Branston, the chaplain there, and stole a cloak, suggests that the chaplain was living in the rector's house; and in 1519 the parish priest of Snitterby was specifically presented because he did not sleep in the rectory, but elsewhere in the town.[3]

The average stipend of these priests was less than £5 at the end of the fifteenth century, and it is hardly surprising that some at least of them should have tried to supplement it, especially as prices rose. A similar situation in the later fourteenth century and a general relaxation of standards after the Black Death led many parochial chaplains into crime, and the rolls of the justices of the peace for 1360 to 1375 are full of accusations of theft and violence committed by chaplains. Thomas Stuther and Robert of Bolingbroke were two Spalding chaplains, for example, who were said to have stolen gold and silver from a house at Whaplode, and two chaplains joined four laymen from Lincoln in beating up the parson of Skellingthorpe in his own church on All Saints' Eve in 1369.[4] The parochial chaplains of the early sixteenth century had different ways of improving their economic position: they often took a lease of the rectorial tithes and, doubtless, being resident, collected them more efficiently than the rector himself. They hired farms and made themselves into farmers; they were merchants, like the curate of Surfleet, who spent all his time trading in hemp, corn, and cattle; and there is even one case of a fisherman curate at Barton on Humber who was "a common fisherman in the Humber, in English wading," and who incidentally "made an attack on the town watch." On the whole complaints about the parochial chaplains are few at any time and they must have done their duty moderately well. There seem to be only five cases in the 1519 visitation when the chaplains were said to be inefficient in the performance of their duties, and genuine accusations of immoral life are certainly few. There is, of course, the occasional spectacular individual like John Wymark, former chaplain of Sutton le Marsh "now hiding in Kesteven," who fathered a child on Margaret of Habrough and after the birth "threw the child into the sea and so killed it," and there are the

[3] LRS 56, pp. 59–60; LRS 33, p. 96.
[4] M. Bowker, *op. cit.*, p. 103; LRS 30, *passim*.

underpaid, unsatisfactory priests hired by the prior of Spalding for the church there.[5]

One thing seems certain: by the end of the fifteenth century the actual numbers of parochial chaplains and other stipendiaries available for the country parishes had undoubtedly shrunk, and a number of the chapels which had been served by a chaplain were now, temporarily or permanently, derelict. In some cases, as at the chapel of St Leonard at Brakenholm in Farlesthorpe parish, the abbot of Louth Park had ceased by 1474 to provide a priest for a chapel which no longer served any population. But this scarcely explains the other cases reported in the early sixteenth century of Sutton St James and St Nicholas, of Sloothby, or of Holdingham and Rigsby, where incumbents of mother churches were refusing to honour their obligations to provide service for chapelries. This was not entirely a new problem: in 1455 a long case had been fought to oblige the parson of West Halton to ensure service in the chapels of Holy Cross Conesby and St Leonard Gunnes, and as early as 1376 the chapel of Sailholme seems to have been derelict. Comparison of the numbers of stipendiaries employed in the late fourteenth century with those of the 1526 subsidy suggests that the effect was not so much shrinkage as redeployment. Beltisloe and Yarborough deaneries each had fewer stipendiaries in 1526 (32 in 1376, 11 in 1526, for Beltisloe; 46 and 37 for Yarborough), but in Holland on the other hand, where the chantry and gild places were numerous and relatively more attractive, 112 in 1376 had become 153 in 1526, the increase being almost entirely in Boston where the curates, gild priests, and cantarists now numbered 32.[6]

The drawback at any time to the employment of such men as this was that, with lack of regular supervision from a rector or vicar, they would behave like the chaplains of Surfleet, Gedney Hill, and Ingoldmells, who neglected to sing their services. On the whole, however, non-residence was not a very large problem in the county in the early sixteenth century, nor presumably earlier. Occasional deprivations of rectors for persistent unlicensed non-residence, as at Scrivelsby in 1467, and the safeguards provided in licences granted by the diocesan and Pope as to proper service, seem to have prevented the more serious effects of persistent non-residence. Moreover, among the 83 non-residents noted by Mrs Bowker in the years 1514–20 (the total number of benefices being reckoned by Hamilton Thompson as 628), many of them held minute or even non-existent parishes such as Cadeby and Coates by Stow, Rand, or Swinhope, where the total income must have been very small and plurality almost a necessity for a reasonable living.

What was perhaps a more serious problem at all periods, and especially

[5] LRS 33, *passim*; LAO Vj/4, f. 34.
[6] LRS 61, pp. 43–4, 119–20; Reg. 21, ff. 173–97.

by 1500, was the number of livings appropriated to religious uses (Hamilton Thompson estimated them as 311, just under fifty per cent of the total of Lincolnshire livings). Here the appropriating house occasionally put in a religious, particularly a canon, and Mrs Bowker has calculated that in the years 1495 to 1520 80 religious were presented to 43 benefices in the county. It seems probable that many houses took this action as a means of saving money during the course of the fifteenth century, when the values of rectories tended to shrink from various economic causes, and at the same time augmentations, or reordinations, of vicarages were being forced on the appropriators as a direct result of ecclesiastical policy. Four such cases, for Alford, Horncastle, North Kelsey, and Navenby, are recorded in the years 1462–7.[7] A fairly typical vicarage was Rauceby (not in Mrs Bowker's list), where the prior and convent of Shelford in Nottinghamshire were proprietors and where in 1500 the parishioners complained that they were accustomed to have a secular vicar, and sought henceforth that religious should not be instituted to their benefice. Only nine beneficed religious figure in the 1519 visitations and the comments on them are generally non-committal. A note added to an entry about Wilksby, which was served by a monk from nearby Revesby, is revealing: "It is a very small value and no secular chaplain is willing to serve it." Similar considerations must have led the canons of Kyme to serve Northolme (Wainfleet St Thomas) by one of their own number, and caused the prior of the Lincoln Carmelites to figure in the 1526 Subsidy as the parish priest of Lincoln St Mark.[8]

The sources of an incumbent's income have already been discussed, but it is important to remember that custom varied much from place to place, that rectories themselves were of widely differing value, and that where in appropriated parishes vicarages were ordained, the vicar's portion might vary very considerably. Mrs Bowker has calculated that the average gross stipend of a rector in 1526 was £12 13s. 8½d., which after the various charges were met was on average net £9 9s. 6¾d. Similarly a vicar had an average gross payment of £9 9s. 1¼d., and net £6 13s. 1½d. The vicar's portion was sometimes a flat payment, but more often a share of the tithe and offerings, and this might vary very considerably with economic conditions and the state of the population. The vicarage of Whaplode, which was appropriated to Crowland, was estimated in the late fifteenth century to be worth £28 18s. 8d., which was partly made up of 67s. 8d. for Cokwax and Romepenny from "eleven score and twelve houses, omitting forty-nine widows' houses, oblations" of twenty-four score and four persons, eight score new communicants

---

[7] Reg. 20, f. 86; *English Clergy*, p. 115; Bowker, *op. cit.*, appendix III; Reg. 20, ff. 56, 82, 86, 163.
[8] LAO Vj/5, *passim.*

at Easter, and offerings in the chapels of Holy Trinity, St Katherine, and St John Baptist. Out of it he found two parish chaplains at £6 each and their keep and chambers, maintained a house, and paid the holy-water carriers during the three days of principal offerings. In 1526 Whaplode's value was estimated at £16 6s. 8d. gross, finding a chaplain at £5 6s. 8d.[9]

The rectory itself might have many components and the large prebendal rectory of Bishop Norton was surveyed in 1323 with very interesting results. It consisted in the tithes of those living in Norton, Atterby, and a fourth part of Spital on the Street, including tithes of sheaves, wool, lambs, cattle, and other animals, a chief house to the south of the church and another little house on its north side, and nine and a half acres of arable on the east side of the town and six on the west, sown in alternate years. The average value of the tithe laid in the barns was sixty marks, and the land at 6d. an acre was worth 7s. 9d. Offerings at the four chief feasts came to 40s. Wax at Candlemas and cerage at Easter were worth 8s. and the lesser offerings 3s. Tithe of geese, eggs, pigs, and chickens brought in 8s., and there was meinport (an offer of bread) at the principal feasts. Tithe of curtilages yielded 6d., of wool and lambs 100s. Profits of corrections (in the prebendal court) were 2s., tithe of mills 4s. Out of this the prebendary paid 3s. for the house where the chaplain lived; the chaplain was paid 6 marks and found drink for those carrying the lance to Lincoln for the Pentecost procession. Out of all this a competent vicarial portion was assigned, and the vicar was given a third part of the house and garden on the north of the church, which had a hall, chamber with solar, kitchen, barn, and stable. This sort of partition of the benefice house between rector and vicar was not unusual, especially in the thirteenth century. At Kingerby for example, at its appropriation to Elsham Priory in 1268, the vicar was assigned the east side of the church house from the gable of the solar, with the hall and other offices in that part, the priory having the west side, with the barn. At Louth, on the other hand, what seems to have been a separate house on the south side of the church, with a kitchen and little close set about with willows and a stone wall, was assigned to the vicar in 1238.[10]

Standards rose in the next two hundred and fifty years, but only as rebuilding became necessary. A rectory built at South Ormsby—not a large benefice—in the mid-fourteenth century had a hall, solar, and an external chamber, while the good living of Coningsby benefited in 1463 from the bequest of one of its rectors, John Croxby, which gave it the handsome house recently investigated by Mr Barley and Dr Rogers. The standards of some vicarage houses rose too. William Stukeley described his vicarage house at All Saints Stamford, which retained medieval features: "a hall with a cove at the upper end for a publick dining

[9] BM Add. 5845, f. 96.   [10] Reg. 4, ff. 13v–14v; LRS 20, p. 30; LRS 11, p. 99.

room many old Latin verses still visible painted on the timber. By a stone staircase we goe up to his lodging room, handsomly covy'd, wainscot ledges along the cornish for Tapestry hangings." By far the best evidence, however, of the social and economic position of the vicar in a community is the detailed description of the house to be built in the late fourteenth century at Theddlethorpe for the vicar of All Saints, appropriated to Revesby: it was to have a hall twenty-four feet long and eighteen feet wide and two chambers above, the whole to be under a single roof and to have two cellars. There was to be a second building containing kitchen, bake-house, and brew-house, and a third for a stable to hold three horses, a haystore, and a sty for twelve pigs. All this was to be roofed with reeds or straw and the glebe on which it was to stand was to be shut in with dikes, *iuxta morem patrie*.[11]

A 'mud and stud' house of the common Lincolnshire type might easily become dilapidated, and ruinous benefice houses reappear continually in the story of the Lincolnshire church. In 1305 the dean and chapter rectory at Glentham was reported to be in a bad state: the south wall of the hall was in ruins, its ceiling was broken, its north porch required attention and so did the timbers and gable of the little room on its south side. The gutter of the principal chamber and its gable, the bake-house, kitchen, servants' chamber, ox-house, cart-house, hay-house, and long sheepfold all needed repair, the private chamber was almost in ruins, the stone and mud walls round the court were decayed, and all the buildings needed rethatching. In 1454 the fruits of the rectory of Withern were sequestrated until the rector Thomas Dunham repaired the chancel and rectory house. The story is repeated endlessly, and it seems that the blame is often, though by no means always, to be laid at the door of a religious house: of thirty-nine parishes whose rectories were ruinous or dilapidated in 1519, only fifteen were in appropriated benefices, and most of the rest belonged to livings so small that a rector could scarcely maintain himself there, or were in the hands of negligent lay farmers, as at Gautby.[12]

An inquisition into the revenues of the two parts of the rectory of Grayingham, made in 1454, shows how complicated and, indeed, wasteful tithe collection could be. The rectors received the tithe as a whole and divided it equally between them: the grain and hay tithe cost 4s. to collect and 6s. 8d. to carry, and each received:[13]

Two quarters of corn worth				10s.
Two	,,	,, rye	,,	6s. 8d.
Twenty	,,	,, barley	,,	33s. 4d.

[11] CCCC ms. 618, p. 91; Reg. 12, f. 461*v*.
[12] LOA D & C A/2/21, f.8; Reg. 20 f. 8. [13] Reg. 20, f. 7.

Ten quarters of peas	worth		20s.
Four ,, ,, hay	,,		4s. 10d.
Twelve tithe lambs	,,		3s.
Six stones of tithe wool	,,		12s.
milk and calves	,,		4s. 6d.
geese	,,		16d.
pigs	,,		6d.
doves	,,		4d.
hemp and flax	,,		6d.
hay	,,		18d.
wax-scot	,,		10d.
Total			£6 17s. 3d.

There seem to have been relatively few disputes in Lincolnshire about *what* tithe was paid on, apart from one or two cases concerning fish (at Sutterton in 1293 and at St Saviour, Clee, in 1306/7) and salt or salt meadow. Before 1534 rape-seed oil seems to have been included among the tithe payments at Tydd St Mary without any dispute. On the other hand there was constant dispute in the thirteenth and fourteenth centuries as to which *lands* should pay tithe, to which parish the tithe of disputed areas on a boundary should belong, and how the tithe should be collected. Many of these disputes were the result of careful exploration by religious houses of the extent of rights which had until then been ill defined and a matter of custom only. A dispute between Bardney Abbey and the men of Winceby in 1252 resulted in a careful enumeration of the mode of tithe payment and an inquiry made in 1336 during a visitation into tithing at Hainton resulted in a report by the "greater of the parish" that "the parish custom is to pay tithe of milk, butter and cheese during the first nine days in May..."[14]

Of the actual collection few traces have remained except when disputes arose and the parishioners came to blows. In 1357 the vicars of Ancaster and Kelby and their two parochial chaplains were all in the street at Ancaster taking up the collection (probably of the personal tithes) in the Tuesday of Whitsun week when certain sons of iniquity laid hands on them. The parochial chaplains must often have been the agents or proctors for the collection: we see John, the proctor of the church of Wyberton in 1278, accused of secretly exporting tithe wool to the continent through Boston, and Walter, the parochial chaplain, and John Sire, his fellow, proctors of Barrowby, hiring a labourer to thresh their tithe corn in 1372.[15] By the fifteenth century however, direct col-

[14] LRS 52, p. 105; Grimsby Court Book i, f. 349; *Val. Eccl.* IV, p. 90; BM Cott. Vesp. E xx, f. 118; LAO D & C A/2/24, f. 2.
[15] Reg. 7, f. 78; *Hundred Rolls*, pp. 308, 383; LRS 30, p. 154.

lection was much rarer. In 1519 many tithes were said to be let out to farm, and the farmers might sometimes be laymen, but might equally well be the vicar or the parochial chaplain. The last of the Stragglethorpe witnesses in the case mentioned above was a lay farmer of tithes—he had tithes of grains, wool, and lambs—for which he paid to the rector of Beckingham eight marks and the chaplain had all the other revenues and offerings for his stipend. At Brigsley, Grainsby, and Swinhope the parish chaplains were farmers of the rectorial tithe; at Humberstone the vicar was the farmer.[16]

As a tithe owner the rector or vicar might often be in a difficult situation vis-à-vis his parishioners, but as a glebe owner the rector at least was a farmer among farmers, in some cases occupying a considerable holding and playing an important part in the agricultural community of his parish. Most rectors conducted themselves irreproachably in this role, but an occasional tendency to presume on their rights, and encroach on or overstock commons, can be detected as early as 1272, when a stint was imposed on the rector of Gate Burton and his successors by Roger of Trehamton. Quite soon after this William de Clifford, rector of Swineshead, had appropriated and enclosed upwards of one hundred acres in the Eight Hundred Fen, and John Huntman, incumbent of Sutton le Marsh, who had been deprived of pasture outside the sea bank by the inundation of the sea, had intruded on the inland commons of the parish, where he had no rights. Conduct such as this was much resented and many cases of ill feeling and actual aggression were reported. In 1274 a pitched battle took place between the men of the parson of North Witham and the entourage of the bailiff of the wapentake, and in the agrarian troubles of the mid-fourteenth century attacks on the glebe and the rectory house were very frequent.[17]

Some personal causes for friction may well have been removed, during the century and a half before the Reformation, by a well-marked tendency to lease the tithe and glebe to laymen in return for a fine and a money rent. The bishop's permission had been needed for this since the practice began in the early thirteenth century, but it is clear that leases were often arranged without his knowledge: in 1519 at least thirty-two rectories, which presumably included land and house as well as tithe, were leased to laymen or clerks. In addition, there emerges from this visitation a general impression of the secularization of many of the clergy. Some might have shed the troubles of tithe collection, but a number of others were themselves holding leases or engaging in mercantile activities, and this is unlikely to have added to the respect in which they were held.

[16] LRS 61, *passim*.
[17] *Hundred Rolls*, p. 305; Magd. Coll. Oxford i, no. 69 (K.M.); *Hundred Rolls*, p. 390.

The tithe owners may have looked keenly after their own interest, but they were not necessarily to blame, for economic pressures were telling against most of them for the whole of the medieval period, and it must sometimes have been particularly hard for vicars to live. As early as 1222 the vicar's portion in the living of Langtoft, which was appropriated to Crowland, was being augmented by a toft and a piece of land. Many vicars must have suffered, like Richard of Coates at West Ravendale in 1298, from lack of meat in a diet provided by the priory, and even the apparent bounty of the Stixwold vicar's weekly provision from the convent of "fourteen gallons of ale, seven prikked loaves, besides eels, cheese, butter, soap, and turf for burning," can scarcely have been sufficient in itself.[18] Then, too, population changes and alterations in agricultural practice must have affected quite seriously the many small parishes of the wold areas, and some town churches, especially in the declining centre of Lincoln. The tithes decreased in value, the glebe may never have been very large and could no longer be profitably farmed. Even where parishes did not disappear completely their incumbents could probably scarcely make a living and this must have brought out all their most acquisitive qualities. In extreme cases, of course, two churches were consolidated as with the Bail churches of All Saints and St Mary Magdalen in Lincoln in 1318, or with Hameringham and Dunsthorpe in 1438, when the latter church was said to be so poor as to be able to provide only one-eighth of a chaplain's stipend. At the same time many parochial chapels, like Humby in Somerby by Grantham, must have lost their own chaplains. In this case, in 1470, the rector of Somerby was licensed to celebrate there himself, instead of providing a chaplain, the twenty-one inhabitants of the two places having deposed that their total tithes amounted to no more than £9 19s. 8d.[19] If individual incumbents looked sharply after their tithes and offerings, the monastic proprietors must have done the same, and the general impression created by the parochial scene after 1350 is one of continual pressure by the tithe owner on the tithe payer.

In such circumstances it is scarcely surprising that there was always a certain amount of anticlericalism and that, in moments of local or national crisis, it should flare up into a series of ugly incidents. There were three principal periods of trouble, when ill feeling seems to have been widespread: the last decade of the thirteenth century, the fifteen or twenty years after the Black Death, and the years from 1420 to 1455.

The earliest incident of the first spell of trouble seems to have been an altercation at Boston in which a merchant, Peter de Cysters, seized John the parish chaplain by his hood. In 1296 a personal attack was made on

[18] Wrest Park, f. 143; LRS 39, pp. 54, 115.
[19] Reg. 3, f. 388; Reg. 20, ff. 77, 102.

the parochial chaplain of Normanby le Wold and his clerk in church on the feast of the Exaltation of the Holy Cross, and in the same year swans belonging to the parson of Gosberton were carried off "in a riotous manner" by Sir Ranulf de Rye and others. Hugh the vicar of All Saints Stamford suffered a similar attack in the town market place on St Edmund's day 1298.[20] Most of the feeling came out in a series of refusals to pay offerings. The earliest incident of this sort was at Langtoft in 1296, where the parishioners tried to reduce the number of offerings required at funerals, marriages, and churchings. There were similar 'strikes' at St James's, Grimsby, and at Moulton and Grantham in 1298, the men of Moulton being determined to remove the funeral candles set round the bier when a corpse was carried to the cemetery so that the ministers of the church should not have them as perquisites. What appears to have been a 'sit-in' took place at Gedney in 1299 and disputes about fees continued sporadically during the next nine or ten years, at Grantham again in 1301, at St Benedict Lincoln in 1309, and throughout the north-eastern deaneries of Grimsby, Yarborough, and Walshcroft in 1314.

These incidents no doubt reflected the general civil discontent of the last years of the thirteenth century, making use of well-established resentments against exactions or personal irritations as an outlet for more generalized unease.[21] The post-Black Death disturbances were less organized and probably indicated no more than unscrupulous men taking advantage of the relaxation of standards which followed the Pestilence. In 1353 and probably on other occasions, the bishop found it necessary to enjoin incumbents to reside and parochial chaplains to perform their duty, and some incumbents and chaplains plainly took advantage of the crisis to indulge in a life of robbery and extortion. Violence and aggression against clerics broke out intermittently, in the Ancaster riot of 1357, in reports of disturbances during the 1356 Pentecost processions, and in the refusal of the men of Holbeach in 1360 to pay their hay tithe in kind; it is perhaps surprising that no more disturbances are reported.[22]

The final period of serious anticlericalism appears to have been associated with the aftermath of the Lollard disturbances and was of no great extent but was again symptomatic of more general unease. In 1424 Walter Atkirk of Welton by Lincoln held meetings of his fellow parishioners, to persuade them to make no offerings to the vicar at funerals and churchings, beyond a single penny called le Mespeny. Robert and Elizabeth Taylour refused to pay their tithe hens and Walter Smithe confessed to burning tithe faggots. Surprisingly few traces of active anticlerical feeling have survived for the next century. If the feeling was

[20] LRS 52, p. 82; LRS 60, pp. 183, 142; LRS 64, p. 125.
[21] LRS 60, p. 190; LRS 64, pp. 78–9, 87–8, 126, 173–4; Reg. 3, ff. 41, 154, 291*v*.
[22] Reg. 8, f. 39*v*; Reg. 7, f. 78, 84*v*, 124; LRS 30, *passim*.

present, it had no opportunity for expression and so far as one can see offerings were collected and tithes paid with no sign of resentment.

Some of the difficulties experienced by the parochial clergy in their relations with their parishioners must have stemmed from the lowness of their educational standards. The numbers of university men, of book owners and book readers, were never very large in the county: in 1376 there were only eighteen Masters of Arts among the parochial clergy. And although, as Mrs Bowker has pointed out, schooling undoubtedly increased in quantity and improved in quality during the fifteenth century, there is nothing to suggest that its effects were as yet very widespread.[23] The parochial chaplains, who were, after all, in the closest and most constant touch with the laity, could presumably read and write, but it is difficult to believe that many of them, seen in the context of undignified squabbles about offerings or candles, can have inspired much respect.

Given all these obstacles to understanding it should be remembered that most wills were witnessed by the parochial clergy, who, moreover, often acted as executors. This is nowhere so marked as in the fourteenth-century Lincoln city wills, but the habit continued to the Reformation and beyond. The time had gone by when the parish chaplain would speak in the name of the vill, as Walter the clerk of Laythorpe did in 1272 in an attempt to bribe a coroner.[24] The lay officials, who had gradually assumed responsibility for the finances of the parish, were now its accepted representatives and would increasingly be so regarded in the new Protestant dispensation, for the parish church had evolved from a territorial chapel dependent on a local landowner, and controlled by him and his priest, into the shrine, meeting place, and possession of all the parishioners.

[23] LRS 49, p. 25; LRS 56, pp. 25, 73, 84, 157; LAO D & C A/2/32 f. 30.
[24] Lincoln Cathedral ms. 169, ff. 75–274; *Hundred Rolls*, p. 248.

APPENDIX 1

Numbers of clergy in 1376 and 1526 in the Deanery of Holland

The 1376 figures are taken from a modern copy in the Foster Library of PRO E179/7/35; those of 1526 from H. Salter's edition, *A Subsidy Collected in the Diocese of Lincoln in 1526*, Oxford 1909, pp. 62–8. The incumbent is not counted in either figure and not all parishes are included in the 1376 returns.

	1376	1526
Crowland	6	2
Fleet	10	1
Gedney	9	8
Gosberton	9	4
Holbeach	7	9
Moulton	8	5
Pinchbeck	8 + 1 subdeacon	5
Quadring	2	4
Spalding	11	6
Surfleet	3	2
Sutton	17	11
Tydd	3	4
Weston	3	1
Whaplode	10 + 1 deacon 2 subdeacons	5

APPENDIX 2

Numbers of religious in 1376

These numbers are extracted from PRO E179/7/35, Foster Library copy.

Alvingham	Prior, 7 canons, 29 nuns, 11 sisters
Bardney	Abbot, 20 monks, one a student in Oxford
Barlings	Abbot, prior, subprior, 25 monks, 5 *conversi*, 8 clerks in the church
Bullington	Prior, 9 canons, 2 *conversi*, 45 nuns, 10 sisters
Cammeringham	Prior and his fellow
Catley	Prior, 2 canons, 1 lay brother, prioress, 18 nuns, 8 sisters
Cotun (Nuncoton)	Prioress, 12 nuns
Eagle	2 brothers
Elsham	Prior, 7 canons
Fosse	Prioress, 5 nuns, 2 sisters
Gokewell	Prioress, 9 nuns, 2 sisters
Greenfield	Prioress, 11 nuns
Grimsby	Prioress, 9 nuns
Hagnaby	Abbot, prior, 10 canons
Heynings	Prioress, subprioress, 13 nuns, 2 sisters
Hough	2 brothers
Humberston	Abbot, 5 monks, 1 *conversus*
Kirkstead	Abbot, prior, 28 monks
Kyme	Prior, 11 canons, parochial chaplain
Legbourne	Prioress, 14 nuns
Limber	2 monks
Lincoln St Katherine	Prior, 10 canons, 3 *conversi*, 6 sisters
Louth Park	Abbot, prior, 16 monks, 5 *conversi*
Markby	Prior, 12 canons
Minting	Prior, a brother, a vicar
Neubo	Abbot, 8 canons
Newhouse	Abbot, 20 canons
Newstead-on-Ancholme	Prior, 6 monks
Ormsby	Prior, 5 canons, 30 nuns, 7 sisters
Ponte Aslaci (Bridgend)	2 brothers
Revesby	Abbot, 27 monks, 4 *conversi*

Semptingham	(incomplete) 56 nuns, 18 sisters
Sixhills	Abbot, 10 canons, prioress, 35 nuns, 8 sisters
Spalding	Prior, subprior, 21 monks
Stainfield	Prioress, 20 nuns
Stixwold	Prioress, 27 nuns
Swineshead	Abbot, prior, 15 monks, 3 *conversi*
Thornholm	Prior, 13 canons
Thornton	Abbot, prior, 24 canons, 5 *conversi*
Torksey	Prior, 4 canons
Tupholme	Abbot, 6 canons
Vaudey	Abbot, 16 monks

APPENDIX 3
Religious houses

This list includes all religious foundations for the existence of which satisfactory evidence has been found: it should be noted that many so-called monasteries omitted from it were no more than granges or large farms in monastic ownership. Much more work remains to be done before a full list of monastic granges for the county can be published. The following abbreviations are used in the list:

A.: abbey; AP.: alien priory; Aust.: Augustinian canon, Austin friar; Ben.: Benedictine; Cam.: *camera*; Carm.: Carmelite; Carth.: Carthusian; Cist.: Cistercian; Coll.: collegiate church; Com.: commandery; Dom.: Dominican; f.: founded; Fran.: Franciscan; Gilb.: Gilbertine; Hosp.: hospital; Hospit.: Hospitallers; Pr.: priory; Prec.: preceptory; Prem.: Premonstratensian; Sack.: Friars of the Sack; Templ.: Templars.

Approximate site references are given in the Ordnance Survey's *Map of Monastic Britain, Southern Sheet*, 2nd edn, 1954.

ALVINGHAM Pr. Gilb. f. 1148–54 by ? Hugh de Scotney
   Site known: to north of two churches
ASLACKBY Prec. Templ. f. c.1164 by Hubert de Rye
   Site known
AXHOLME Pr. Carth. f. 1397–8 by Thomas Mowbray, Earl of Nottingham
   Includes Priory in the Wood (Melwood)
   Site known: moat and stones at Low Melwood. Description by De La Pryme
BARDNEY A. Ben. f. 1115–16 by Gilbert de Gant
   Originally a cell of Charroux. Includes cells of Partney, Skendleby, Hartsholme
   Site known: excavated 1909–11 (*Arch. J.* 79 (1922), pp. 1–92)
BARLINGS A. Prem. f. 1154 by Ralf de Haya
   Site known: fragment of tower
BARTON ON HUMBER Hosp. f. 1259
   (R. M. Clay, citing *Cal. Pat. Rolls, 1248–66*, p. 12)
BELWOOD Cam. Templ. f. c.1145 by Roger de Mowbray

BENNINGTON, LONG   AP.   Cist.   f. 1163   by Ralf de Fougères
   A cell or grange of Savigny
BONBY   AP.   Ben.   f. before 1216
   A grange of St Fromund
BOOTHBY PAGNELL   Hosp. (lepers)   f. late 12th century   by John Paynel or Hugh de Bobi
   Site ? near churchyard
BOSTON   Pr.   Ben.   f. *c.*1098
   A cell of St Mary York (Pishey Thompson)
BOSTON   Friaries   Aust.   f. 1316–17
               Dom.   f. before 1288   Some remains
               Fran.   f. before 1268   by German merchants
               Carm.   f. 1293
BOTTESFORD   Cam.   Templ.
   A cell of Willoughton
BOURNE   A.   Aust. (Arrouasian) Canons   f. 1138   by Baldwin FitzGilbert
   Acquired Wilsford Priory in 1401
   Site known: conventual church adapted for use as parish church
BRAKENHOLME   Pr.   ?   f. before 1139
   Acquired by Louth Park
BRIDGEND (Holland Bridge)   Pr.   Gilb.   f. before 1199   by Godwin the Rich of Lincoln
   After 1445 it became a cell to Sempringham. Charged with the upkeep of Holland Bridge causeway
   Site known
BULLINGTON   Pr.   Gilb.   f. 1148–54   by Simon de Kyme
   Tunstal united to it
   Site known: moat and foundations
BURWELL   AP.   Ben.   f. early 12th century   by Ansgot de Burwell
   Cell of La Sauve Majeure near Bordeaux, acquired by Tattershall Coll.
   Site known
BYTHAM   A.   Cist.   f. 1147   by William, Earl of Albemarle
   Transferred to a new site at Vaudey within a year
CAMMERINGHAM   AP.   Prem.   f. before 1192   by Robert de Haya
   Cell of either L'Essay (Coutances) or Blanchelande
   Site known
CARLEDALE (also known as Keddington or Hallington)   Pr.   Cist. nuns
   Predecessor of Legbourne
CARLTON LE MOORLAND   Hosp. (lepers)   f. *c.*1180   by Elias de Amundeville
   Controlled by Burton Lazars; (male) anchorite on the site in 1437
CATLEY   Pr.   Gilb.   f. 1148–54   by Peter de Billinghay
   Site known

COVENHAM   AP.   Ben.   f. 1082   by King William I
   Cell of St Carileph (Le Mans); sold to Kirkstead in 1303
CROWLAND   A.   Ben.   f. before Norman Conquest
   Includes cell of Freiston
   Site known: abbey church partly adapted as parish church
DEEPING   Pr.   Ben.   f. 1139   by Baldwin FitzGilbert
   Cell to Thorney
   Site known: house built on it in 17th century. Portions of priory church adapted for parish church
EAGLE   Prec.   Templ.   f. before 1154   by King Stephen
   Site known
EDENHAM   ?   Pr.   Aust.
   Cell to Bridlington
   Site known
   (R. M. Clay describes this foundation as a *hospital* on doubtful evidence)
ELSHAM   Hosp. and later Pr.   Aust.   f. before 1166   by Beatrice de Amundeville
   Ceased to be a hospital before 1200
FOSSE   Pr.   Cist. nuns   f. before 1201   by the men of Torksey
FREISTON   Pr.   Ben.   f. *c.*1114   by Alan de Creoun
   Cell of Crowland
   Site known: east of parish church
GAINSBOROUGH   Hosp. (aged poor)   f. 1495
   (R. M. Clay, p. 332)
GAINSBOROUGH   Cam.   Templ.
GEDNEY FEN   Hosp.   f. late 12th century
   A dependency of Creake Abbey (Norfolk); disused before 1345
GLANFORD BRIGG (Wrawby)   Hosp. (poor)   f. late 12th century   by Adam Paynel
   Cell of Selby Abbey
GLANFORD BRIGG   Hosp. (poor)   f. 1422   by Sir William Tyrwhitt
GOKEWELL   Pr.   Cist. nuns   f. before 1148   by William de Alta Ripa
   Site known: in Broughton by Brigg; no remains
GRANTHAM   Hosp. of St Margaret & St Leonard   f. temp. Henry I
GRANTHAM   Cam.   Templ.
   Site known: the Angel
   (A.H.T. *Memorials*, p. 136)
GRANTHAM   Friary   Fran.   f. before 1290
   Site known
GREENFIELD   Pr.   Cist. nuns   f. before 1153   by Eudo de Grainsby
   Site known: a farmhouse
GRIMSBY   Hosp. (lepers)   f. before 1291

APPENDIX 3

GRIMSBY St Leonard Pr. Aust. nuns f. before 1184
    Site known: junction of Laceby and Scartho roads
GRIMSBY Friaries Aust. f.1293
              Fran. f. before 1240
HAGNABY A. Prem. f. 1175 by Agnes de Orreby
    Site known: moats and foundations
HARTSHOLME St Magdalen Pr. or Hosp. f. early 12th century by Ranulf, Earl of Chester, and others
    Cell of Bardney
HAUGHAM AP. Ben. f. before 1086 by Hugh, Earl of Chester
    Cell of St Sever (Coutances); acquired by pr. of St Anne, Coventry
HAVERHOLME A. Cist. f. 1137–9 by Bishop Alexander
    Removed to Louth Park
HAVERHOLME Pr. Gilb. f. 1139 by Bishop Alexander
    Site known: recently excavated by M. U. and W. T. Jones
HENES in Axholme Pr. Ben. f. mid-12th century by William de Warenne
    ? A cell of St Mary York, later annexed to Monks' Abbey, Lincoln
HEYNINGS Pr. Cist.   monks and nuns   f. after 1135   by Rayner de Evermu
    Site known: conventual church perhaps converted for use as parish church
HOLBEACH Hosp. (poor) f. 1351 by Sir John de Kirton
    Site known: Chequers Inn
HOLLAND MARSH(Wyberton) St Thomas the Martyr Pr. Gilb. f. *c.*1180 by Ralf, son of Stephen
    Cell of Sempringham for two canons
HORKSTOW Cam. Templ.
    Cell of Willoughton
HOUGH AP. Aust. f. *c.*1164
    Cell of St Mary de Voto (Cherbourg); acquired by Mountgrace Pr.
HUMBERSTONE A. Ben. (Tironian) f. *c.*1160 by William, son of Drogo
    Site known: near church (A. E. Kirkby, *Humberstone*, p. 57)
HYRST in Axholme Pr. Aust. f. early 12th century by Nigel d'Albini
    Cell of Nostell, probably for a single canon
    Site known: some moats and a modern house
IRFORD Pr. Prem. nuns f. temp. Henry II by Ralf d'Albini
    Site known: priory mill survives
KIRKSTEAD A. Cist. f. 1139 by Hugh, son of Eudo
    Site known; considerable remains including gate chapel
KYME Pr. Aust. f. before 1169 by Philip of Kyme
    Site: probably north of parish church of S. Kyme, which was part of conventual church

LANGWORTH   Hosp. (lepers)   f. before 1313
   Barlings undertook responsibility for chapel there in 1267 (LRS 20, p. 24); Bishop Dalderby granted indulgence to it, 1313 (Reg. 2, f. 248v).
LEGBOURNE   Pr.   Cist. nuns   f. c.1150   by Robert FitzGilbert
   Site known: modern house
LIMBER, GREAT   AP.   Cist.   f. before 1157   by Richard de Humet
   Cell or grange of Aunay; acquired by pr. of St Anne, Coventry
LIMBER, GREAT   Cam.   Templ.
LINCOLN   Cam.   Hosp.   f. before 1257
LINCOLN   Holy Innocents or la Malanderie   Hosp. (lepers)   f. c.1090–1100 by Bishop Robert Bloet
   Site known
LINCOLN   Holy Sepulchre   Hosp.   f. 1094–1123   by Bishop Robert Bloet
   Incorporated in St Katherine
   Site known
LINCOLN   St Bartholomew   Hosp. (lepers)   f. before 1314
   Site known
LINCOLN   St Giles   Hosp. (poor and aged, travellers)   f. 13th century
   Assigned by Bishop Sutton to the support of the vicars-choral
   Site known
LINCOLN   St Katherine   Pr.   Gilb.   f. c.1148   by Bishop Robert de Chesney
   Site known
LINCOLN   St Leonard outside the Castle   Hosp. (lepers)   f. before 1300
LINCOLN   St Mary Magdalen   Hosp.   f. before 1311
LINCOLN   St Mary Magdalen   Pr.   Ben.   f. before 1150
   Cell of St Mary's York
   Site known: slight remains of chapel (Monks' Abbey)
LINCOLN   Friaries   Aust.   f. 1269–70
               Dom.   f. before 1238
               Fran.   f. c.1230   by William of Benniworth   Church survives
               Carm.   f. 1269   by Odo of Kilkenny   Site known: slight remains
               Sack.   f. before 1266   Site known: at Stamp End
LOUTH   Hosp. (lepers)   f. before 1314
LOUTH PARK   A.   Cist.   f. 1139   by Bishop Alexander
   Transferred from Haverholme; includes Brakenholm Pr.
   Site known: foundations of church survive (Venables, *Chronicon*)
MALTBY by Louth   Com.   Hospit.   f. 1135–54   by Ranulf, Earl of Chester
   Site known

MARKBY   Pr.   Aust.   f. 1154–87   by Ralf FitzGilbert
  Site known: parish church probably part of priory church
MELWOOD   "Priory in the Wood"   Date and founder unknown
  Incorporated in Axholme
MERE (Dunston)   Hosp. (poor)   f. *c.*1220–30   by Simon of Ropsley
  Site known
MERE   Cam.   Templ.
MINTING   AP.   Ben.   f. before 1129   by Ranulf, Earl of Chester
  Cell of Fleury (St Benoît sur Loire); acquired by Mountgrace Pr.
NEUBO   A.   Prem.   f. *c.*1198   by Richard de Malebisse
  Site probably known (Barrowby and Sedgebrook)
NEWHOUSE   A.   Prem.   f. 1143   by Peter of Goxhill
  Site known: north of Brocklesby Park
NEWSTEAD next Stamford   Hosp. before 1247, and later Pr.   Aust.   f. *c.*1163
  by William d'Albini
  Site known
NEWSTEAD-on-Ancholme   Pr.   Gilb.   f. before 1164   by King Henry II
  Site known: farmhouse incorporates crypt of chapter house
NOCTON PARK   A.   Aust.   f. 1135–54   by Robert Darcy
  Site known: Stukeley drawing of remains
NUNCOTON   Pr.   Cist. nuns   f. 1135–54   by Alan de Moncels
  Site known: east of Brocklesby Park
NUNORMSBY (in N. Ormsby)   Pr.   Gilb.   f. 1148–54   by Gilbert FitzRobert of Ormsby
  Site known: farm buildings incorporate some stones
PARTNEY   Hosp.   f. *c.*1115   by Abbot of Bardney
  Cell of Bardney after 1318
  Site known (G. G. Walker, *History of Partney*)
POINTON   Hosp. (lepers)   f. before 1276   by Alexander of Pointon
RAVENDALE, WEST   AP.   Prem.   f. 1202   by Alan. son of Earl Henry of Brittany
  Cell of Beauport (Brittany); acquired by Southwell Coll.
REVESBY   A.   Cist.   f. 1142   by William of Romara
  Site known: moats and ditches excavated by E. B. Stanhope
SAILHOLME (Wainfleet)   ? Pr.   Ben.   f. *c.*1165   by Matthew de Praeres
  Cell of Bury St Edmund
SALTENEYA (Holland)   ? Hosp.   f. ? later 12th century
  (Wrest Park Cart. f. 192*v*)
SANDTOFT   ? Pr.   Ben.   f. 1147–87   by Roger de Mowbray
  Cell of St Mary's York, later annexed to Monks' Abbey
SEMPRINGHAM   Pr.   Gilb.   f. *c.*1131   by Gilbert of Sempringham
  Includes Holland Bridge priory
  Site known: excavated 1938

SIXHILLS Pr. Gilb. f. 1148-54 by ? Robert de Gresley
  Site known: moat and farmhouse incorporating masonry
SKENDLEBY ? Pr. Ben.
  Cell of Bardney
SKIRBECK Hosp. (poor); after 1230 Com. Hospit. f. by Sir Thomas Moulton
  Site known
SPALDING Pr. Ben. f. *c.*1087 by Thorold of Bucknall
  At first a cell of St Nicholas Angers
  Site known: dormitory, turret, and part of moat survive
SPALDING St Nicholas Hosp. f. before 1313
SPILSBY Coll. f. 1347 by John, Lord Willoughby
SPITAL ON THE STREET Hosp. (poor) f. before 1322; augmented by Thomas Aston
  Site known
STAINFIELD Pr. Ben. nuns f. 1154 by William or Henry de Percy
  Site known approximately
STAMFORD All Saints Hosp. f. 1485 by William Brown
STAMFORD St Leonard Pr. Ben. f. 1082 by William Carileph, Bishop of Durham
  Site known: west end of church and one arcade survive
STAMFORD Friaries Aust. f. 1341-2 by Robert de Wodehouse
      Dom. f. before 1241
      Fran. f. before 1236
      Carm. f. before 1268
      Sack. f. before 1274
  (Religious houses in Stamford Baron, Northants., are omitted from this list)
STIXWOLD Pr. Cist. nuns f. *c.*1135 by Lucy, Countess of Chester
  Site known
SWINESHEAD A. Cist. f. *c.*1148 by Robert de Gresley
  Site known: modern farmhouse
TATTERSHALL Almshouse f. 1438 by Ralph, Lord Cromwell
TATTERSHALL Coll. f. 1439 by Ralph, Lord Cromwell
TEMPLE BRUER Prec. Templ. f. late Henry II by William of Ashby
  Site known: tower and foundation of round church
TETFORD St Bartholomew ? Hosp. linked with Lincoln Malandry
THORNHOLME Pr. Aust. f. 1135-54 by King Stephen
  Site known: mounds and foundations
THORNTON A. Aust. f. 1139 by William, Earl of Albemarle
  Cell at Thwaite in Welton-le-Marsh
  Site known: extensive remains
THORNTON St James Hosp. f. before 1322

THWAITE in Welton
    Cell to Thornton
    Site known
TORKSEY   Pr.   Aust.   f. 1154–87   by ? King Henry II
    Site known: north side of parish church
TUNSTAL   Pr.   Gilb.   f. before 1164   by Reginald de Crevequer
    United to Bullington before 1189
TUPHOLME   A.   Prem.   f. 1155–6   by Gilbert de Neville
    Site known: fragment of refectory survives
VAUDEY   A.   Cist.   f. 1147   by William, Earl of Albemarle
    Originally sited at Bytham
    Site known: in Grimsthorpe Park, partly excavated in 1850
WALCOT   Hosp. (lepers)   f. before 1261
WELLOW (Grimsby)   A.   Aust.   f. after 1118   by ? King Henry I
    Site known: to north-west of parish church of St James
WENGALE   AP.   Ben.   f. before 1086
    Cell of Sées, Normandy; acquired by Trinity College, Cambridge
WHAPLODE   Fr.   Crutched Friars   f. *c.*1246–7
WILLOUGHTON   Prec.   Templ.   f. 1135–54   by Roger de Builli
    Cells at Bottesford and Horkstow
    Site known
WILLOUGHTON   AP.   Ben.   f. *c.*1140   by Empress Maud
    Cell of St Nicholas Angers; acquired by King's College, Cambridge
WILSFORD   AP.   Ben.   f. 1135–54   by Hugh Wake
    Cell of Bec Hellouin; acquired by Bourne A.
WINSTOWE (Fleet)   Hosp.   f. before 1230
    Transferred to Skirbeck Hospit.
WITHAM, SOUTH   Prec.   Templ.   f. before 1164
    Site known

APPENDIX 4
The medieval bishops of Lincoln

Reprinted, by permission of the Royal Historical Society, from F. M. Powicke and E. B. Fryde, *Handbook of British Chronology*, 2nd edn, 1961, pp. 235-6. The following abbreviations are used in this list: a.: *ante*; conf.: confirmed; cons.: consecrated; d.: died; el.: elected; nom.: nominated; post.: postulated; prov.: provided; qua.: quashed; res.: resigned; temp.: temporalities; trs.: translated; x: between two dates.

Remigius	cons. 1067	d. 6 May 1092

(Remigius transferred his see from Dorchester to Lincoln, 1072)

Robert Bloet	nom. Mar. 1093, cons. 12 Feb. 1094	d. 9 Jan. 1123
Alexander	nom. Apr., cons. 22 July 1123	d. 20 Feb. 1148
Robert de Chesney	el. 13 Dec., cons. 19 Dec. 1148	d. 27 Dec. 1166
Geoffrey	el. late Apr. 1173, temp. 1173, conf. 1 Jul. 1175	res. 6 Jan. 1182
Walter of Coutances	el. 8 May, cons. 3 July 1183	trs. Rouen 17 Nov. 1184
Hugh of Avalon	el. May, cons. 21 Sept. 1186	d. 16 Nov. 1200
William of Blois	el. a. 6 July, cons. 24 Aug. 1203	d. 10 May 1206
Hugh of Wells	el. a. 14 Apr., cons. 20 Dec. 1209, temp. 1 June 1213	d. 7 Feb. 1235
Robert Grosseteste	el. 19 Feb. x 5 Apr., temp. 16 Apr., cons. 3 or 17 June 1235	d. 9 Oct. 1253
Henry Lexington	el. 30 Dec. 1253, temp. 1 Apr., cons. 17 May 1254	d. 8 Aug. 1258
Richard Gravesend	el. 30 Sept., temp. 17 Oct., cons. 3 Nov. 1258	d. 18 Dec. 1279
Oliver Sutton	el. 1 Feb., cons. 19 May 1280	d. 13 Nov. 1299
John Dalderby	el. 15 Jan., temp. 18 Mar., cons. 12 June 1300	d. 12 Jan. 1320
[Anthony Bek	el. 3 Feb. 1320	qua. 1320]

APPENDIX 4

Henry Burghersh	prov. 27 May, cons. 20 July, temp. 5 Aug. 1320	d. Dec. 1340
Thomas Bek	el. a. 1 Mar. 1341, prov. 26 June, cons. 7 July, temp. 17 Sept. 1342	d. 2 Feb. 1347
John Gynwell	prov. 23 Mar., temp. 2 June, cons. 23 Sept. 1347	d. 5 Aug. 1362
John Buckingham (Bokyngham)	el. a. 20 Oct. 1362, prov. 5 Apr., temp. 23 June, cons. 25 June 1363	res. Mar. x July 1398 d. 10 Mar. 1399
Henry Beaufort	prov. 27 Feb., cons. 14 July, temp. 19 July 1398	trs. Winchester 19 Nov. 1404
Philip Repingdon	prov. 19 Nov. 1404, temp. 28 Mar., cons. 29 Mar. 1405	res. 20 Nov. 1419
Richard Fleming	prov. 20 Nov. 1419, cons. 28 Apr., temp. 23 May 1420	d. 25 Jan. 1431
William Gray	trs. London, prov. 30 Apr., temp. 4 Aug. 1431	d. 10 x 18 Feb. 1436
William Alnwick	trs. Norwich, post. a. 23 May, prov. 19 Sept. 1436, temp. 16 Feb. 1437	d. 5 Dec. 1449
Marmaduke Lumley	trs. Carlisle, prov. 28 Jan., temp. 14 Mar. 1450	d. a. 1 Dec. 1450
John Chedworth	el. a. 11 Feb. 1451, prov. 3 May, temp. 2 June, cons. 18 June 1452	d. 23 Nov. 1471
Thomas Rotherham or Scot	trs. Rochester, prov. 8 Jan., temp. 10 Mar. 1472	trs. York 7 July 1480
John Russell	trs. Rochester, prov. 7 July, temp. 9 Sept. 1480	d. 30 Dec. 1494
William Smith	trs. Lichfield, prov. 6 Nov. 1495, temp. 6 Feb. 1496	d. 2 Jan. 1514
Thomas Wolsey	prov. 6 Feb., temp. 4 Mar., cons. 26 Mar. 1514	trs. York 15 Sept. 1514
William Atwater	prov. 15 Sept., temp. 6 Nov., cons. 12 Nov. 1514	d. 4 Feb. 1521
John Longland	prov. 20 Mar., cons. 5 May 1521	d. 7 May 1547

Fig. 8. *Token of the Good Rood at Boston*

GENERAL INDEX

Chapelries and hamlets are indexed under the name of the mother parish, with a cross-reference. Counties are given for places outside Lincolnshire.

Addlethorpe, 81, 110, 112
advowson, 4
Aethelred II, king of England, 1
Alan, Count, *see* Brittany
Albertini, 125
Alexander, archdeacon of Lincoln, 30
   'the Magnificent', bishop of Lincoln, 13, 27, 29, 38, 41, 50, 75
   III, Pope, 25
   the vintner, 124
Alford, 135
   Rigsby in, 14, 50, 133-4
   Robert de, 103
Algarkirk, 124
alms, 33, 53, 71, 96
almshouse, 101
Alnwick, William, bishop of Lincoln, 20
altar, bequest to, 14, 92
Alvingham, priory, 49, 65-6, 72, 77, 144
   parish church of, 72
Amcotts, William, 99
Amundeville, family, 8
   Beatrice de, 52
   Elias de, 51, 55, 123
Ancaster, 1, 115, 138, 141
Ancholme, river, 19, 55
Andrew the clerk, 124
Angers abbey, Normandy, 15
Angus, earl of, *see* Umfreville
anti-clericalism, 139-42; *see also* tithe
Anwick, 108
archdeacon, court of, 35-6
   functions of, 35, 75, 117-18
   visitation by, 35, 120
Arsic, fee of, 49
Arundel, Thomas, archbishop of Canterbury, 36
Asgarby, 122
Ashby, by Partney, 10
   de la Launde, 62-3, 70, 109

Ashingdon, *see* Willoughby le Marsh
Aslackby, 65
   chapel of St John in, 18
Aslacoe deanery, 121
Aswick, *see* Whaplode
Atkirk, Walter, 141
Atterby, *see* Norton, Bishop
Atwater, William, bishop of Lincoln, 122
Aukborough, 71, 121
Aunby, *see* Castle Bytham
Aunsby, Crofton in, 100
Austin canons, 48, 55, 75, 77
Austin friars, order of, 52
Avalon, St Hugh of, bishop of Lincoln, 29-31, 34, 39-42, 45, 50, 107
Awnesby, Walter, 99
Axholme, 51
   Charterhouse in, 53, 80
Aylesby, 116, 121

Babynton, Brother, 70
Bagworth, John, clerk, 122
banners, parochial, 107, 117
baptism, sacrament of, 16, 102-3
Bardney, 120
   abbey of, 48-9, 56-7, 60, 63, 65-6, 71, 75, 78-83, 138, 144
   abbot of, 27
Barholme, 57
Barkston, 17
Barlings abbey, 53, 55, 63, 66, 71, 80, 144
Barrowby, 116, 138
Barthorpe, *see* Swineshead
Barton on Humber, 1, 39, 130, 133
Bassingham, Rodemill in, 18, 65, 125
   see Scremby
Bassingthorpe, 39
Baston, 57
   Boycote Green in, 69

GENERAL INDEX

Basuin, Roger, 39
Baudellzinus, Friar, 88
Baumber, 122
    Great Sturton in, 6, 13, 66
Bayard's Leap, extra-parochial, 60
Bayeux, De Baiocis, family of, 8
    Adam of, 60
    bishop of, 47
    Ranulf of, 49
    William of, 60
Beauport abbey, Brittany, 54
Beckingham, 97
    Stragglethorpe in, 16, 132–3, 139
bede-roll, 104, 122
Bégar abbey, Brittany, 58
Bek, family of, 19, 57
    Thomas, bishop of Lincoln, 33
Belleau, 95
Bellers, Roger, 100
bells, church, 119
Beltisloe, deanery of, 7, 8, 105, 134
Belvoir priory, co. Leicester, 65
Benedictine order, 48, 57, 75, 77, 79, 81
benefice, residence in, 26
    value of, 135–6
Bennington, Long, priory, 54
Bernard, St, 79
Berners, William, 14
Beverley, co. York, E.R., 37
Bicker, 26, 124
Billinghay, Dogdike in, 19, 93
    Walcot in, 57
Bilsby, 4, 25
Binbrook, 4
Black Death, 25, 77, 140–1
Blankney, Lindwood grange in, 15, 57, 60
Bloet, Robert, bishop of Lincoln, 13, 14, 21, 27, 55
Blois, William of, bishop of Lincoln, 42
Blount, Thomas, 100
Bolebec, Ralph, 125
Bolingbroke, 85, 105
    castle of, chapel in, 19
    Robert of, clerk, 133
Bonby priory, 54
Bonthorpe, *see* Willoughby le Marsh
books, church, 118–19; *see also* religious houses
Boothby, *see* Welton le Marsh
Boston, 31, 64, 68, 106, 110–12, 124, 127–31, 138, 140

    friaries at, 52, 85, 89–90
    friars at: Carmelite, 90; Dominican 80, 85, 89–91; Franciscan, 52, 85–6
    gilds in, 95, 98, 100–1
    Shodfriars Lane in, 85
Bottesford, Burringham in, 6
    Holme in, 61–2
Boultham, 114, 127
boundaries, *see* parish
Bourne, 109
    abbey, 57, 66, 79
Boycote Green, *see* Baston
Bradley, 17
Brakenholme, *see* Farlesthorpe
Branston, John of, clerk, 133
Brantyngham, John of, monk of Louth, 82
bricks, tithe of, 115; *see also* religious houses
Bridgend, *see* Holland Bridge
Bridlington priory, co. York, E.R., 5, 8, 15, 54, 56, 65, 68, 74
Brigg, Glanford, *see* Wrawby
Brigsley, 139
Bristol, 86
Brittany, Alan, son of Henry earl of (Count Alan), 54, 58
Broughton, Brant, Little Stapleford in, 28
    by Brigg, 61
Brown, Edward, 87
Broxholme, 26
Bruman, Robert son of, 124
Brumby, 122
Buchart, John, 124
Bucke, John, clerk, 93–4, 100
Buckingham, archdeaconry, 122
    John, bishop of Lincoln, 17, 25, 29–30, 91
Bulby, *see* Irnham
Bullington priory, 14, 15, 47, 63, 66, 77, 144
Burgh le Marsh, 10, 119, 125, 128
Burghersh, Henry, bishop of Lincoln, 25
burial, offering for, 16
    rites of, 103–4, 128
    see also funeral, obit
Burringham, *see* Bottesford
Burton, Gate, 139
    Lazars, co. Leicester, 55
    Pedwardine, 92, 99, 114
    Stather, 93, 110, 113; Normanby in, 93
    on Trent, co. Stafford, 115

Burwell, 120
　Ansgot of, 49, 125
　priory of, 48-9, 54
Bury St Edmunds abbey, Suffolk, 18, 51, 65, 74
Bytham, Castle, 2, 8, 19; chapels of, 8, 19; Aunby in, 2, 8; Counthorpe in, 8
　Little, 8

Cadeby, 134
Caistor, 1, 2, 37, 39
Calceworth, Edmund, dean of, 36
Cambridge, Carmelites at, 88
　University, colleges in: Buckingham, 81; King's, 54
Cammeringham priory, 48, 144
candles, 14, 119-20
Candlesby, 10
Canterbury, archbishop of, 41; *see also* Arundel, Reynolds, Theobald, Walter—H, Winchelsey
　pilgrimage to, 121, 126
Canwick, Sheepwash in, 58, 63
Careby, 109
Carlisle, bishop of, 2
Carlton, Castle, 19
　le Moorland, hospital at, 51, 55, 123
Carmelite order, 52, 81
Castleacre priory, Norfolk, 5, 72
Catley priory, 49, 57, 66, 144
causeway, repair of, 51
Cawode, Thomas, clerk, 129
Cawthorpe, Little, 87
celebration of mass, licence for, 27
Chambers, Henry, 119
chancel, repair of, 72, 113
chantry, 53, 93-101
　aisle built for, 97
　decayed, 95
　plate given to, 97
　see also alms, chapel—manorial, citizen, gild, merchant, music
chapel, bridge, 16, 19
　built by hermit, 100
　chantry, 12
　free, 6
　gild, 10
　manorial (private, demesne), 5, 8, 12, 14, 16, 22, 93; served by canon, 54
　market, 19
　parochial, 5-6, 8, 10-11; service of, 1-20, 99-100, 132, 134, 140
chaplain, parochial, 100, 132-42; stipend of, 133, 136
Chedworth, John, bishop of Lincoln, 122
cheese manufacture, *see* religious houses
Chesney, Robert de, bishop of Lincoln, 17, 29, 41, 65
Chester, earl of, *see* Lupus
Chittok, Elizabeth, 119
choir, 102
　provided by chantry, 102
chrism pennies, 17
church, collegiate, 8, 99-100
　mother, 1, 5
　parish, 102-31; *see also* altar, bell, book, chancel, consecration, light, nave, vestment, window
　building: agreement, 115; by monasteries, 114-15; by gilds, 114; indulgence for, 114; wooden, 113
　fabric, 110, 112-16; fund, 33
　furnishings, 117-18
　lay proprietors of, 22
　meetings in, 104-5
　secular courts in, 104
　served by religious, 135
　valuables stored in, 104
church ales, 17, 32, 105, 128
church path, 10
church-scot, 2
churchwarden, 116-17, 131, 141; *see also* kirkmaster
churchyard, fairs and markets in, 32, 105
Cîteaux, order, 8, 18, 48, 50-1, 57, 64-6, 68, 71, 75-7
citizen, chantry founded by, 94
Claxby by Alford, 10
Claypole, 110
Clee, Old, 27, 109, 111
　St Saviour, 138
clergy, parochial, 132-42
clerk, examination of, 26
　parish, 105-6
Clifford, William de, clerk, 139
Cnut, king of England, 1
Coates by Stow, 110, 134
　Richard of, 73, 140
Cockerington, 64, 77
'Cokwax', 135
Coleby, 118

GENERAL INDEX

common of pasture, dispute about, 60, 62-3
Compostella, pilgrimage to, 51, 125-6
Conesby, *see* Halton, West
Coningsby, 136
consecration, of church, 13, 27
conversi, *see* religious houses
Corby, 122
Corringham, 132
  deanery of, 121
corrody, *see* religious houses
Counthorpe, *see* Castle Bytham
Coutances, bishop of, 47
  Walter of, bishop of Lincoln, 24
Covenham, priory, 47, 54
  St Mary, 27
Cowbit, *see* Spalding
Craon, Guy de, 123
Creake abbey, Norfolk, 12, 56
Crevequer, honour of, 49
Croft, 110, 125
Crofton, *see* Aunsby
Cromwell, Maud, 99
  Thomas, 50
cross, 2; *see also* procession, sermon
  week, *see* procession
Crowland, 143
  abbey of, 4, 47-8, 50, 57, 60, 64-6, 69, 71, 75-83, 115-16, 118, 126-7, 135, 140; *see also* Aswick
  abbot of, *see* Litlington
Crowle, 117
  Geoffrey, 99
Croxby, 125, 132
  John, clerk, 136
crusade, crusader, 48, 51, 123-5; *see also* pilgrimage
Cumberworth, Sir Thomas, 94, 123
Cuping, William, 124
Cysters, Peter de, 140

Dalderby, John, bishop of Lincoln, 25, 40, 89, 105, 126
  Robert, 94
De Baiocis, *see* Bayeux
dean, rural, 28, 36; chapter of, 36; extortion by, 36
Deeping, East (St James), 13, 27, 57, 128, 130-1; Frognal in, 5, 15-16; priory in, 48, 51, 66, 73, 80, 117
  Market (St Guthlac), 15
  West, 57

De la Mare, Ralf: Bercelina mother of, 15
De la Pryme, Abraham, 120
Denton, 132
Denys, Roger, 115
Dogdike, *see* Billinghay
Dominican order, 52
Donington in Holland, 112
  Wykes in, 6
Dorchester, co. Oxford, 1, 20, 37
Dorrington, 111
D'Oyry, John, 12
  Robert, 103
Dunham, Richard, abbot of Louth, 64, 72
  Thomas, clerk, 137
Dunsthorpe, 140
Dunston, 65
Durham, bishop of, 47
  cathedral priory, 81
Dyklon, Richard, president of the consistory of Lincoln, 31
Dymmok, Roger, O.P., 91

Eagle, 18, 95, 144
  preceptory of, 48
  Barnsdale, extra-parochial, 60
Eaudike, *see* Quadring
Edenham, 6, 8, 15, 65, 74-5, 100, 110, 132
  cell at, 54
  Elsthorpe in, 8, 15
  Grimsthorpe in, 8, 15, 75
  Scottlethorpe in, 8, 75, 93-4
  Southorpe in, 6, 8, 75
Edlington, 27, 115
Edward (the Confessor), king of England, 50
Eight Hundred Fen, 139
Elsham priory, 55-6, 72, 136, 144
Elsthorpe, *see* Edenham
Eltruth, Lambert son of, 124
enclosure, 61-2
Epworth, 95, 97-8, 120
Eresby, 19
Ernis, William son of, 5
Eustace, clerk, 26
Everard, Master, 82
Eynsham, co. Oxford, 47

faculty, 28
Farlesthorpe, 18
  Brakenholme in, 18, 56, 134
farthings, smoke, *see* pentecostals

Fenhall, *see* Whaplode St Katherine
festival, observance of, 110–11; *see also* Sunday
Fishtoft, Scraine in, 69
Fitzgilbert, Ralf, 49
Flaye, Eustace de, 110
Fleet, 10, 14, 72, 88, 110, 120, 143
  Hargate, 10
  hospital of Winstow in, 10–11, 52, 56
  John of, clerk, 118
Fleming, Richard, bishop of Lincoln, 32
Fleury (St Benoît sur Loire), abbey of, 48
Folceby, Ralph de, 81
Folkingham, 117
Fontinello, Geoffrey de, 26
Fool-feast, 111
Fosse priory, 79, 144
Frampton, 95, 112, 128
  chapel at Moulton manor in, 95
Franciscan order, 52
fraternity, 53; *see also* gild
Freiston priory, 48, 71, 80
friars, 16, 84–91; *see also* Austin, Carmelite, Dominican, Franciscan
  and bishop, 91
  church of, 85–6; anniversary in, 87; burial of layman in, 90; play in, 86; sanctuary in, 86
  collectors for, 86–7
  conduit of, 85
  confessors, 85, 89
  confraternity of, 87
  education of, 86
  heresy among, 84
  pastoral care by, 91
  popularity of, 52
  sermons of, 84, 87–9, 91, 110
  tithes denounced by, 89
  treason fomented by, 89
Friesthorpe, 111, 121
Friskney, 14
Frognal, *see* Deeping, East
Fulbeck, 15, 50
Fulstow, 125, 132
  Fulstowmarsh or Marshchapel in, 18, 32, 110, 120
  Robert, parson of, 53
funeral of St Hugh, 40
Furness abbey, co. Lancaster, 68

Gainsborough, 49, 57, 97, 100, 114, 121
  Stockwith in, 6
Gant, Gilbert of, 48, 49
  honour of, 49, 57
  Walter of, 54
Gartree wapentake, 65
Gautby, 137
Gayton, le Wold, 58, 64
  South, 86
Gedney, 4, 10, 88, 125, 141, 143
  Emecina of, 4
  Fen, hospital in, 12, 56
  Hill, 12, 134
  John, sacrist of Humberstone, 78
  St Thomas, 12
Gelston, *see* Hough on the Hill
Gerald, *pincerna*, 13
Gilbertine canons, 48, 51, 57–8, 64, 65–6, 68, 77, 81
gild, parochial, 53, 95, 127–31; chantry founded by, 95; church rebuilt by, 114; church porch built by, 114; church windows given by, 114
Gimer, Hugh son of, 124
Giraldus Cambrensis, 38
Girsby, Henry of, 66
glebe, 4, 12–14
Glen, river, 8
Glentham, 42, 137
Godefeld, Robert, 53
Gokewell priory, 66, 79, 144
Gosberton, 114, 120, 124, 141, 143
Goxhill, Peter of, 6, 49
Grainsby, 139
  Eudo of, 49
grange, *see* religious house
Grange de Lings, extra-parochial, 58, 60
Grantham, 1, 2, 39, 106, 111, 122, 128, 130, 141
  chantry at, 94, 100–1
  friary at, 52, 80, 85–6, 91
  hospital at, 48
  Towthorpe in, 5
Gravesend, Richard, bishop of Lincoln, 45, 132
Grayingham, 14, 121, 137–8
Grebby, *see* Scremby
Greenfield, priory, 49, 53, 144
  Margaret, prioress of, 103
Gregory VII, Pope, 24
Grim, William, 49

GENERAL INDEX

Grimblethorpe, extra-parochial, 60
Grimsby, 68, 75, 85, 106, 110–11, 125, 127–30
  deanery of, 105, 141
  friary at, 52, 80
  friars, Austin, at, 87, 90
  priory of St Leonard at, 56, 66, 144
  St James, 87, 90, 114, 141
  St Mary, 109, 115
Grimsthorpe, *see* Edenham
Grosseteste, Robert, bishop of Lincoln, 5, 17, 30, 32–3, 40, 52, 73, 84, 103–5, 107, 109, 111, 120, 126, 132
Gudred, Gerald son of, 124
Gulburn, Margery, 92
Gunby le Marsh, 10
Gunnes, *see* Halton West
Guy, Hubert son of, 124
Gynwell, John, bishop of Lincoln, 25, 27, 110

Habertoft, *see* Willoughby le Marsh
Habrough, 14, 105
  Margaret of, 133
Hacconby, 125
Hagnaby abbey, 52, 53, 64, 66, 80–1, 83, 144
Hagworthingham, 111, 113, 116, 118, 130
Hainton, 45, 121
Haldin, John, 119
Hale, Great, 14, 55, 98, 100
  Sir Simon of, 14
  Little, 5
Halpeny, Henry, 121
Halton, East, 64
  West, 29, 103; Conesby in, 134; Gunnes in, 103, 134
Hamelin the dean, 72
Hameringham, 140
Hamo the chancellor, 38
Hanby, *see* Welton le Marsh
  Roger de, 69
Harby, Joan, 123
Hardene, John, 78
Hardres, Robert of, archdeacon of Lincoln, 35
Harrington, 94, 97, 100, 109, 122
  Mr John of, 94, 97
Harrowby, Robert of, 51
Hartsholme, 13, 48, 56
Haugham priory, 47, 54

Haverholme priory, 49, 51, 66, 80
Hawthorpe, *see* Irnham
Haxey, 106, 117
Hayles, abbey, co. Gloucester, 126
  Robert of, archdeacon of Lincoln, 35
Healey, Arnold, 93
Heckington, 55, 113
Helpon, Jocelin son of, 72
Helpringham, 57
Hemswell, 1
Henry I, king of England, 48
  VI, king of England, 99
Henry, Simon son of, 62
Heoldefen, *see* Sutton in Holland
heresy, presentment of, 122
  see also friars
hermit, *see* chapel
hermitage, 127
Hervey the clerk, 51
  Elyas son of, 124
Heydour, 45
Heynings priory, 66, 144
Hibaldstow, 35
High Dike, the, 2, 3
Hill, William, 105
Hogsthorpe, 114
Holbeach, 10, 12, 15, 31–2, 75, 104, 110, 112, 121, 124, 127, 141, 143
  Hurn, 10
  Hurnfleet in, 12
  St Nicholas, 98
Holdingham, *see* Sleaford
Holflet, Thomas of, 124
Holland, parts of, 51
  deanery, 134
  Ralf son of Stephen of, 54
  Bridge, 19; priory, 51, 144
  Marsh, chapel in, 54
Holles, Gervase, 131
Holme, *see* Bottesford, Wainfleet
Holtzmann, Dr Walther, 25
holy water, 102–3
  carrier of, 106, 117, 136
Holywell, 8
Honington, 17, 57
Horncastle, 1, 2, 119, 127, 130–1, 135
  St Laurence, 95
Horsington, 51
hospital, 10, 48, 51–2, 54–6
Hospital of St John, order of, 48, 54, 69–70
hospitality, exercise of, 71

Hough on the Hill priory, 54, 144
  Gelston in, 2
Hoyland, Gilbert, abbot of Swineshead, 79
Humberstone, 139
  abbey, 66, 71, 73, 78, 80, 144
Humby, see Somerby
Humphrey the Subdean, 40
Huntingdon, Henry, archdeacon of, 38
Huntingfield, family of, 8
  Roger of, 6
  William Lord, 89, 91
Huntman, John, clerk, 139
Hurn, Hurnfleet, see Holbeach
Hykeham, North, St Katherine's grange in, 6
Hyrst in Axholme priory, 48

indulgence, see church
Ingleby, William of, 53
Ingoldmells, 110, 134
Ingulph, 80
Innocent III, Pope, 26
Irnham, 8, 99, 121
  Bulby in, 8; Woodgrange in, 58
  Hawthorpe in, 8

Jerusalem, pilgrimage to, 125
John le Borne, 124
Jolyf, John, 103
Jordan, Jordan son of, 62–3

Kay, Joan, 92
Keal, Ketelbern of, 4
  East, 4
  West, 4
Keddington, 13
Kelby, 138
Kelsey, North, 114, 135
  South, 5; St Mary, 119
Kelstern, 17
Ker, Neil, 80
Kesteven, 37, 51
Ketel, Alan son of, 50
  William son of, 50
Killingholme, Fredissande of, 53
Kingerby, 72, 136
Kinnard's Ferry, see Owston
Kirkby, cum Osgodby, 114, 131
  on Bain, 15, 17
  East, 63, 97, 99, 114, 120

Laythorpe, 31, 142
  William of, 124
kirk-loaf, 102; see also pain bénit, singing bread
kirk-master (churchwarden), 116–17
Kirkstead, abbey, 5, 18, 54, 57–8, 60, 63–6, 68–9, 72, 77, 80–1, 83, 144
  abbot of, 75
Kirmington, Gilbert of, 53
Kirton, in Holland, 95, 100, 112–13, 124
  Lindsey, 37, 45, 116, 130–1
knighthood, conferment of, 104
Kyme, Philip of, 49
  priory, 19, 52, 80–2, 118, 135, 144

Lacy, Edmund de, 53
  John de, 53
  Margaret de, 53
Lake, Alice de la, 104
Lamkyn, John, 121
Langtoft, 17, 57, 116, 140
Langton by Spilsby, 26
Langwath, William of, 6
Langworth, bridge, 19
  chantry chapel, 53, 55
La Sauve Majeure, Bordeaux, 48–9, 125
Lawres deanery, 121
Laythorpe, see Kirkby
Leadenham, 15, 125
Leasingham, Roxholme in, 6
Legbourne priory, 144
Legsby, 60
Leicester, archdeaconry, 122
Leland, John, 80
Lenton, 57
  Osgodby in, 27
leper, see hospital
L'Essay, Coutances, 48
Leverton, 117, 120, 131
lights, 53, 92, 119–20
Lilford, alias Deeping, William, O.P., 89
Limber priory, 144
Lincoln, 31, 39, 68, 133
  archdeacon of, 29, 34–5; see also Alexander, Thornaco, Hardres, Hayles
  bishop of, chapter 2 passim, 47; see also Alexander, Atwater, Avalon, Bek, Bloet, Blois, Burghersh, Chesney, Chedworth, Dalderby, Gravesend, Grosseteste, Gynwell, Remigius, Repingdon, Sutton, Wells

GENERAL INDEX

Lincoln, bishop of (*cont.*)
    administration, 20–36, 39; commissary, 3; courts, 30–2; estates, 20–1; legislation, 30; official, 31, 34; probate by, 31; registrar of, 39; *sede vacante*, 41; synod, 40; visitation, 32–4
    cathedral, 2, 4, 29, 37–46, 107, 111, 118, 126; bequests to 42; building of, 41; chancellor, 39, *see also* Hamo; chantries, 44; chapter, 38; choristers, 45; common fund, 42; fabric fund, 43; liberty, 45–6; library, 38, 88; Mariecorn, 37; Old Minster fee, 37; peculiar of, 45; pilgrimages to, 40; plays in, 46; prebendal estates, 42–3; prebendal house, 43; prebendal residence, 44; processions, 46; schools, 38; statutes, 37; subdean, *see* Humphrey; vicars choral, 44
    Close, 43–5
    consistory, 31
    earl of, 64
    episcopal palace at, 21
    friaries, 52, 80, 85; Carmelite, 87, 135; Dominican, 86; Franciscan, 85
    gilds, 95, 127, 129
    hospitals: St Giles, 44; Holy Innocents (Malandry), 48, 55; Holy Sepulchre, 48, 55
    John of, O. Carm., 86
    Le Batailplace, 87
    miracle plays, 112
    parishes: All Saints, 140; St Benedict, 94, 141; St Laurence, 37; St Margaret, 45; St Mark, 135; St Martin, 37; St Mary, 37, 39, 47; St Mary Magdalen, 45, 140; St Paul in the Bail, 114; St Peter at Arches, 92, 123
    priory of St Katherine, 14, 55, 66, 80, 144
    Thorngate, 68
    vice archdeacon of, 27, 35
    Wigford, 43
Lindsey, archdeacon of, 22
    cathedral of, 37
Lindwood, *see* Blankney
Litlington, John, abbot of Crowland, 82
London, Osbert of, 53
Longchamp, Henry of, 92
Lound, *see* Witham on the Hill

Louth, 2, 21, 37, 39, 102, 104, 106–7, 111–16, 128, 130–2, 136
    gilds in, 95, 100–1
    Park Abbey, 18, 56, 61, 64–6, 71–2, 74, 77, 80, 82, 144; abbot of, 134; *see also* Dunham
Louthesk wapentake, 65
Lucius III, Pope, 24
Ludborough wapentake, 65
Lupus, Hugh, earl of Chester, 47
    Robert, 19
Lutton, *see* Sutton in Holland, St Nicholas
Lymm, river, 10
Lynn, Norfolk (King's Lynn), 115
    Carmelites of, 88

Malet, Hugh, 72
Maltby, by Louth, commandery of, 48
    le Marsh, 80
Malton priory, co. York, E.R., 68
Manby, 61
Manlake, deanery, 121
    Gregory, dean of, 36
Mannyng, Robert, 79, 88, 110, 111
Manthorpe, *see* Witham on the Hill
Manton, 61
Mareham, Marome, John, 49, 74
Markby, priory, 49, 64, 66, 68, 71, 73, 80, 144
    prior, 25
marriage, clerical, 22
    sacrament, 16, 103
Marsh, Andrew, 15
Marshchapel, *see* Fulstow
Marston, 92
measures, monastic, 63
'meinport', 17, 136
merchant, chantry founded by, 94
Messingham, 61–2
Metheringham, 50
    William son of Walter of, 50
minsters, head, 1
    old (mother churches), 1
Minting priory, 48, 144
miracle, 126–7
Morton, by Bourne, 57
mortuary, 2, 5, 16
Moulton, 10, 71, 105–6, 113, 117–19, 124, 141, 143
    St James, 12
    Thomas son of Lambert of, 125

Mowbray, John, 98
　Lord, 95
　Roger, 49, 51
　Thomas, earl of Nottingham, 52
Mumby, 116
music, church, 96
Mustel, Musteile, Roger, 50
　William, 15, 47

nave, repair of, 72, 113-14
Navenby, 135
Nettleham, 17, 21, 40, 111
Neubo abbey, 52, 144
Neville, family, 8
　Jollan de, 50; Eustachia daughter of, 51, Oliva daughter of, 51
　Robert de, 61
Newark, co. Nottingham, 21
Newhouse, abbey, 18, 49, 53, 56, 58, 65-6, 80-1, 144
　St Martial, 27
Newstead, by Stamford, priory, 56, 80
　on Ancholme, priory, 66, 71, 144
Newton, William, 100
Nocton, 60, 65-6, 80
　prior of, 61
non-residence, 134-5
Normanby, *see* Burton Stather
　le wold, 141
Northdike causeway, *see* Stickney
Northolme, *see* Wainfleet
Norton, Bishop, 17, 118, 135; Atterby in, 136
　Disney, Rodemill in, 18
Nostell priory, co. York, 48
Nottingham, earl of, *see* Mowbray
　John of, 53
Nuncoton priory, 30, 66, 68, 79, 144
　master of, 29
Nun Ormsby priory, 56, 65-6, 77, 80, 144

obit, 92-3
　celebrated by gild, 130
offerings, parochial, 12, 16, 22, 72, 74-5, 135-6, 141-2; *see also* church-scot, mortuary, plough-scot, soul-scot, chrism penny, 'meinport'
Orby, 10
ordination, 28
organ, 102, 120

organist, provided by chantry, 100
Ormsby, Arthur, esquire, 125
　North, 125
　South, 120, 125, 136
Osbert, Alexander son of, 50; Nigel son of, 50
Osgodby, *see* Kirkby, Lenton
Otley, Reginald of, 26
Otby, *see* Walesby
Otto, cardinal deacon of St Nicholas *in carcere*, 117
Owersby, 114
Owston, Kinnard's Ferry in, 99
Oxford University, Durham college in, 81; Gloucester college in, 81

paganism, 25, 32
pain bénit, 90, 102; *see also* kirk loaf, singing bread
papal, court, appeals to, 24
　judgments, 24-5
parish, boundaries, 2, 15, 17, 75
　priests, revenues of, 22
　see also church
parochia, 37
Partney, 10, 39, 110
　hospital in, 10, 48, 56
Paynel, Adam, 52, 54, 56
Peak Hill, *see* Spalding
Peckbridge, *see* Spalding
penance, sacrament of, 103
pentecostals, smoke farthings, 42, 107
Peterborough, co. Northampton, 115
　abbey, 4, 13, 16, 29, 47, 61-2, 64
Peterspence, *see* Romepenny
Pilat, Thomas, 10
pilgrimage, 50-1, 125-7; *see also* Canterbury, Compostella, crusade, Hayles, Jerusalem, Lincoln, token, Walsingham
Pinchbeck, 124, 143
　Huscord the steward of, 72
pittance, *see* religious house
plays, parochial, 111-12, 130-1; *see also* Lincoln cathedral
plough dinner, 130
plough-scot, 2
Pointon, Alexander of, 5
Poitou, Roger of, 47
Ponton, Great, 114
Porter, John, 105

Portmore, Alice of, 77
Potter, John, 122
Praeres, Matthew de, 18, 51
Premonstratensian canons, 48, 57, 66, 77
priests, stipendiary, 22; *see also* chantry, chaplain, parochial
primer, bequest of, 123
priories, alien, 47-8, 54
processions, parochial, 107
  pentecostal, 107, 136
  Rogation, 16, 70, 108-9
psalter, bequest of, 123
purification (churching), sacrament of, 103
Pygot, Sir John, 79

Quadring, 120, 143
  Eaudike, 14, 103
Quarrington, 2
quarry, *see* religious house

Raithby by Spilsby, 4
Ralph, Gilbert son of, 61
  Henry son of, 61
Ramsey abbey, co. Huntingdon, 47
Ranby, 17
Rand, 2, 134
Rasen, Market, Walter son of Walter of, 72
Rauceby, South, 74, 135
Ravendale, West, 73, 140; priory, 54, 56
Raventhorpe, 61-2
  Norman, priest of, 62
  Twigmore in, 61-2, 64
rectory house, *see* residence
religious houses, 47-83; *see also* individual houses
  books, 80-1
  brick-making, 83
  buildings, 82-3
  chapels at gates, 71-2, 82, Plate VI
  cheese trade, 68
  chronicles, 79-80
  churches granted to, 47, 72-3, 135; *see also* offerings, vicarages
  conversi (lay brothers), 58, 65-6
  corrody, 77-8
  domestic life, 78-9
  feudal links of, 49-50
  foundation gifts to, 49
  granges, 51, 57-65
  laity disputing with, 60, 62-3, 69-70
  lands held by, 56-7, 64-5
  learning, 79-81
  numbers, 76 and Appendix 2
  pittance, 53
  prayers by, 50-1
  reclamation by, 49, 51, 57-8, 60, 69; *see also* grange, drainage
  road repair, 69
  salt trade, 68-9
  schools, 81
  tanning, 68
  tithe barn, 50-1, 72; dispute, 65; gift of, 51, 72
  visitation, 76
  wool trade, 66-8
  worship in, 82
religious orders, agreement between, 65
Remigius, bishop of Lincoln, 20, 37, 41, 47
Repingdon, Philip, bishop of Lincoln, 36, 75
reredos, alabaster, 120
residence house, 136-7
Revesby abbey, 18, 27, 49, 57-8, 65-6, 68-9, 72, 77, 80-1, 83, 135, 137, 144
  perch of, 63
Reynolds, Walter, archbishop of Canterbury, 117
Richard I, king of England, 123
Richmond, honour of, 49
Rigsby, *see* Alford
Rippingale, 126
Robert the butcher, 124
  the potter, 124
Rodemill, *see* Bassingham, Norton Disney
Rogation, *see* procession
Romepenny, 135
rood-loft, 120
Ropsley, 114
rosary, prayer beads, bequest of, 123
Rothwell, 72
  manorial chapel at, 72
Roughton, 60
Roumara, honour of, 49
  William of, 4, 49, 51
Routhe, Joan de [fetys Jonet], 78; William son of, 78
Roxholme, *see* Leasingham
Russell, William, O.F.M., 89
Rye, Sir Ranulf de, 141

GENERAL INDEX

sacrament, sale of, 32
Sailholme, *see* Wainfleet St Mary
St Albans abbey, 42
St Carileph, Le Mans, abbey, 47
St Ives, co. Huntingdon, 68
St Lazarus, order of, 55
Saleby, 31
    Edmund, vicar of, 36
Salisbury, 2
    bishop of, 47
salt, tithe, 65; *see also* religious house
Saltby, Richard de, 94
Saltfleethaven, *see* Skidbrook
Saltney, *Salteneia*, gate, 12
    hospital, 12, 52, 56
sanctuary, 32, 121–2; *see also* friar
Sapperton, 123
Saturday, Dike, 12
    observance, 32
Sausthorp, 122
Scampton, 1, 63, 121
Scawby, 61
Schalby, John of, 39, 43
school, 39, 99; *see also* Lincoln, religious house
    provided by chantry, 100–1; by gild, 101
Schorwood, Joan of, 36
Scopwick, 109
Scotter, 120
Scottlethorpe, *see* Edenham
Scotton, 16
Scraine, *see* Fishtoft
Scredington, 113
Scremby, 10
    Bassingham in, 10
    Grebby in, 10
Scrivelsby, 26, 134
Sedgebrook, 132
Selby abbey, co. York, W.R., 54, 56
Sempringham, 32
    priory, 19, 39, 48, 50, 54, 58, 64, 66, 77, 79–80, 82, 110, 126, 145
    St Gilbert of, 39, 48, 50
sepulchre, Easter, 120
sermon, 108–10; *see also* friar
sewers, commissioners of, 51
Shavelock, Joan, 126
    Richard, 126
Sheepwash, *see* Canwick
Shelford priory, co. Nottingham, 74, 135
Sibsey, Benedict of, 124

sick, visitation of, 102
singing bread, 14; *see also* kirk-loaf, *pain bénit*
Sixhills, priory, 49–50, 66, 72, 145
    prior, 60
Skellingthorpe, 133
Skidbrook, 33
    Saltfleethaven in, 18, 99
Skirbeck, 124
    commandery of, 52, 56
Slackholme, *see* Willoughby le Marsh
Sleaford, 21, 37, 75, 112, 128, 130
    chantry at, 94, 100
    Holdingham in, 134
    Old, 2, 31
Sloothby, *see* Willoughby le Marsh
Smith, Smithe, Walter, 141
    William, 122
Snitterby, 133
Somerby, by Brigg, 104
    by Grantham, Humby in, 140
Somercotes, North, 110
    South, 110
sorcery, 121
soul-scot, 2, 16
Southorpe, *see* Edenham
Southrey, 78
Southwell, co. Nottingham, 37
Spalding, 10, 124, 133–4, 143
    Cowbit in, 6, 12
    Peak Hill in, 12
    Peckbridge in, 51
    priory, 47, 51, 57, 60, 66, 68–9, 71–2, 80–1, 145
Spilsby (originally in Eresby), 10, 99
    St James, 19
Spridlington, 121
Stainfield, 105
    priory, 66, 145
Stallingborough, 66, 125
    William son of Umfrid of, 125
Stamford, 4, 31, 39, 68, 115, 123, 130; *see also* Newstead
    friaries, 52, 80, 85; Austin, 52; Carmelite, 86; Dominican, 87, 89, 91; Franciscan, 89
    gilds, 95, 100
    parishes: All Saints, 136, 141; St Paul, 123
    priory of St Leonard, 80
    schools, 68

Stapleford, 113
　Little, see Brant Broughton
Steeping, Great, 49
　Little, 64
Stather, see Burton Stather
Stephen, clerk, 62
　king of England, 48, 95
Stickney, Northdike causeway in, 19, 35, 51, 109
Stigedbi, William of, clerk, 27
Stixwold, 140
　priory, 14, 17, 19, 29, 39–40, 50–1, 53, 57, 63, 65–6, 68, 71, 73–4, 77, 92, 145
　Thorald son of Ralf of, 39
Stockwith, East, see Gainsborough
　William of, 6
Stoile, Roger, 124
Stoke Rochford, 114
Stow, archdeaconry, 29, 35
　Green, see Threekingham
　in Kesteven, 57
　in Lindsey, 2, 21, 40, 47, 121
Stragglethorpe, see Beckingham
Streyl, Robert, canon of Kyme, 81
Strubby, 116
Stukeley, William, 1, 8, 113, 136
Sturton, Great, see Baumber
Stuther, Thomas, clerk, 133
Sudbrooke, 133
Sunday, observance, 110, 121
　trading, 32, 110
superstition, 25; see also paganism
Surfleet, 72, 113, 115, 124, 133–4, 143
Sutterton, 112, 116, 124, 138
Sutton, John of, 43
　Oliver, bishop of Lincoln, 17, 20, 25, 31, 33, 39, 44, 89, 95, 125
Sutton, in Holland [Long Sutton], 5, 10, 104, 113, 119, 143
　chapels: St Edmund, 12; St James, 12, 134; St Katherine, 12; St Nicholas, 10, 134; St Thomas Martyr, 12; Holy Trinity, 12
　Heoldefen in, 5
　le Marsh, 133, 139
Swaby, 4
Swift, William son of, 124
Swinderby Moor, 18
Swineshead, 112, 117, 124, 130, 139, 145
　abbey, 66, 79–80; see also Hoyland Barthorpe in, 6

Swinhope, 134, 139
Swinstead, 2
Syngar, Edward, 122
synod, 28–30

Talbot, William, 74
tanning, see religious house
Tattershall, 15, 102, 110, 114, 117
　castle, 83, 115
　college, 54, 99–101, 125
　Robert son of Hugh of, 6, 8
Taylour, Elizabeth, 141
　Robert, 141
Temple, order of the, 48, 54, 57, 62–3, 65
　Bruer, 62–3, 70
Tenell, John, O.P., 87
Tergisius, 62
Tetford, 48
Theddlethorpe, All Saints, 27, 110, 125, 137
Theobald, archbishop of Canterbury, 65
Thimbleby, 119
Thomas, archbishop of York, 21
Thoresby, South, 64
Thorganby, 36
Thornaco, William de, archdeacon of Lincoln, 29
Thorney abbey, co. Cambridge, 48
Thornholme priory, 66, 79, 80, 145
Thornton abbey, 56, 64, 68, 76, 80–1, 83, 105, 145
Thorpe St Peter, 112
Threekingham, 55
　Stow Green chapel in, 19
Thurgarton priory, co. Nottingham, 94
Thurlby by Bourne, 4, 13, 27
Thurstan, Richard son of, 124
Tisun, William of, 49
Tithe, 3, 12, 14–15; see also brick, friar, religious house, salt
　barn, 14
　collection, 137–9
　composition, 14
　demesne, 14–15
　of newland, 15–16
　produce of, 136
Toft, see Witham on the Hill
token, pilgrim, 127 and Fig. 8
Tong, Emma, 123
Torksey, 21, 68
　priory, 145

Torre, co. Devon, abbot and convent of, 33
Torrington, East and West, 15, 47
Totheby, Joan the widow of Gilbert of, 123
Towthorpe, *see* Grantham
Toynton, unidentified, 125
Trehamton, Roger of, 139
Tupholme abbey, 63, 65–6, 80, 145
turbary, 60
Turketin, Robert son of, 18
Twigmore, *see* Raventhorpe
Tydd St Mary, 88, 138, 143

Ulceby, Joan of, 36
Umfreville, Gilbert of, earl of Angus, 82, 93, 118
Utterby, 13

Vaudey abbey, 8, 15, 49, 65–6, 75–6, 80–2, 94, 145
Vavasour, Sir Henry, 64
Venice, 125
vernacular sermon, 33, 89
vestments, church, 118
vicarage, augmentation of, 140
  house, *see* residence
  ordination of, 26–7, 73–4
Villein, Ralf the, 49
visitation, by bishop, 120–1; *see also* archdeacon, religious house
  correction during, 30
  injunctions after, 28

Wainfleet, 69, 122
  All Saints, Northolme, 19, 33, 135
  St Mary, 19, 110; Holme in, 19; Sailholme in, 18, 19, 51, 65, 74, 126, 134
Wake, Baldwin, 5, 13, 57
Walcot, *see* Billinghay
Walesby, Otby in, 69
Walshcroft deanery, 141
Walsingham, Norfolk, pilgrimage to, 126
Walter, Hubert, archbishop of Canterbury, 124
  the smith, 124
  William son of, 51
Waltham, 95
  soke of, 57
  Essex, abbot of, 114
Wax-scot, 16

Welby, Adlard, clerk, 115
  Richard, esquire, 118
Welle, John of, 53, 103
  John, canon of Hagnaby, 80–1
Wellingore, 13, 37, 121, 125
Wellow abbey, 48, 66, 78, 83, 90
Wells, Hugh of, bishop of Lincoln, 26, 27, 73, 76
Welton, by Lincoln, 37, 42, 96, 141
  by Louth, Richard of, monk of Louth, 82
  le Marsh, 10; Boothby in, 10; Hanby in, 10
Wengale priory, 47, 54
Were, John, 71
Westby, 51
Weston, 143
Westminster abbey, 15, 47, 75
Whaplode, 4, 10, 12, 15, 31, 75, 112, 116, 119, 122, 133, 135, 143
  Aswick, 12
  chantry of St John, 12
  Drove, 12, 113
  friary, 85
  Marsh, 103
  St Katherine of Fenhall, 12
Whitby abbey, co. York, E.R., 68, 72
Whytebrede, John, 114
Wigtoft, 124
Wildmore fen, 65
Wilksby, 135
William, the baker, 125
  the diker, 124
  king of Apulia, 124
  I, king of England, 1, 37, 47
  II, king of England, 21
  the skinner, 124
Willoughby le Marsh, 10; Ashingdon in, 10; Bonthorpe in, 10, 103; Habertoft in, 10; Slackholme in, 10; Sloothby in, 10, 134
  [Wilughby], Sir John de, 103
  William, Lord, 100, 125
Willoughton, preceptory, 71
  priory, 54
Wilsford, 115, 122
  priory, 95
Winceby, 138
Winchelsey, Robert, archbishop of Canterbury, 117
window, church, 83, 99, 114–15, 131

Winstow, *see* Fleet
Wisbech, co. Cambridge, 81
Witham, river, 18, 19, 58
 on the Hill, 8; Lound in, 8; Manthorpe in, 8; Toft in, 8, 113
 John, 19
 North, 139
Withern, 113, 137
Wolhede, William, 92
Wolsthorp, Roger de, 94
Woodhall, Roland of, 60
Wortley, Thomas, 122
Wraggoe, wapentake, 65
Wrangle, 5, 114

Wrawby, Glanford Brigg in, 19; hospital at, 52, 55–6
Wryde, Robert of, 15
Wulfwig, bishop of Dorchester, 37
Wyberton, 4, 113–15, 124, 138
 Marsh, 18
Wyga, John, 114
Wykes, *see* Donington in Holland
Wymark, John, clerk, 133

Yarborough, deanery, 134, 141
 wapentake, 56
York, archbishop of, 47; *see also* Thomas
 Roger of, 62